gotta**hike**®
BC

Voice in the Wilderness Press

▶ Boot-tested and written by Skye and Lake Nomad

▷ ▷ ▷ the **premier** trails in southern British Columbia, Canada

Mt. Sir Donald, from Bald Mountain (Trip 21)

Dedicated to helping people
more easily appreciate
mountain grandeur, in hope
that it will enrich their lives
and inspire their commitment
to preserve what little
wilderness remains.

Photos by authors
Cover design by Matthew Clark
Typesetting by Angela Lockerbie

Published in Canada by
Voice in the Wilderness Press, Inc.
P.O. Box 30, Riondel, British Columbia V0B 2B0
Fax: (250) 225-3377   E-mail: explore@wild.bc.ca   Website: www.wild.bc.ca

Canadian Cataloguing in Publication Data

Nomad, Skye, 1959-
    Gotta hike B.C.

Includes index.
    ISBN 0-9698016-8-8

    1. Hiking--British Columbia--Guidebooks. 2. Trails--British Columbia--Guide-
books. 3. British Columbia--Guidebooks. I. Nomad, Lake, 1955- II. Title.
GV199.44.C22B7468 2001   917.1104'4   C2001-910568-1

Front cover photo: Lake of the Hanging Glacier (Trip 25)
Back cover photo: Macbeth Icefield cascades (Trip 23)

Contents

Your Safety is Your Responsibility

Hiking and camping in the wilderness can be dangerous. Experience and preparation reduce risk, but will never eliminate it. The unique details of your specific situation and the decisions you make at that time will determine the outcome. This book is not a substitute for common sense or sound judgment. If you doubt your ability to negotiate mountain terrain, respond to wild animals, deal with medical emergencies, or handle sudden, extreme weather changes, hike only in a group led by a competent guide. The authors and the publisher disclaim liability for any loss or injury incurred by anyone using information in this book.

WHERE YOU'VE GOTTA HIKE

See At-A-Glance (page 3) for trip names.

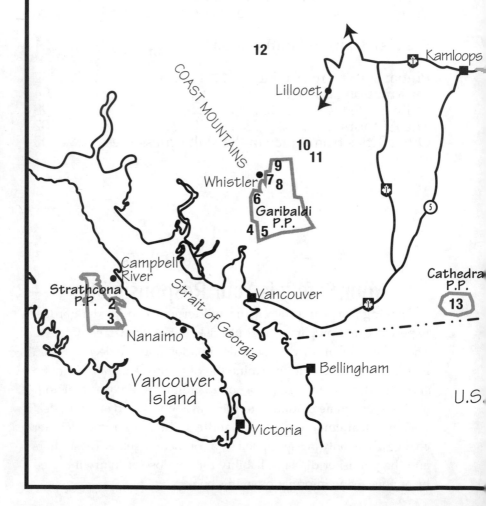

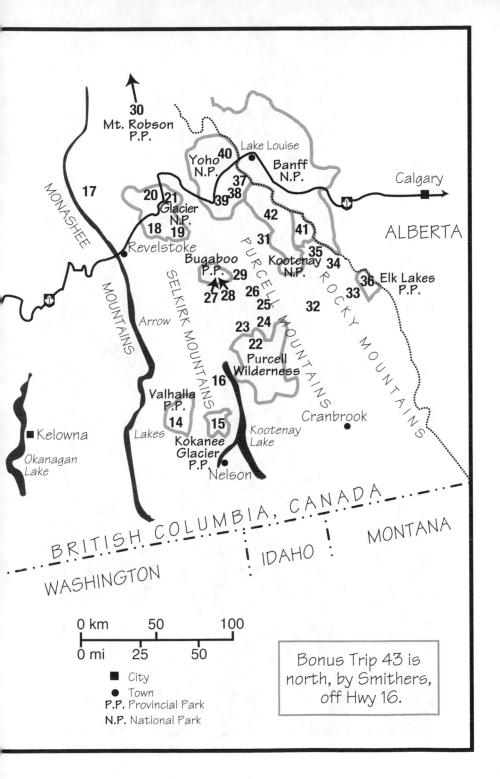

30
Mt. Robson
P.P.

Lake Louise

Yoho 40
N.P.

37
39 38

Banff
N.P.

Calgary

17

20 21
Glacier
N.P.
18 19

Revelstoke

42

41

ALBERTA

MONASHEE

31

35
Kootenay 34
N.P.

36 Elk Lakes
P.P.

Bugaboo
P.P. 29

27 28 26
25

33

32

Arrow

MOUNTAINS

SELKIRK MOUNTAINS

23 24

22
Purcell
Wilderness

PURCELL MOUNTAINS

ROCKY MOUNTAINS

16

Valhalla
P.P.

14 15

Cranbrook

Kelowna

Lakes

Kokanee
Glacier
P.P.

Kootenay
Lake

Nelson

Okanagan
Lake

BRITISH COLUMBIA, CANADA

COLUMBIA

WASHINGTON

IDAHO

MONTANA

0 km   50   100

0 mi   25   50

■ City
● Town
P.P. Provincial Park
N.P. National Park

Bonus Trip 43 is
north, by Smithers,
off Hwy 16.

The large glaciers in the Coast Mountains testify to the area's abundant snowfall and short summers. (Trip 7)

From the Pacific Ocean to the Canadian Rockies

If you're a hiker, you've gotta hike B.C. We say that with confidence, because we've hiked a lot of the world: 20,000 kilometers (12,400 miles) of it as of May, 2001, and no place has impressed us quite like British Columbia, Canada. Where else can you find so much mountain wilderness, such dramatic scenery, and so many trails? And of all the trails in the province, these are the ones that you've gotta hike. We're certain of that, too, because we've written four other guidebooks on B.C. mountain ranges. The trails in this book are those that dazzled us, that continue inspiring fervent memories, and that we'll return to zealously.

You now hold in your hands the only book that will guide you to premier hiking trails throughout southern B.C., from the Pacific Ocean to the Canadian Rockies. After completing several of these selected trips, if you want to explore more thoroughly, read our *Don't Waste Your Time*® hiking guidebooks. They offer bold opinions and specific advice to help you get the most from southern B.C.'s magnificent wilderness areas.

Volume One of *Gotta Hike B.C.*® covers the bottom quarter of the province: south of the Trans-Canada Highway. It's an area the size of Arizona or France. There are six major mountain ranges here: the Vancouver Island Ranges, the Coast Mountains (extending north from Vancouver), the Cascades (a continuation of Washington's North Cascades), the Selkirk and Purcell ranges (in B.C.'s southeast corner), and the Canadian Rockies (along the Alberta border). Each comprises numerous sub-ranges.

Every trail in this book leads to sensational scenery. The rapture you'll experience on these hikes trivializes the effort you'll expend. The drama usually unfolds soon: the rewards generously dispensed well before arrival at the destination. You'll be inspired by ancient forests, piercing peaks, tumbling glaciers, sheer cliffs, rowdy creeks, sprawling meadows, psychedelic wildflowers. The climactic vistas have startling impact. Most of the dayhikes are quickly gratifying because they start high. The backpack trips lead to alplands as splendid as any on the planet.

A few querulous hikers will dispute our choice of trails. Granted, we consulted nobody about our opinions. They're simply that: our opinions. But they're based on widely shared, common-sense criteria. "What about the Yabadabadoo trail?" someone will indignantly ask. The answer: if we didn't include it, we didn't think it afforded most hikers a premier experience. In all likelihood, we too enjoyed the trail in question; just not as much as you did, and not as much as those we selected for *Gotta Hike® B.C.* We never intended this to be an exhaustive compendium. Our goal was to write a handy, friendly guide that most B.C. residents who hike, and any hiking visitor, will find helpful and enjoyable.

The one omission we should explain is the West Coast Trail—B.C.'s most popular multi-day backpack trip. Does it need more publicity? No. Several books are dedicated to the subject. The number of hikers per day is restricted. Bookings fill months in advance. Could the West Coast Trail benefit from a few hikers directed elsewhere? Yes. That's true for many trails, but this one in particular. Unceasing hordes churn the path into calf-deep slop every year. Might hikers who go elsewhere also benefit? Definitely. Premier trails abound in B.C. Perpetuating an undue fixation would be a disservice. So the West Coast Trail isn't one we believe you've gotta hike.

We hope *Gotta Hike® B.C.* compels you to get outdoors more often and stay out longer. Do it to cultivate your wild self. It will give you perspective. Do it because the backcountry teaches simplicity and self-reliance, qualities that make life more fulfilling. Do it to remind yourself why wilderness needs and deserves your protection. A deeper conservation ethic develops naturally in the mountains. And do it to escape the cacophony that muffles the quiet, pure voice within.

Lake Lovely Water and the Tantalus Range (Trip 4)

> **Trips at a Glance**
>
> *Trips are listed according to geographic location: starting in the south and moving roughly from west to east, then north. After the trip name, the round-trip distance is listed, followed by the elevation gain.*

VANCOUVER ISLAND

1	East Sooke Coast	10 km (6.2 mi)	305 m (1000 ft)
2	Forbidden Plateau	22 km (13.6 mi)	380 m (1246 ft)
3	Strathcona Provincial Park		
	Bedwell Lake	12 km (7.4 mi)	600 m (1968 ft)
	Flower Ridge	14 km (8.7 mi)	1182 m (3877 ft)

COAST MOUNTAINS

4	Lake Lovely Water	10 km (6.2 mi)	1128 m (3700 ft)
5	Elfin Lakes / Mamquam Lake	22 km (13.6 mi)	915 m (3000 ft)
6	Garibaldi Lake / Panorama Ridge	18 km (11.2 mi)	875 m (2870 ft)
7	Musical Bumps	19 km (11.8 mi)	727 m (2385 ft)
8	Russett Lake	14.5 km (9 mi)	1280 m (4200 ft) loss
9	Wedgemount Lake	14 km (8.7 mi)	1160 m (3805 ft)
10	Joffre Lakes	11 km (6.8 mi)	370 m (1214 ft)
11	Stein Divide	28.6 km (17.7 mi)	1265 m (4150 ft)
12	Southern Chilcotin	37 km (23 mi)	1340 m (4400 ft)
13	Cathedral Lakes	32 km (19.8 mi)	1200 m (3936 ft)

SELKIRK MOUNTAINS

14	Gwillim Lakes	11.6 km (7.2 mi)	847 m (2780 ft)
15	Glory Basin	24 km (15 mi)	6160 m (2000 ft)
16	Mt. Brennan	14.6 km (9 mi)	1463 m (4800 ft)
17	Keystone and Standard basins		
	14.6 to 22 km (9 to 13.6 km)	400 m (1312 ft) to 608 m (1994 ft)	
18	Glacier Crest	10.4 km (6.4 mi)	1005 m (3296 ft)
19	Perley Rock	11.4 km (7.1 mi)	1162 m (3810 ft)
20	Hermit Basin	5.6 km (3.5 mi)	770 m (2525 ft)

PURCELL MOUNTAINS

21	Bald Mountain	35.2 km (21.8 mi)	1354 m (4440 ft)
22	Earl Grey Pass	61 km (37.8 mi)	1525 m (5000 ft)
23	MacBeth Icefield	15.6 km (9.7 mi)	874 m (2867 ft)
24	Jumbo Pass	8.4 km (5.2 mi)	686 m (2250 ft)
25	Lake of the Hanging Glacier	16 km (10 mi)	700 m (2296 ft)
26	Thunderwater Lake	12 km (7.4 mi)	455 m (1492 ft)
27	Bugaboo Spires	10 km (6.2 mi)	660 m (2165 ft)
28	Cobalt Lake	17.4 km (10.4 mi)	930 m (3047 ft)
29	Chalice Ridge	13 km (8.1 mi)	655 m (2148 ft)

ROCKY MOUNTAINS

30	Mt. Robson/Berg Lake	39.2 km (24.3 mi)	786 m (2578 ft)
31	Diana Lake/The Judge	12 km (7.4 mi)	600 m (1968 ft)
32	Pedley Ridge/Mt.Aeneas	4.2 km (2.6 mi)	440 m (1444 ft)
33	Limestone Lakes	34 km (21 mi)	1345 m (4400 ft)
34	Ralph and Queen Mary lakes	10 km (6.2 mi) 25 km (15.5 mi)	834 m (2736 ft) 1644 m (5392 ft)
35	Aurora Creek/ Marvel Pass	15 km (9.3 mi)	760 m (2493 ft)
36	Elk Lakes/Petain Basin	22 km (13.6 mi)	595 m (1950 ft)
37	Lake O'Hara Alpine Circuit	9.8 km (6 mi)	495 m (1625 ft)
38	Lake O'Hara Region	numerous choices	
39	Goodsir Pass	29 km (18 mi) by bike, plus 21.4 km (13.3 mi) on foot 335 m (1100 ft) by bike, plus 775 m (2542 ft) on foot	
40	Iceline/Whaleback	12.8 km (8 mi)	690 m (2265 ft)
41	Mt. Assiniboine Region	56.4 km (35 mi)	482 m (1580 ft)
42	The Rockwall	54.8 km (34 mi)	1490 m (4887 ft)

BONUS TRIP

43	Hudson Bay Mountain	13 to 22 km (8 to 13.6 mi), 284 m (930 ft) to 980 m (3214 ft)

Mountain Climate

The volatility of the southern B.C. mountain climate will have you building shrines to placate the weather gods.

Summer is pitifully short. Don't count on more than two-and-a-half months of high-country hiking. Most of these trails aren't snow-free until early July. High passes can be blanketed in white until later that month. Snowfall is possible on any day, and likely at higher elevations after August. Contact Park Info Centres (listed under *Information Sources* at the back of this book) for weather forecasts and trail-condition reports.

Regardless of the forecast, always be prepared for heavy rain, harsh winds, plummeting temperatures, sleet, hail: the whole miserable gamut. Likewise, allow for the possibility of scorching sun and soaring temperatures. The weather can change dramatically, with alarming speed. A clear sky at dawn is often filled with ominous black clouds by afternoon. Storms can dissipate equally fast.

Throughout the mountain ranges covered in this book, statistics indicate that you can generally expect a third of summer days to be rainy. The average monthly maximum and minimum temperatures reveal the following. July is usually the hottest month. August can be almost as hot as July, but generally isn't. September tends to be slightly warmer than May. In the Coast Mountains, the mercury can soar up to 33° C (92° F) in summer. The Purcells and Selkirks have summer highs near 30° C (86° F), lows near 10° C (50° F). These inland ranges have September highs just over 20° C (68° F), and lows just below 8° C (45° F). Summer highs in the Rockies average 24° C (75° F), lows average 7° C (45° F). By September, highs in the Rockies are about 17° C (65° F), while the lows hover just above freezing.

Fall is touted by many as the ideal time to hike in southern B.C. Bugs are absent then, crowds diminish, larch trees turn golden. Most of the hikes in this book should be available until early October. But the days are shorter, the nights noticeably colder. We prefer the long days and warm nights of mid-summer.

Backcountry Permits

Upon entering the **Canadian Rocky Mountain national parks**, everyone must pay a User Fee. Parks Canada also charges for all camping. In 2001, a backcountry camping permit cost $6 per person, per night, up to a maximum of $30 per trip. The alternative is to buy a Wilderness Pass allowing you unlimited backcountry camping for one year. It cost $42 per person in 2001. Even with a Wilderness Pass, you must obtain permits to reserve campsites.

Backcountry campsites in the national parks are 100% reservable. You can make reservations up to 90 days in advance by writing or calling the appropriate park info centre. This service costs an additional $10. You can also change your reservations by phone or mail, but this too costs $10 each time. Bookings fill early for campgrounds on all the Gotta Hike national-park trails, so making reservations is a necessary form of trip insurance. Hey, the world's just too crowded.

Plan your itinerary before you call the park info centre, so you can ask for specific campgrounds along your intended route. The centre will mail you the permit if you purchase it at least two weeks in advance.

British Columbia Provincial Parks charge $5 per person per night for backcountry camping. No reservations are required. Bring cash in your backpack because fees are usually collected by a warden (ranger) at each backcountry campground. As of 2001, Tantalus and Elk Lakes provincial parks do not charge a camping fee. Expect this to change.

Maps, Elevations, Distances

There is no definitive source for accurate trail distances and elevations. Maps, brochures, and trail signs state conflicting figures more often than they agree. But the discrepancies are usually small. And most hikers don't care whether an ascent is 715 m (2345 ft) or 720 m (2362 ft), or a trail is 8.7 km (5.4 mi) or 9 km (5.6 mi). Still, we made a supreme effort to ensure accuracy. Our directions are also extremely detailed. So topographical maps are unnecessary. This book is all you need.

You might want topo maps, however, for several reasons. (1) After reaching a summit, say Mt. Brennan (Trip 16), a topo map will enable you to interpret the surrounding geography. (2) On particularly rough hikes, such as Limestone Lakes (Trip 33), or long backpack trips, such as the Southern Chilcotin (Trip 12), a topo map will make it even easier to follow our directions. (3) Off-trail scrambles, like the one over Lucifer Pass from Gwillim Lakes (Trip 14), are safer and more efficient with a topo map. (4) If you're intrigued by the country through which you're hiking, a topo map ensures a more fulfilling experience.

Ascending steep gully to Wedgemount Lake (Trip 8)

The Surveys & Mapping Branch of the Department of Energy, Mines and Resources (DEMR) prints 1:50,000 topographic maps covering the province. They're sold at government agent offices, as well as some outdoor shops and bookstores. We've listed the applicable DEMR topo maps for each trip in this book. They're the most helpful maps for hikers. These maps can be frustrating, however, because DEMR doesn't update all the information, such as trail locations. Narrower, less popular trails are not always indicated, even though the trails themselves are distinct on the ground. DEMR maps are also expensive, and you'll often need two or three for a single backpack trip. Earl Grey Pass (Trip 22), for example, stretches across three DEMR maps: Lardeau 82 K/2, Duncan Lake 82 K/7, and Toby Creek 82 K/8.

Request provincial park brochures from the district offices. The contact numbers are listed under *Information Sources* at the back of this book. Or pick up the brochures from a roadside Tourist Infocentre or trailhead kiosk. The maps in these brochures are simplistic and will give you only a general sense of direction, distance and elevation.

Modestly priced B.C. road maps are available at Tourist Info Centres in towns and cities throughout the province. If you live out-of-province, the SuperNatural British Columbia tourism office will mail you a B.C. Road Map and Parks Guide. Call 1-800-633-6000 from anywhere in North America, (604) 387-1742 from overseas.

For Coast Mountain hikes, you'll often see ITM maps listed in the trip information boxes. They're published by International Travel Maps in Vancouver. The 1:50,000 *Whistler and Region*, and the 1:100,000 *Garibaldi Region* are more useful than the government maps because they indicate the trails.

Gem Trek Publishing of Calgary, Alberta, prints topographic maps of the mountain parks. The contour intervals are 50 or 100 meters. All trails and distances are indicated. The Gem Trek Lake Louise & Yoho map has handy, enlarged 1:25,000 maps for the Lake O'Hara area. Most of their maps are printed on water- and tear-resistant paper. Buying one Gem Trek map saves you the expense of several DEMR maps. They're sold at outdoor shops, bookstores, and park info centres.

The *Arrow and Kootenay Lake Forest District Recreation Map* provides an excellent overview of the West Kootenays. The *Invermere Forest District Recreation Map* displays the Purcell Mountains of the East Kootenays. In addition to showing Forest-Service roads, the maps indicate the general location of many hiking trails. Call the

Forest Service offices (listed in the back of this book) to find out the most convenient way to buy their map.

The Valhalla Society prints two brochures: *A Visitor's Guide to the Valhalla Provincial Park*, and *Visitor Guide to the White Grizzly Wilderness*. Both contain 1:125,000 maps. The first brochure covers Valhalla and Kokanee provincial parks. The second shows Goat Range Provincial Park. Both are full of valuable information, but maps of this scale are useful only as a general guide. These also tend to be optimistic. Some of the indicated routes and trails can be difficult, even impossible, for the average hiker to follow. Both brochures are available directly from the Valhalla Society (250-358-2333) as well as at some West Kootenay outdoor shops and bookstores.

Wilderness Ethics

We hope you're already conscientious about respecting nature and other people. If not, here's how to pay off some of your karmic debt load:

Let wildflowers live. They blossom for only a few fleeting weeks. Uprooting them doesn't enhance your enjoyment, and it prevents others from seeing them at all. We've heard parents urge a string of children to pick as many different-colored flowers as they could find. It's a mistake to teach kids to entertain themselves by killing nature.

Give the critters a break. The wilderness isn't a zoo. The animals are wild. Recognize that this is their home, and you are an uninvited guest. Behave accordingly. Allow all of them plenty of space. Most are remarkably tolerant of people, but approaching them to take a photograph is harassment and can be dangerous. Some elk, for example, appear docile but can severely injure you. Approaching any bear is suicidal. Read our Bears section.

Stay on the trail. Shortcutting causes erosion. You probably won't save time anyway, unless you're incredibly strong. When hiking cross-country in a group, spread out to soften your impact.

Roam meadows with your eyes, not your boots. Again, stay on the trail. If it's braided, follow the main path. When you're compelled to take a photo among the wildflowers, try to walk on rocks.

Traversing Tabletop Mountain, Stein Divide (Trip 11)

Leave no trace. Be aware of your impact. Travel lightly on the land. At campgrounds, limit your activity to areas already denuded. After a rest stop, and especially after camping, take a few minutes to look for and obscure any evidence of your stay. Restore the area to its natural state. Remember: tents can leave scars. Pitch yours on an existing tentsite whenever possible. If none is available, choose a patch of dirt, gravel, pine needles, or maybe a dried-up tarn. Never pitch your tent on grass, no matter how appealing it looks. If you do, and others follow, the grass will soon be gone.

Avoid building fires. They're prohibited in national and provincial parks, except at a few places where there are established fire rings and firewood is supplied. Even where allowed, fires are a luxury, not a necessity. Don't plan to cook over a fire; it's inefficient and wasteful. If you pack food that requires cooking, bring a stove. In forest districts and wilderness areas, if you must indulge in a campfire, keep it small. Use an existing fire ring made of rocks. If no rings are present—which is rare—build yours on mineral soil or gravel, not in the organic layer. Never scorch meadows. Below a stream's high-water line is best. Garbage with metal or plastic content will not burn; pack it all out. Limit your wood gathering to deadfall about the size of your forearm. Wood that requires effort (breaking, chopping, dragging) is part of the scenery; let it be. After thoroughly dousing your fire, dismantle the fire ring and scatter the ashes. Keep in mind that untended and unextinguished campfires are the prime cause of forest fires.

Be quiet at backcountry campgrounds. Most of us are out there to enjoy tranquillity. If you want to party, go to a pub.

Pack out everything you bring. Never leave a scrap of trash anywhere. This includes toilet paper, nut shells, even cigarette butts. People who drop butts in the wilderness are buttheads. They're buttheads in the city too, but it's worse in the wilds. Fruit peels are also trash. They take years to decompose, and wild animals won't eat them. If you bring fruit on your hike, you're responsible for the peels. And don't just pack out your trash. Leave nothing behind, whether you brought it or not. Clean up after others. Don't be hesitant or oblivious. Be proud. Keep a small plastic bag handy, so picking up trash will be a habit instead of a pain. It's infuriating and disgusting to see what people toss on the trail. Often the tossing is mindless, but sometimes it's intentional. Anyone who leaves a pile of toilet paper and unburied feces should have their nose rubbed in it.

Poop without impact. Use the outhouses at trailheads and campgrounds whenever possible. Don't count on them being stocked with toilet paper; always pack your own in a plastic bag. If you know there's a campground ahead, try to wait until you get there.

In the wilds, choose a site at least 60 meters (66 yards) from trails and water sources. Ground that receives sunlight part of the day is best. Use a trowel to dig a small cat hole—10 to 20 cm (4 to 8 inches) deep, 10 to 15 cm (4 to 6 inches) wide—in soft, dark, biologically active soil. Afterward, throw a handful of dirt into the hole, stir with a stick to speed decomposition, replace your diggings, then camouflage the site. Pack out used toilet paper in a plastic bag. You can drop the paper (not the plastic) in the next outhouse you pass. Always clean your hands with anti-bacterial moisturizing lotion. It's sold in drugstores.

Urinate off trail, well away from water sources and tent sites. The salt in urine attracts animals. They'll defoliate urine-soaked vegetation, so aim for dirt or pine needles.

Keep streams and lakes pristine. When brushing your teeth or washing dishes, do it well away from water sources and tent sites. Use only biodegradable soap. Carry water far enough so the waste water will percolate through soil and break down without directly polluting the wilderness water. Scatter waste water widely. Even biodegradable soap is a pollutant; keep it out of streams and lakes. On short backpack trips, you shouldn't need to wash clothes or yourself. If necessary, rinse your clothes or splash yourself off— without soap.

Respect the reverie of other hikers. On busy trails, don't feel it's necessary to communicate with everyone you pass. Most of us are seeking solitude, not a social scene. A simple greeting is sufficient to convey good will. Obviously, only you can judge what's appropriate at the time. But it's usually presumptuous and annoying to blurt out advice without being asked. "Boy, have you got a long way to go." "The views are much better up there." "Be careful, it gets rougher." If anyone wants to know, they'll ask. Some people are sly. They start by asking where you're going, so they can tell you all about it. Offer unsolicited information only to warn other hikers about conditions ahead that could seriously affect their trip.

Hiking With Your Dog

Dogs are not allowed in the B.C. provincial park backcountry. You can bring your dog to Elk Lakes Park, but you must keep it on a leash.

All the Canadian Rocky Mountain national parks, at the time of this writing, allow dogs in the backcountry with the stipulation that they be physically restrained the entire time. But before you take your dog hiking, ask the appropriate park info centre about their current policy regarding dogs, particularly in backcountry campgrounds. Dogs are a controversial issue, and policies might change. Keep in mind that if your destination is Lake Magog, in Mt. Assiniboine Park, you'll hike through Banff Park.

But before you take your dog when you go hiking, think about it. Most dog owners believe their pets are angelic. Other people rarely agree, especially hikers confined overnight in a backcountry campground where someone's brought a dog. The reasons are numerous. A barking dog can be outrageously annoying. A curious dog, even if friendly, can be a nuisance. An untrained dog, despite its owner's hearty reassurance that "he won't hurt you," can be frightening. Many owners ignore their responsibility to keep dogs from polluting streams and lakes, or fouling campgrounds.

Dogs in the backcountry are a danger to themselves. For example, they're likely to be spiked by porcupines that prowl campgrounds at night. Even worse, they can endanger their owners and other hikers, because dogs infuriate bears. If a dog runs off, it might reel a bear back with it.

Leave your dog at home. If you must hike with a dog, never unleash it.

Physical Capability

Until you gain experience judging your physical capability and that of your companions, these guidelines might be helpful. Anything longer than an 11-km (7-mi) round-trip dayhike can be very taxing for someone who doesn't hike regularly. A 425-m (1400-ft) elevation gain in that distance is challenging but possible for anyone in average physical condition. Very fit hikers are comfortable hiking 18 km (11 mi) or more and gaining 950-plus meters (3100-plus feet) in a single day. Backpacking 18 km (11 mi) in two days is a reasonable goal for most beginners. Hikers who backpack a couple times a season can enjoyably manage 27 km (17 mi) in two days. Avid backpackers should find 38 km (24 mi) in two days no problem. On three- to five-day trips, a typical backpacker prefers not to push beyond 16 km (10 mi) a day. Remember it's always safer to underestimate your limits.

Wildlife

It's possible to see all kinds of animals—big and small—throughout B.C.'s mountains. Deer, chipmunks, squirrels, raccoons, skunks, bats and owls, you might expect. But also be on the lookout

Watch for moose in boggy, marshy areas.

for eagles, elk, mountain goats, bighorn sheep, moose, coyotes, black bears and grizzlies. In the evening, watch for porcupines waddling out of the forest and beavers cruising ponds. On alpine trails, you're likely to see pikas and marmots. It's a rare and fortunate hiker who glimpses a wolf, wolverine, or cougar.

About those porkies. Selkirk and Purcell mountain trailheads are infamous for car-eating porcupines. Seriously. They munch tires, hoses and fan belts. Their voracious appetite for rubber could leave you stranded. Don't want to hitchhike down the mountain to call a tow truck? Wrap chicken wire around your vehicle and secure it with rocks and pieces of wood. Chicken wire is available at the Gibson Lake trailhead in Kokanee Glacier Park and the Bugaboo Spires / Cobalt Lake trailhead in Bugaboo Provincial Park. Elsewhere you'll have to bring your own. Mothballs, liberally scattered beneath and around a vehicle, are also rumoured to deter the critters. It's worth a try, but consider yourself a test case. Just remember to pick up every single mothball before you drive away. You're not backpacking? Don't worry. Porcupines are nocturnal, so dayhikers don't have to erect a fortress.

Bears

Bears are rarely a problem in these mountain ranges. But oblivious hikers can endanger themselves, other people, and the bears. If you're prepared for a bear encounter and know how to prevent one, you can hike confidently, secure in the understanding that bears pose little threat.

Only a couple hundred grizzly bears roam the Canadian Rocky Mountain Parks. The black-bear population is comparable. You're more likely to see a bear while driving the Icefields Parkway than while hiking most backcountry trails. National park info centres post trail reports that include bear warnings and closures. Check these before your trip; adjust your plans accordingly.

Grizzlies and blacks can be difficult for an inexperienced observer to tell apart. Both species range in colour from nearly white to cinnamon to black. Full-grown grizzlies are much bigger, but a young grizzly can resemble an adult black bear, so size is not a good indicator. The most obvious differences are that grizzlies have a dished face; big, muscular shoulder humps; and long, curved front claws. Blacks have a straight face; no hump; and shorter, less visible front claws. Grizzlies are potentially more dangerous than black bears, although a black bear sow with cubs can be just as aggressive. Be wary of all bears.

If you see a grizzly bear this close, hope you're in your vehicle.

Any bear might attack when surprised. If you're hiking, and forest or brush limits your visibility, you can prevent surprising a bear by making noise. Bears hear about as well as humans. Most are as anxious to avoid an encounter as you are. If you warn them of your presence before they see you, they'll usually clear out. So use the most effective noisemaker: your voice. Shout loudly. Keep it up. Don't be embarrassed. Be safe. Yell louder near streams, so your voice carries over the competing noise. Sound off more frequently when hiking into the wind. That's when bears are least able to hear or smell you coming. For further suggestions and detailed strategies, listen to the audio cassette *Bears Beware: Warning Calls You Can Make to Avoid an Encounter*. It's described in the back of this book.

Bears' strongest sense is smell. They can detect an animal carcass several kilometers (miles) away. So keep your pack, tent and campsite odor-free. Double or triple-wrap all your food in plastic bags. Avoid smelly foods, especially meat and fish. On short backpack trips, consider eating only fresh foods that require no cooking or cleanup. If you cook, do it as far as possible from where you'll be sleeping. Never cook in or near your tent; the fabric might retain odor. Use as few pots and dishes as you can get by with. Be fastidious when you wash them. At night, hang all your food, trash, and anything else that smells (cooking gear, sunscreen, bug repellent, toothpaste) out of bears' reach. Use the metal food caches provided at some provincial-park backcountry campgrounds. Elsewhere, a tree branch will suffice. Bring a sturdy stuffsack to serve as your bear bag. Hoist it at least 5 meters (16 feet) off the ground and 1.5 meters (5 feet) from the tree trunk or other branches. You'll need about 12 meters (40 feet) of light nylon cord. Clip the sack to the cord with an ultralight carabiner.

Backpackers who don't properly hang their food at night are inviting bears into their campsite, greatly increasing the chance of a dangerous encounter. And bears are smart. They quickly learn to associate a particular place, or people in general, with an easy meal. They become habituated and lose their fear of man. A habituated bear is a menace to any hiker within its range.

If you see a bear, don't look it in the eyes; it might think you're challenging it. Never run. Initially be still. If you must move, do it in slow motion. Bears are more likely to attack if you flee, and they're fast, much faster than humans. A grizzly can outsprint a racehorse. And it's a myth that bears can't run downhill. They're also strong swimmers. Despite their ungainly appearance, they're excellent climbers too. Still, climbing a tree can be an option for escaping an aggressive bear. Some people have saved their lives this way. Others been caught in the process. To be out of reach of an adult bear, you must climb at least 10 meters (33 feet) very quickly, something few people are capable of. It's generally best to avoid provoking an attack by staying calm, initially standing your ground, making soothing sounds to convey a nonthreatening presence, then retreating slowly.

What should you do when a bear charges? If you're certain it's a lone black bear—not a sow with cubs, not a grizzly—fighting back might be effective. If it's a grizzly, and contact seems imminent, lie face down, with your legs apart and your hands clasped behind your neck. This is safer than the fetal position, which used to be recommended, because it makes it harder for the bear to flip you over. If you play dead, a grizzly is likely to break off the attack once it feels you're no longer a threat. Don't move until you're sure the bear has left the area, then slowly, quietly, get up and walk away. Keep moving, but don't run.

Arm yourself with pepper spray as a last line of defense. Keep it in a holster, on your hip belt or shoulder strap, where you can grab it fast. Many people have successfully used it to turn back charging bears. Cayenne pepper, highly irritating to a bear's sensitive nose, is the active ingredient. Without causing permanent injury, it disables the bear long enough to let you escape. But vigilance and noise making should prevent you from ever having to spray. Do so only if you really think your life is at risk. You can buy pepper spray at outdoor stores. Counter Assault and Bearguard are reputable brands.

Remember that your safety is not the only important consideration. Bears themselves are at risk when confronted by humans. Anytime they act aggressively, they're following their natural instinct for self preservation. Often they're protecting their cubs or a food source. Yet if they maul a hiker, they're likely to be killed or captured and moved by wildlife management officers. Protecting these beautiful, magnificent creatures is a responsibility hikers must accept.

Merrily disregarding bears is foolish and unsafe. Worrying about them is miserable and unnecessary. Everyone occasionally feels afraid when venturing deep into the mountains, but fear of bears can be restrained by knowledge and awareness. Just take the necessary precautions and don't let your guard down. Experiencing the grandeur of B.C.'s mountains is certainly worth risking the remote possibility of a bear encounter.

Intimidating trailhead warning

Cougars

You'll probably never see a cougar. But they're present in B.C., and they can be dangerous, so you should know a bit about them.

Elsewhere referred to as a puma, mountain lion, or panther, the cougar is an enormous, graceful cat. An adult male can reach the size of a big human: 80 kilos (175 pounds), and 2.4 meters (8 feet) long, including a 1-meter (3-foot) tail. In B.C., they tend to be a tawny grey.

Nocturnal, secretive, solitary creatures, cougars come together only to mate. Each cat establishes a territory of 200 to 280 square kilometers (125 to 175 square miles). They favour dense forest that provides cover while hunting. They also hide among rock outcroppings and in steep canyons.

Habitat loss and aggressive predator-control programs have severely limited the range of this mysterious animal that once lived throughout North America. Still, cougars are not considered endangered or threatened. Cougars appear to be thriving in British Columbia.

Cougars are carnivores. They eat everything from mice to elk, but prefer deer. They occasionally stalk people, but rarely attack them. In folklore, cougars are called ghost cats or ghost walkers, and for good reason. They're very shy and typically avoid human contact. Nevertheless, cougar encounters continue to occur near North Vancouver neighbourhoods that have grown up forested mountainsides. During the winter of 2000/01, two cougar-attack incidents occurred in the Canadian Rockies. Both were near townsites and involved lone victims.

Cougar sightings and encounters are increasing, but it's uncertain whether that's due to a larger cougar population or the growing number of people visiting the wilderness. If you're lucky enough to see a cougar, treasure the experience. Just remember they're unpredictable. Follow these suggestions:

Never hike alone in areas of known cougar sightings. Keep children close to you; pick them up if you see fresh cougar scat or tracks. Never approach a cougar, especially a feeding one. Never flee from a cougar, or even turn your back on it. Sudden movement might trigger an instinctive attack. Avert your gaze and speak to it in a calm, soothing voice. Hold your ground or back away slowly. Always give the animal a way out. If a cougar approaches, spread your arms, open your jacket, do anything you can to enlarge your image. If it acts aggressively, wave your arms, shout, throw rocks or sticks. If attacked, fight back. Don't play dead.

Lightning

Many of our recommendations take you to high ridges, open meadows and mountain peaks where, during a storm, you could be exposed to lightning. Your best protection is, of course, not being there. But it's difficult to always avoid hiking in threatening weather. Even if you start under a cloudless, blue sky, you might see ominous, black thunderheads marching toward you a few hours later. Upon reaching a high, thrilling vantage, you could be forced by an approaching storm to decide if and when you should retreat to safer ground. Try to reach high passes early in the day. Rain and lightning storms tend to develop in the afternoon.

The power of nature that makes wilderness so alluring often presents threats to your safety. The following is a summary of lightning precautions recommended by experts. These are not guaranteed solutions. We offer them merely as suggestions to help you make a wiser decision on your own and reduce your chance of injury.

A direct lightning strike can kill you. It can cause brain damage, heart failure or third-degree burns. Ground current, from a nearby strike, can severely injure you, causing deep burns and tissue damage. Direct strikes are worse but far less common than ground-current contact.

To avoid a direct strike, get off exposed ridges and peaks. Even a few meters off a ridge is better than right on top. Avoid isolated, tall trees. A clump of small trees or an opening in the trees is safer.

To avoid ground current, stay off crevices, lichen patches, or wet, solid rock surfaces, and away from gullies with streams in them. Loose rock, like talus, is safer.

Crouch near a highpoint at least 10 meters (33 feet) higher than you. Sit in the **low-risk area**: near the base of the highpoint, at least 1.5 meters (5 feet) from cliffs or walls.

If your hair is standing on end, there's electricity in the air around you. Get outa there! That's usually down the mountain, but if there's too much open expanse to traverse, look for closer protection.

Once you choose a place to wait it out, squat with your feet close together. To prevent brain or heart damage, you must stop the charge from flowing through your whole body. It helps to keep your hands and arms away from rocks. Several books say to insulate yourself by crouching on a dry sleeping pad, but we wonder, how do you do this if it's raining and you're not in a tent or cave?

Stay at least 10 meters (33 feet) from your companions, so if one is hit, another can give cardiopulmonary resuscitation.

Deep caves offer protection, but stay out of shallow or small caves because ground current can jump across openings. Crouch away from the opening, at least 1.5 meters (5 feet) from the walls. Also avoid rock overhangs. You're safer in the low-risk area below a highpoint.

Hypothermia

Many deaths outdoors involve no obvious injury. "Exposure" is usually cited as the killer, but that's a misleading term. It vaguely refers to conditions that contributed to the death. The actual cause is hypothermia: excessive loss of body heat. It can happen with startling speed, in surprisingly mild weather—often between 0 and 10° C (30 and 50°F). Guard against it vigilantly.

Cool temperatures, wetness (perspiration or rain), wind, or fatigue, usually a combination, sap the body of vital warmth. Hypothermia results when heat loss continues to exceed heat gain. Initial symptoms include chills and shivering. Poor coordination, slurred speech, sluggish thinking, and memory loss are next. Intense shivering then decreases while muscular rigidity increases, accompanied by irrationality, incoherence, even hallucinations. Stupor, blue skin, slowed pulse and respiration, and unconsciousness follow. The heartbeat finally becomes erratic until the victim dies.

Avoid becoming hypothermic by wearing synthetic clothing that wicks moisture away from your skin and insulates when wet. Read *Preparing For Your Hike*, in the back of this book, for an explanation of the clothing and equipment that will help keep you warm and dry. Food fuels your internal fire, so bring more than you think you'll need, including several energy bars for emergencies only.

If you can't stay warm and dry, you must escape the wind and rain. Turn back. Keep moving. Eat snacks. Seek shelter. Do it while you're still mentally and physically capable. Watch others in your party for signs of hypothermia. Victims might resist help at first. Trust the symptoms, not the person. Be insistent. Act immediately.

Create the best possible shelter for the victim. Take off his wet clothes and replace them with dry ones. Insulate him from the ground. Provide warmth. A prewarmed sleeping bag inside a tent is ideal. If necessary, add more warmth by taking off your clothes and crawling into the bag with the victim. Build a fire. Keep the victim conscious. Feed him sweets. Carbohydrates quickly convert to heat and energy. In advanced cases, victims should not drink hot liquids.

PREMIER TRAILS IN SOUTHERN B.C.

Coast Mountains, Mt. Garibaldi in background.

Trip 1

East Sooke Coast

Location	Vancouver Island, south coast
Round trip	10 km (6.2 mi)
Elevation gain	305 m (1000 ft)
Time required	6 to 8 hours
Difficulty	Easy to Moderate
Maps	Sooke 92 B/5; Capital Regional District Parks brochure

OPINION

In a book full of remote mountain trails, here's an exception: a coastal hike just outside Victoria. Rarely can you devote all day to a premier outdoor adventure, then spend the evening partaking of cosmopolitan conviviality. The East Sooke coast trail makes that possible. And you can hike it all year. Mountain snowpack be damned.

Now dispel all thoughts of urbanity. This is a wild stretch of Vancouver Island's south coast, well protected by 1422-hectare (3512-acre) East Sooke Regional Park. The coast trail is the most scenic portion of the park's 50-km (31-mi) trail network. The elevation stated above—305 m (1000 ft)—is an estimate. At trail's end, you might feel you climbed more than that. Ups and downs are constant. Though most are small, many are steep, and they add up fast. The rugged terrain intensifies the challenge by occasionally blurring the distinction between hiking and scrambling.

The trail plays along the south edge of East Sooke Peninsula. It bounds over rocky bluffs, dodges windswept trees, runs past crashing surf, tiptoes around coves and ravines, darts into shadowy rainforest, then pops back into the sunlight at the edge of the sea. The flora is wonderfully varied. The arboreal melange includes Sitka spruce, Douglas fir, western hemlock, and arbutus (smooth reddish bark). Slightly inland are mosses, ferns, and salmonberry (bushes with orange fruit). Kinnikinnick, Oregon grape, and salal thrive along much of the trail. The only constant on this trip is the Pacific Ocean. Though the trail nips down to the water's edge only a few

East Sooke Coast trail

times, Juan de Fuca Strait is often in view and usually audible. You'll probably see harbour seals. You might see a humpback whale, or a school of dolphin.

If possible, hike the East Sooke coast trail with friends. Bring two cars and arrange a shuttle. The route described below is the optimal trip: one way, generally southeast, starting at Pike Road trailhead, on the peninsula's west side, to Aylard Farm trailhead, on the peninsula's east side. Only have one vehicle? Hitchhiking here is difficult. But it's not impossible. We've done it. After completing the one-way trip, try getting a ride near Aylard Farm. Thumbing from Pike Road trailhead in late afternoon is almost hopeless. If you insist on hiking out and back, start at Aylard Farm, because it's on the ocean. From Pike Road trailhead, you'll hike 3.2 km (1.9 mi) just getting to and from the actual coast trail. Also, Aylard's sandy beaches and spacious pasture invite apre-tromp relaxation.

Recent heavy rain means the already demanding trail will, in places, be uncomfortably slippery. Still, it's distinctly mud-free compared to Vancouver Island's more famous ocean-edge paths. The Juan de Fuca and West Coast trails are notoriously sloppy. Otherwise it's difficult to compare the East Sooke and West Coast trials; they're completely different. The West Coast Trail is a multi-day backpack trip so popular that several guidebooks are dedicated to the subject, the number of hikers per day is limited, and bookings fill months in advance. The Juan de Fuca Trail, however, requires no reservations and can be broken into three dayhikes, so it bears comparison with the East Sooke coast trail. Our opinion is that East Sooke is vastly superior in every way: frequency of ocean views; beauty, diversity and integrity of the forest; variety of terrain; quality of the trail itself; and overall capacity to intrigue and motivate. Hiking the Juan de Fuca Trail is worthwhile, but it's not a premier experience. Too muddy. Too much slippery boardwalk. Too many clearcuts. Too often away from the ocean.

Finally, East Sooke Peninsula's history is worth noting. Coast Salish natives left their mark here in the form of petroglyphs. In the late 1800's, everything from stately square-riggers to dugout canoes plied Juan de Fuca Strait, bringing supplies to and from Fort Victoria. Loggers, miners and fishermen have all exploited the area. At Iron Mine Bay and Mt. Maguire, copper and iron were mined for nearly a century. At Cabin Point, near the coast trail's midpoint, a restored trap shack hunkers on rock just above the surging sea. From the late 1800s until 1958, fishermen lived in shacks like these and tended fishtraps. In July 1928, 70,000 pounds of salmon were caught at Otter Point. Today, the shack serves as a shelter for hikers. It's a comfortable place to stop for a lunch break and gnosh your living-light-on-the-land tofu sandwich.

FACT

Before your trip

Contact Capital Regional District Parks (250-478-3344; www.crd.bc.ca/parks) to request their East Sooke Regional Park brochure. It has a handy map. Also, be aware that the park allows day use only; backpacking is prohibited.

By Vehicle

The trail is on East Sooke Peninsula, which is 27 km (16.7 mi) west of Victoria. Drive the Old Island Hwy to Sooke Road, Hwy 14. From Colwood Corners, follow Hwy 14 west 14 km (8.7 mi) to Gillespie Road. This is just west of the 17-Mile Pub and 8 km (5 mi) from Sooke. Turn left (south) and reset your trip odometer to 0.

0 km (0 mi)

Turning off Hwy 14 onto Gillespie Road, signed for East Sooke Park.

5.5 km (3.4 mi)

Reach a junction. Go right on East Sooke Road for Pike Road trailhead; directions continue at the 13.4-km (8.3-mi) point. For Aylard Farm trailhead, turn left. Go 2 km (1.2 mi), then turn right and follow Becher Bay Road 1.3 km (0.8 mi). Bear right where the marina entrance forks left. Descend into the parking lot. It's open sunrise to sunset. There are toilets and an information kiosk here.

13.4 km (8.3 mi)

Turn left onto Pike Road and continue 200 meters (220 yards) to arrive at Pike Road trailhead amid tall Douglas firs. There are toilets and an information kiosk here.

On Foot

Starting at Pike Road trailhead, hike south through heavy timber. In 10 minutes, reach a junction. Bear right (south) for Iron Mine Bay. Left leads northeast to 272-m (892-ft) Mt. Maguire and continues inland across the park to East Sooke Road and Anderson Cove.

The trail soon forks again. Bear left (south) for Iron Mine Bay. Right leads south/southwest, ending in another 1 km (0.6 mi) on Pike Point. Reach the **Iron Mine Bay** overlook at 1.6 km (1 mi). There are toilets and a shelter here. Follow the coast trail left (southeast). This will remain your general direction of travel for most of the trip, until Beechey Head.

Shortly after the trail goes inland through a forested gully full of alders, reach a junction at 2.6 km (1.6 mi). The Coppermine road/trail forks left (northeast). Continue on the coast trail. Reach another junction at 3.8 km (2.4 mi), where the park Heights road/trail forks left (northeast). Again, continue on the coast trail. The shoreline here offers a cormorant-roost viewpoint.

Nearing Cabin Point, ascend a steep, rocky outcropping. The trail then veers inland to round a gorge. Thick salal bushes make it difficult to recognize where you must descend. Watch closely for a worn path and yellow blaze. Don't go too far inland. Stay aware, in case you have to backtrack and try again.

At 5 km (3.1 mi) arrive at **Cabin Point**, where a restored trap shack serves as a comfortable shelter. Most hikers will be here about 2.5 hours after leaving Pike Road trailhead. A minute beyond Cabin Point, ignore the left fork leading inland to Aylard Farm. Proceed on the coast trail.

Pass a rectangular cove with stone walls and a black pebble beach. Approaching **Beechey Head**, an island is visible in Juan de Fuca Strait. At 7.6 km (4.7 mi), where the trail curves along the bay just west of Beechey Head, there's a picnic table and a shelter with benches.

After rounding Beechey Head, your general direction of travel is northeast for the rest of the trip. Alldridge Point is visible ahead. Pause there to appreciate Coast Salish petroglyphs on a boulder at water's edge. From here, it's about a 20-minute hike to Aylard Farm trailhead.

At 10 km (6.2 mi), about 15 minutes past Alldridge Point, reach a junction in **Becher Bay**. Fork left to arrive at **Aylard Farm trailhead** in a couple minutes. Proceed right to follow the coast trail slightly farther. It curves west to **Creyke Point**. From there you can quickly circle back to the trailhead.

Trip 2
Forbidden Plateau

Location	Strathcona Provincial Park, Vancouver Island
Round trip	22 km (13.6 mi) to subalpine ridge below Mt. Albert
Elevation gain	380 m (1246 ft) to subalpine ridge below Mt. Albert
Time required	8 hours for subalpine ridge below Mt. Albert; 11 hours for Mt. Albert summit; 2 days for Mt. Albert summit and Frink/Castlecrag traverse
Difficulty	Easy to Challenging
Maps	Forbidden Plateau 92 F/11; BC Parks brochure; *Mt. Washington Marmot Forbidden Plateau* tabloid

OPINION

The name *Forbidden Plateau* comes from Native legend. Throughout history, people have labeled *taboo* those areas they'd yet to explore because the physical and mental challenges seemed overwhelming. World leaders as recently as 510 years ago accepted as gospel maps that stated "Here there be dragons." Haven't gone? Looks threatening? Must be a bogeyman there. Thus, aboriginal people once believed that these forbidding mountains in what is now Strathcona Provincial Park concealed evil spirits that would devour women and children who dared trespass.

Apparently, the spirits are no longer terrorizing the neighbourhood. Maybe they folded their tents and skedaddled. Today, the only hazard you'll encounter on Forbidden Plateau is the cantankerous terrain itself. Beyond the initial boardwalk, the trails are rough, because the land is rocky, rooty and muddy. But that's nothing to complain about, considering where you are. These island mountains are a primeval breed. Unruly. Craggy. Staggeringly steep. Which makes Forbidden Plateau a welcome anomaly. It is, after all, a plateau. Here you'll find Strathcona Provincial Park's

Moat Lake, below Castlecrag Mountain

easiest hiking and most extensive trail network. And this is the park's only subalpine-zone trailhead. It saves hikers several hours of sweaty toil through viewless forest. It's even accessed by paved road. Within minutes of leaving your vehicle, you'll enjoy level hiking through luxurious meadows fringed by graceful western hemlock and Douglas fir. The Canadian Rockies this ain't. The epidemically popular adjective *awesome* has no use here. But you will see some of Vancouver Island's loveliest backcountry.

Many dayhikers feel they've adequately sampled the plateau's atavistic atmosphere by the time they reach Circlet Lake junction— a 19.4-km (12-mi) round trip from Paradise Meadows trailhead. The junction doesn't afford a climactic view because it's below treeline, but shortly beyond, the trail deteriorates to a gnarly route and steepens dramatically, heading for Mt. Albert Edward.

Mt. Albert (let's abbreviate that tiresome name) is the area's highest peak. From Circlet Lake junction, it's just 1.3 km (0.8 mi) to a subalpine ridge with a panorama that includes Mt. Albert above and Moat Lake below. But the short distance is deceptive. Allow at least half an hour to claw your way up this demanding stretch that comprises a steep, muddy slope and an even steeper scree gully. If you have the time and energy, go. The vista will make your dayhike complete.

Atop the subalpine ridge, scramblers can continue without difficulty to Mt. Albert's 2094-m (6868-ft) summit. From the trailhead, it's a 30.4-km (18.8-mi) round trip gaining 994 m (3260 ft). Dynamos who start early can pull it off in an 11-hour dayhike. Carry the topo map to guide your ascent.

Want an even longer option? Traverse Mt. Frink and Castlecrag Mtn, then continue around Moat Lake. Include an excursion to the summit of Mt. Albert, and your total circuit distance from the trailhead will be 32.8 km (20.3 mi). Total elevation gain: about 1124 m (3687 ft). That would be a monster dayhike in light of how rugged the terrain is beyond Circlet Lake junction. So break it into a two-day backpack trip, spending the night at Circlet Lake.

However long you intend to hike on Forbidden Plateau, be aware that these mountains snag foul weather. Even in mid-summer, the plateau can be engulfed in cloud and drizzle, while the sun shines on Courtenay. So try to wait for a brilliant forecast. But bring warm clothes and a full set of raingear, regardless.

FACT

Before your trip

Study the Strathcona Provincial Park brochure/map, as well as *The Mt. Washington Marmot*—an annual, advertising tabloid containing a Forbidden Plateau map/trail guide. Call Strathcona Park (250-337-2400) to receive one by mail. Or pick them up at the trailhead ranger cabin.

If backpacking, check the map for core-area boundaries. Within the Forbidden Plateau core area, camping is permitted only at Kwai Lake, Circlet Lake, and Lake Helen Mackenzie. The fee is $3 per person, per night. As of 2001, there's no charge for random camping outside the core area.

By Vehicle

From Hwy 19 at **Courtenay**, drive west on Strathcona Parkway. Follow signs to Mount Washington Ski Area. At the junction where a sign points left (straight) for Forbidden Plateau, go right (northwest) on Condensory Road for Mt. Washington. Set your trip odometer to 0.

0 km (0 mi)
Starting northwest on Condensory Road.

8 km (5 mi)
Cross the Island Hwy.

8.6 km (5.3 mi)
Bear Left.

9.8 km (6.1 mi)
Proceed straight through the junction and begin ascending.

24 km (14.9 mi)
Arrive at Mt. Washington Ski Area. Continue ascending on paved road.

25.1 km (15.6 mi)
Fork left to Paradise Meadows parking lot, signed for Strathcona Park.

26.8 km (16.6 mi)
Bear left into the trailhead parking lot. There's a ranger cabin here, at 1100m (3608 ft.)

On Foot
The trail initially descends, heading generally southwest. In the first 0.3 km (0.2 mi) bear right, passing two left forks for Paradise Meadows loop. Extensive boardwalk reduces hikers' impact on these moist, subalpine meadows.

At 3 km (1.9 mi) arrive at a junction near the north shore of **Lake Helen Mackenzie**. Turn right, gradually curving south around the west side of the lake, which is barely visible through the dense, mature forest of alpine fir and mountain hemlock. Left leads 1.2 km (0.75 mi) east to Battleship Lake where another left turn leads north—back to the trailhead.

Passing Lake Helen Mackenzie, the trail rises over a low ridge, then drops into meadows. Reach a **map/sign and ranger hut** at 6.1 km (3.8 mi), 1264 m (4146 ft). Strong hikers will be here 1½ hours after leaving the trailhead. Five minutes beyond, reach a signed junction. Left leads south to Kwai Lake. Stay right (west) and ascend, heading toward Circlet Lake—3.9 km (2.4 mi) distant. In a few minutes, bear right again. Left is **Hairtrigger Lake** and a view southwest to Mounts Albert and Regan.

Reach a junction at 8.1 km (5 mi), 1180 m (3870 ft). Left loops back to Kwai Lake. Go right for Circlet Lake. From here, it's 2.2 km (1.4 mi) to Circlet Lake and 7 km (4.3 mi) to the summit of Mt. Albert.

At 9.7 km (6 mi), 1220 m (4000 ft) reach **Circlet Lake junction**. Fast dayhikers will be here in 2½ hours, moderately-paced backpackers in 3½ hours. Go left for Moat Lake, Mt Albert, and the Frink/Castlecrag traverse. Right immediately passes an unnamed lakelet, then drops northwest, arriving at Circlet Lake campground in 0.6 km (0.4 mi). A rough trail rounds the north end of Circlet, crosses the outlet stream, then heads generally northwest, descending 80 m (262 ft) to reach Amphitheatre Lake in 1.3 km (0.6 mi). The unnamed lakelet just north of Circlet Lake junction is a good place to rest before starting the steep climb to Mt. Albert. From the junction, the summit is still 5.4 km (3.3 mi) distant and 874 m (2867 ft) higher. Allow 3½ to 4 hours one way.

About 200 meters (220 yards) southwest of Circlet Lake junction, reach **Moat Lake junction** in a marshy clearing. Left (south) is a rough route to Moat Lake. If you complete the Frink/Castlecrag traverse described below, you'll return that way. For now, bear right. The trail soon deteriorates to a seriously steep, rugged, rocky, rooty route. At 1378 m (4520 ft), about 25 minutes from the Moat Lake junction, reach a junction in a **very steep scree gully**. For Mt. Albert, go left and assault the gully. Right leads to 1820-m (5970-ft) Jutland Mtn.

It takes about 10 minutes to surmount the gully. Immediately above, attain a revelatory vantage atop a **subalpine ridge** at 11 km (6.8 mi). The outlier of Mt. Albert is visible west/southwest. Assess the ascent route from here. Proceed a short way across the ridge to overlook Moat Lake southeast. Dayhikers not intending to summit Mt. Albert should turn around now.

From the alpine ridge, hike west about 20 minutes to the base of Mt. Albert's outlier. Ascend it. On top, turn left (south/southwest). Follow the crest roughly 2 km (1.2 mi) to about 1860 m (6100 ft). Then go right (west) 1.7 km (1.1 mi) up the ridge to reach the 2094-m (6868-ft) **summit of Mt. Albert**. Mt. Regan is visible nearby north. Hope and Charity lakes are south, far below.

At the 1860-m (6100-ft) point, turn left (south) to traverse Mt. Frink and Castlecrag Mtn, loop counterclockwise around Moat Lake, and return to Moat Lake junction. In 1.4 km (0.9 mi), reach the 1940-m (6363-ft) **summit of Mt. Frink**. Descend 380 m (1246 ft) southeast toward the south side of Castlecrag Mtn. Fortunately, you don't have to regain all that elevation. Resuming the ascent, climb only to 1610 m (5281 ft) on the eastern outlier of 1760-m (5773-ft) **Castlecrag Mtn.** Then descend moderate slopes northeast. Finally, hike north along the east side of **Moat Lake.** Intersect established trail at **Moat Lake junction.** Total circuit distance since departing the junction: 13 km (8.1 mi). Or 16.4 km (10.2 mi) if you summited Mt. Albert.

To see more of Forbidden Plateau, don't retrace your steps to the trailhead. Instead, turn right (southwest) at the junction before Hairtrigger Lake. Return via Kwai, Croteau, Lady and Battleship lakes. Though the distance is comparable, the scenery doesn't change significantly, and the descent to Kwai and Croteau necessitates a climb to Paradise Meadows that you won't incur if you simply go back the way you came.

Trip 3
Strathcona Provincial Park

Location	central Vancouver Island
Round trip	12 km (7.4 mi) to Bedwell Lake;
	14 km (8.7 mi) to Flower Ridge
Elevation gain	600 m (1968 ft) to Bedwell Lake;
	1182 m (3877 ft) to Flower Ridge
Time required	6 to 8 hours for Bedwell Lake;
	8 to 9 hours for Flower Ridge
Difficulty	Moderate to Challenging
Maps	Bedwell River 92 F/5; Buttle Lake
	92 F/12, Forbidden Plateau
	92 F/11; BC Parks brochure

OPINION

Much of Strathcona Provincial Park is accessible only to robust, intrepid, experienced mountaineers. These shaggy-walled mountains and incisive canyons will thwart hikers of only average motivation and endurance. Cross-country routefinding is necessary to reach most of the premier scenery. The park's few trails are generally grueling—steep, rocky, muddy, brushy—and demand a long hike before reaching worthwhile destinations. Because the valleys plunge nearly to sea level, trekkers face colossal climbs through forest to attain views in the subalpine zone. A couple trailheads are boat access only, adding hassle and expense to the ordeal.

There are, however, three trails that you gotta hike in Strathcona—even if you'll never make the Canadian Mt. Everest Team. All are suitable for keen, strong, intermediate hikers. All afford reasonable access to desirable goals: meadows, subalpine lakes, alpine ridges. And all are in the park's developed core areas. One is Forbidden Plateau (Trip 2), from Mt. Washington Ski Area. The others—Bedwell Lake and Flower Ridge—are described here. Both start near the south end of Buttle Lake.

Still, Flower Ridge is decidedly steep. Only the Bedwell Lake trail is free of heart-pounding ascents and knee-grinding descents. And from Bedwell, you might want to forge on to Cream Lake.

Flower Ridge, viewed from Phillips Ridge

So get fit. And bring trekking poles. They give you 4WD torque on the way up; anti-lock-brake traction on the way down.

Visiting Vancouver Island? Devoting a single day to the mountains? Hike up Flower Ridge if you're ambitious, Bedwell Lake if you're less so. We rank Forbidden Plateau third among the island's high-country hikes. But be aware that mainland B.C. offers immeasurably superior mountain hiking. What distinguishes the island are coastal trails. Our favourite is just outside Victoria, on East Sooke peninsula (Trip 1).

Planned and built by BC Parks, Bedwell Lake trail is deluxe by Strathcona standards. It even has steel stairways. So it's a relatively easy way to sample the rugged beauty of the park's subalpine backcountry. From Bedwell, a bootbeaten route continues to photogenic Cream Lake. It's an additional 10-km (6.2-mi) roundtrip gaining 527 m (1730 ft). Accessing Cream this way is saner than via Price Creek trail, which climbs 1200 m (3936 ft) in 8.5 km (5.3 mi), including 500 m (1640 ft) in the final 1.4 km (0.9 mi). Another Strathcona misery march.

Speedy zealots can tag Bedwell and Cream on a dayhike. Allow four hours for the round trip to Bedwell, five hours for the Bedwell to Cream round trip, plus a couple hours for resting and wandering. That totals eleven hours. It's feasible late-July through mid-August, if you start by 8 a.m. Otherwise, visiting Cream necessitates backpacking to Bedwell, then dayhiking from there. Keep in mind: Bedwell is prime black-bear habitat. Listen to the audio cassette *Bears Beware*, described in the back of this book. Camp only in a designated site.

Flower Ridge is a breathtaking hike, literally: you'll climb 1160 m (3805 ft) in 6.5 km (4 mi). But there are reprieves. And the trail culminates with an aerial view of Buttle Lake and a panorama that sweeps across the heart of Strathcona Park. On the crest, you can stride freely and gaze at distant peaks. Camping on top is appealing, but the steep ascent and a lack of water makes backpacking here unfeasible for most people. Even dayhikers must carry all the water they'll need.

FACT

Before your trip
Read *Backcountry Permits*, on page 6.

By Vehicle
On Vancouver Island, drive Hwy 19 north to Campbell River. Then go west on Hwy 28, signed for Gold River and Strathcona Provincial Park. In 48 km (29.8 mi), turn left (south) on Strathcona Road. Set your trip odometer to 0.

0 km (0 mi)
Starting south on Strathcona Road.

26 km (16.1 mi)
Pass Ralph River Campground, on the right.

29.6 km (18.4 mi)
Reach the parking lot for Flower Ridge trail, on the left, just north of Henshaw Creek. The trailhead is just southwest of the creek. Elevation: 228 m (748 ft).

34.4 km (21.3 mi)
After crossing the shallow south end of Buttle Lake at Thelwood Creek, turn left (south) onto Jim Mitchell Lake road. Pavement ends. It's rough but passable in a 2WD car.

41.2 km (25.5 mi)
Reach **Bedwell Lake** trailhead parking lot, at 500 m (1640 ft).

On Foot

Bedwell Lake

Follow the trail south. Soon cross a bridge to Thelwood Creek's east side. Begin ascending the forested valley. Near 1.5 km (0.9 mi) the trail jogs left (southeast). Contouring south, the ascent eases. Near 2.5 km (1.6 mi) cross a bridge to the creek's southwest side and continue ascending. At 3.3 km (2 mi), 1000 m (3280 ft), most of the elevation gain is behind you. Proceed south through subalpine meadows. Reach a junction at 4 km (2.5 mi). Right leads 300 meters (330 yards) to Baby Bedwell Lake and a campground with 6 tent platforms and a pit toilet.

The main trail continues along the southeast shore of Baby Bedwell Lake to reach the northeast shore of 68-hectare **Bedwell Lake** at 4.5 km (2.8), 953 m (3125 ft).

Reach Bedwell Lake campground at 5.7 km (3.5 mi), on the southeast shore. It has 10 tent platforms, a food-hanging pole, and a pit toilet. Just southwest of Bedwell Lake are two smaller lakes. To find them, follow the route around Bedwell's northwest shore, then head south.

From Bedwell Lake campground, a route leads generally east 5 km (3.1 mi) to **Cream Lake**. Follow it with the help of a topo map and compass. It begins with a steep climb east to a cascade. Just beyond, pass the north shore of Little Jim Lake at 1240 m (4067 ft). Continue ascending southeast, then contour into Drinkwater/Bedwell Pass. Wildflowers are profuse here in summer. Ascend northeast, top out at 1370 m (4495 ft), then drop southeast to reach Cream Lake's south shore at 1260 m (4133 ft).

Flower Ridge

After a steep start, the trail ascends gently, heading southeast. Hike through open forest of western red cedar, western hemlock, and Douglas fir. Mountain hemlock and subalpine fir thrive above.

At 1 km (0.6 mi) the trail grazes Henshaw Creek. After a brief level stretch, ascend steeply south. About an hour up, watch for spurs leading west to views of Buttle Lake and distant peaks.

Near 3 km (1.9 mi), 660 m (2165 ft), reach a bench. Camping is feasible here because water is available. The trail then jogs southwest before continuing the steep ascent south. From a burn, attain a view southwest to 1814-m (5950-ft) Mt. Myra.

South of another short, level reprieve, the trail deteriorates. You're still on the west side of the ridge. A steep route leads to the top. Crest the ridge at 5.5 km (3.4 mi), 1220 m (4002 ft). The going is now much easier. Views are constant. Backpackers will soon arrive at suitable campsites in a broad flat area.

Follow the ridge south. Proceed as far as your energy and the daylight will allow. Near 6 km (3.7 mi), the crest rises to a 1410-m (4625-ft) knoll. Go over the top to continue to the next flat area at 6.5 km (4 mi). Hiking remains easy for a couple more kilometers. Price Creek canyon is far below to the right (west). Eventually, Cream Lake is visible southwest, above the end of the canyon.

Trip 4

Lake Lovely Water

Location	Tantalus Provincial Park, near Squamish
Round trip	10 km (6.2 mi)
Elevation gain	1128 m (3700 ft)
Time required	4 to 5 ½ hours up, 2 ¾ to 4 hours down
Difficulty	Challenging
Maps	ITM Garibaldi Region; Cheakamus River 92 G/14; BC Parks handout

OPINION

The Tantalus Range has chutzpah. Starting nearly at sea level, wearing glaciers like armor, these bold peaks rear their heads as high as 2575 meters (8450 feet). Visible from Highway 99 and the Squamish Valley road, their defiant stance goads hikers to venture closer. This trail is one of the few allowing people of average strength and normal pain threshold to respond to that intimidating invitation.

At trail's end is a resplendent mountain cirque cupping a high sub-alpine lake that lives up to its name. It's the Coast Mountain equivalent of the Canadian Rockies' Lake Louise. The difference is that here you have to pay. The price of admission is a wickedly steep ascent. Though fit hikers can make this a rigorous day trip, it's worth hauling a full pack so you can make the most of your accomplishment.

The trail to Lake Lovely Water is even steeper than that to Wedgemount Lake (Trip 9). In places, you can look down and see the hiker behind you—between your legs. The trail is narrow, often no wider than two boots, but it's almost brush-free, and despite the radical grade it's in decent condition. Otherwise this trip would be a climb instead of a hike. Still, some hikers might be uncomfortable traversing the steepest slopes next to the creek gorge, where you have to grab hold of roots and haul yourself up.

Unless you have muscles like Popeye, the way to experience anything approximating pleasure on a hike this demanding is to clear your mind. Eliminate discomfort by relinquishing judgment and comparison. Hike with a zen attitude of calm alertness. If you're fully aware of each moment, nothing more, the duration or difficulty of the hike is not

Lake Lovely Water

an issue. The child in the back of your mind asking "When are we gonna get there?" disappears. You stop nagging yourself with progress reports and simply hike, one step at time. You just know you'll get there when you get there. Observe each beautiful, ancient tree in this lush rain forest, and your impatience to escape the trees will subside. (Good thing, since even the lakeshore is treed.) By not precluding enjoyment until you reach the destination, you might experience something even deeper en route.

About 1 ½ hours up, the trail is near Lovely Water Creek and crosses several tributaries. You'll occasionally see the creek cascading through the mossy gorge. Approaching the lake, you'll climb beside powerful falls generating a refreshing blast of mist. It's one of the few places on the entire trip where you can truly relax, without being annoyed by flies. Start preparing for them now. Practice flapping your arms around your head. Or bring a head net.

The hut is an inviting one—solid, spacious, clean, comfortable. And it has two rowboats. If you're an Alpine Club member, or if no members are around to use them, you could row into the middle of the lake for an IMAX perspective of this incredible setting. Also consider hiking to Lambda Lake. Round trip from the hut takes only half a day. Or you can camp there. From Lambda, continue exploring northwest into the basin beneath 2317-m (7600-ft) Serratus Mountain. Allow a full day for that if you're staying at the hut.

Omega, Pelops, Niobe, Pandareus, Ionia, Serratus, and Alpha peaks surround Lake Lovely Water. Like Sirens, they lure climbers onto the rock and ice. Hiking to the lake seems an impressive feat, until you look up and imagine scaling higher. Alpha and Omega mountains are favourites. Superheroes also travel the ridges from Iota Mountain to Mounts Sedgwick and Roderick.

In addition to all the little bugs, you might have some big bugs flying in. Currently three helicopter companies are licensed by BC Parks to land on the lake. But the frequent fly-overs by commercial and private planes are more bothersome.

FACT

Before your trip

To reach the trailhead, on the west bank of the Squamish River, you must canoe across. If you don't own a boat, you'll have to rent one or pay somebody to ferry you. Jay Bicknell of Kodiak Adventures in Squamish will take you across and meet you for the return at an appointed time. Cost: approximately $25 (2001) per person, round trip.

His pager (604-975-1275) is toll-free within B.C.

If you want to stay in the hut, make reservations with Roy Royston of the Alpine Club of Canada: 604-687-2711. Ask the BC Parks Garibaldi / Sunshine Coast District office (604-898-3678) for the park hand-out.

By Vehicle

From **Squamish**, at the traffic light by Esso and McDonald's, drive Highway 99 north 10 km (6.2 mi). Or, if you're heading south on Highway 99, continue 31.6 km (19.6 mi) past **Brandywine Falls** Provincial Park. For either approach, turn west onto Squamish Valley Road, across from the Alice Lake Provincial Park turnoff. Just over 2 km (1.3 mi) from Highway 99, stay straight (right) toward Cheekeye. Left leads into Squamish. At 3.7 km (2.3 mi) cross the Cheakamus River. About 100 meters beyond is a junction. Stay left on Squamish Valley Road.

You'll then drive through Native reserve. Look for a dirt road on the left at 6 km (3.7 mi), as the road curves then straightens out. Turn left here. It might be posted NO TRESPASSING. Continue in 2 km (1.9 mi). Park by the BC Hydro right-of-way, where powerlines cross the road and a cable spans the river. The elevation here is 30 m (100 ft). There's no ladder up to the cable car, and the car is locked to prevent the public from using it. This trailhead access might change in the future. Call BC Parks (604-898-3678) for confirmation.

On Foot

After canoeing to the west bank of the Squamish River, pick up the trail near the cable car tower. Follow it upstream (north), paralleling the river. Immediately stay left of an aluminum shed. In 30 minutes, cross a dry creekbed. Look for flagging on the other side. Clamber steeply over rocky terrain. The trail then improves and is frequently blazed. Soon reach the edge of a clearcut where you turn sharply left (southwest) and ascend.

Within 1½ hours, you'll see raging Lovely Water Creek. Within 2½ hours, at about 565 m (1850 ft), a path forks right, dropping 10 meters to a good rest spot beside slick rock and a waterfall. This is roughly where you enter Lake Lovely Water Recreation Area.

Within 3¼ hours, **cross a couple streams**. The trail soon tilts skyward again. If you're ascending on a clear day, you'll be thankful you're not in the sun on the other side of the gorge. Thirty minutes after the last stream, reach a gentle waterfall. Several minutes farther, there's another good rest spot where you again cross a stream. The elevation here is about 975 m (3200 ft).

You'll cross one more stream before attaining the first view over the Squamish and Cheakamus river valleys. Diamond Head is just a bit north of east. The Black Tusk is northeast. Here, the Lovely Water Creek gorge is a deep gash. The falling water pounds explosively.

Reach **Lake Lovely Water** at 1160 m (3800 ft). The Alpine Club hut is 200 meters to the right, across the mouth of the creek. Visit the hut's lake frontage for an unobstructed view of the water and surrounding mountains. Starting right (northwest) and continuing counterclockwise, you're looking at Alpha, Serratus, Ionia, Pandareus, and Niobe. To your left (south and a bit east) is nearby Omega Mountain.

You have a choice of **five campsites**: behind the hut; on a sandspit on Lovely Water's southeast shore; above Lovely Water's north shore, near Lambda Lake; at the northwest end of Lovely Water, or in the basin above.

Where you arrived at the lake, the rough, blazed trail left (south) leads to the sandspit in about 20 minutes. Hike up and down through dense forest (gaining 60 m / 197 ft) to the top of a boulder field. Scramble down the boulders to the sandspit, visible below. There's room for several tents, but you'll have no privacy. A creek originating in **Omega Bowl** flows into the lake here. The impressive bowl—buggy meadows, steep walls, no camping allowed—is a 10-minute scramble up the east side of the creek.

The **Lambda Lake basin**, above where Lake Lovely Water narrows, is easy to recognize. To get there, pick up the path from the hut and travel above Lovely Water's north shore. On the way, about 10 minutes from the hut, you'll pass a small sandy beach ideal for swimming. Reach Lambda Lake in about 1¼ hours.

Trip 5
Elfin Lakes / Mamquam Lake

Location	Garibaldi Provincial Park, near Squamish
Round trip	22 km (13.6 mi) to Elfin Lakes; 44 km (27.2 mi) to Mamquam Lake
Elevation gain	763 m (2500 ft) to Elfin, plus 152 m (500 ft) out; 1082 m (3550 ft) to Mamquam Lake, plus 473 m (1550 ft) out
Time required	6 ½ hours to 2 days for Elfin; 2 to 3 days for Mamquam
Difficulty	Moderate
Maps	ITM Garibaldi and Region; BC Parks brochure; Cheakamus River 92 G/14, Mamquam Mtn. 92 G/15

OPINION

Awe. Annoyance. Joy. Disgust. Relief. Peace. At-one-ness. You might experience all these feelings here.

Starting as close to treeline as any Coast Mountain trailhead allows, you'll quickly cruise into the subalpine zone. Soon, the fearsome snow-capped Tantalus Range, west across the valley, shouts for attention. The scenic intensity escalates on Paul Ridge, as colossal Mt. Garibaldi and mammoth Mamquam Mountain roar into your life. Beyond, the rocky, glacier-swept, creek-sliced barrens speak to the clarity that resides in us all.

The tiny Elfin Lakes, however, draw hikers from Vancouver like an Electrolux sucks dust. It often gets so crowded that a solitudinous soul can feel oppressed, alienated, claustrophobic. Sound like you? Trek past the lakes, where most people turn around. On a typical, teeming weekend, it wasn't until reaching glacier-fed Ring Creek that we felt liberated from the clutches of civilization. There, with nobody else in sight, we relished a moment of catharsis. Beyond: wilderness.

You can't expect tranquility at an alpine destination as beautiful and accessible as Elfin, unless you come mid-week. Easy backpack trips like this are scarce near Vancouver. The other obvious choice, Garibaldi Lake, is also inundated on weekends. Three-day weekends are worse, so stay away unless you're a Westender who only hopes to diminish the

Ring Creek

noise level a decibel and reduce the human factor by a few thousand faces. Use the extra time to drive farther into the mountains. Arrange to visit these places when most people are at work in the city. It's a hassle, but a private audience with the mountain gods will more than compensate.

Another disappointment here is the road-walk most of the way to Elfin. The rough trail cutting off 15 minutes along is no better; it's more difficult and locked in trees. The scar of the road is ugly, but lift your eyes: roads provide views. This one also enables hikers and bikers to accommodate one another. Yes, bikers. BC Parks allows them to pedal as far as Elfin. It's phenomenal cycling country—another reason you'll have to forego any sense of hinterland until after the popular lakes.

Next problem. There are only two desirably-located campgrounds. One is just below Elfin Lakes, the other at Mamquam Lake. On weekends, the Elfin campground can be a hikers' ghetto. If it's full, you'll be exiled to an overflow lot where you and other refugees must pitch your tents next to each other. You're likely to find a vacant site at distant Mamquam Lake, but if your time is limited, camping there might preclude the side trip to Little Diamond Head, which starts near Elfin. Backpacking all the way to Mamquam in a day is a challenge, but possible if you're exceptionally fit.

The Mamquam campground is in a wonderfully wild setting. Getting there you'll traverse a fascinating moonscape. So at least dayhike from Elfin to the ridge above Mamquam Lake for Holy Cow! views of the lake, Mt. Garibaldi and skyscraping Pyramid Mountain. If you have time and energy on your way back, dash up the Opal Cone, remnant of an extinct volcano.

Okay, lecture time. Since this is a busy area, go out of your way to give others a little space. On the trail, turn your conversation volume down. At campgrounds, lower the cone of silence. And after dark, shut up!

FACT

Before your trip

Call the BC Parks Garibaldi District office (604-898-3678) and ask about the snow level along Paul Ridge. It could be snowbound through July if there's been heavy spring snowfall.

By Vehicle

From **Squamish**, at the traffic light by Esso and McDonald's, drive Highway 99 north 3.1 km (2 mi). Cross the Mamquam River and watch for the BC Parks sign (GARIBALDI) DIAMOND HEAD. At the traffic light, turn east (right) onto Mamquam Road. About 10 km (6.2 mi) from the highway, bear left at the sign. Arrive at the trailhead parking lot at 15 km (9.3 mi). The elevation here is 914 m (3000 ft).

On Foot

First, a geographic clarification. Diamond Head is the southernmost major peak on the Mt. Garibaldi massif. The main summit of 2679-m (8787-ft) Mt. Garibaldi is farther north. Atwell Peak is between them. From Paul Ridge, you can see Diamond Head nearby to the north. The trail curves around its southeast side to the moraine near Ring Creek. Mt. Garibaldi is visible from there. You're hiking in the Diamond Head area, which comprises Elfin and Mamquam lakes.

From the trailhead parking lot, start walking northwest on the logging road. Soon turn northeast, ascending moderately. The short, regrowing forest offers no protection from sun or rain. Within 20 minutes, the Tantalus Range is visible west. Eventually bigger trees line the road. Cross a creek 45 minutes up. After 1 hour, views of the Tantalus are better. At 5 km (3.1 mi), after about 1¼ hours, arrive at the tidy **Red Heather shelter**. It has tables and a woodstove. You're now in subalpine meadows punctuated by western hemlock. The **Red Heather campground** is 100 meters past the shelter. It has 6 tent platforms, a line for hanging food, and a brook nearby. Diamond Head is visible north.

Reach a junction at 1455 m (4775 ft). Hikers go left on trail, bikers go right on road. Elfin Lakes are 6 km farther. The trail ascends more gradually than the road did below the shelter. Soon, you can see the Lake Lovely Water cirque, west beneath Omega and Alpha mountains. After 1 km (0.6 mi) on trail, rejoin the road and continue northeast along the northwest slope of **Paul Ridge**. Sky Pilot Mountain, Mt. Habrich, and Goat Ridge are visible, all slightly west of south. After rising to 1677 m (5500 ft) on Paul Ridge, the road drops 150 m (500 ft) to Elfin Lakes. Descending, you'll see clearcuts up Cheekeye Ridge (northwest) and throughout Mamquam valley (south). The Elfin campground is in the green basin below. About 1 km down Paul Ridge, you can look north and pick out a trail—a possible side trip from Elfin—climbing a meadowy slope to the saddle between Columnar Peak and the Gargoyles.

Reach **Elfin Lakes** at 11 km (6.8 mi). Total hiking time: about 3 hours. The lakes are on the edge of a little plateau. Swimming is allowed in the first, larger lake. Only use the second, smaller lake for drinking water; definitely purify it. The moraines and glaciers of Garibaldi are north. Mamquam mountain and icefield dominate east across Skookum Creek valley. The **Diamond Head Ranger Station** and an old lodge are beside the lakes. The Elfin Lakes shelter (34 bunks, propane and wood stoves) is 200 meters beyond. There's a fee for sleeping there: $10 per person per night, or $25 for a family. From the ranger station, the campground is 1.2 km (0.7 mi), Mamquam Lake 11.2 km (6.9 mi), the Saddle trail 1.5 km (0.9 mi), and the Opal Cone 6 km (3.7 mi).

The road descends northwest from Elfin Lakes to the campground turnoff (left). Five minutes past that turnoff, the signed Saddle trail forks left (northwest), gaining 457 m (1500 ft) in 2.5 km (1.6 mi) to the saddle between the Gargoyles and Columnar Peak—about a 2-hour round trip. To make it more challenging, ascend 170 m (558 ft) above and beyond the Gargoyles to 2100-m (6888-ft) **Little Diamond Head**.

Continuing north to Mamquam Lake, stay straight, still on an old road. Gradually descend along subalpine slopes into Ring Creek canyon, bounded by steep lateral moraines. The view of Mt. Garibaldi improves here. Orange posts in cairns atop boulders show where to rockhop across a fork of Ring Creek, at 1402 m (4600 ft). You're on trail now. Head north, descending 107 m (350 ft) to a bridged **crossing of Ring Creek**—roughly the halfway point between Elfin and Mamquam lakes. Fuschia monkey-flower and yellow asters flourish in the moraine soil.

Above the east side of Ring Creek, 17 km (10.5 mi) from the trailhead, reach a cairned junction. The smaller trail left leads north

Mamquam Mountain, from Paul Ridge

20 minutes on the barren, rocky slopes to a viewpoint of the Garibaldi Névé and the 1738-m (5700-ft) volcanic Opal Cone. For Mamquam Lake, stay right on the main trail. Proceed generally east.

Soon, cross flat, open barrens scratched clean by glaciers. Snow might linger here until mid-August, but there should be no difficulty hiking over it. From atop the next major moraine, at 1463 m (4800 ft), the trail drops to Zig Zag Creek at 1372 m (4500 ft). Continue 30 meters upstream for a narrower place to rockhop across. Then gain 152 m (500 ft) in about 30 minutes to **crest the last moraine** near 1524 m (5000 ft). The best views yet of Mt. Garibaldi (northwest) are from this moraine. The Rampart Ponds are a short distance north on the plateau. East are nearby Pyramid and Mamquam mountains. A steep talus slope on Pyramid drops to the forested shore of **Mamquam Lake**, visible below. To the south, clearcuts encroach on Garibaldi and Pinecone-Burke parks. From a cairned saddle on the moraine, the trail switchbacks 250 m (820 ft) down to the lake. The campground is at the south end, 22 km (13.7 mi) from the trailhead.

Trip 6

Garibaldi Lake / Black Tusk / Panorama Ridge / Helm Creek

Location	Garibaldi Provincial Park, near Squamish
Round trip	35 km (22 mi), includes the ridge on Black Tusk, and Panorama Ridge
Elevation gain	2450 m (8035 ft) total
Time required	2 to 4 days (3 to 4 hours one way to the lake)
Difficulty	Moderate
Maps	ITM Whistler and Region; BC Parks brochure; Cheakamus River 92 G/14, Whistler 92 J/2, Brandywine 92 J/3

OPINION

Wilderness with the edges sanded off. That's Garibaldi Park. The beauty is raw, but it's easily accessible on gently graded, well maintained trails. Signposts are frequent but unnecessary; the park is so popular, there will always be someone you can ask for directions. The major campgrounds are huge, accommodating dozens of tents. There's even a contingent of rangers here all summer. That's the way it is with areas of outstanding natural beauty, like Yosemite, Chamonix, Banff. They draw crowds, which require management, which diminishes the qualities that made the place appealing to begin with. Diminish but not destroy. Garibaldi Park is still magnificent. Go. Whether you need those edges sanded off or want to rough them up, you'll be witnessing one of the world's strongholds of alpine grandeur.

The scenery here is what we're all after on a Pacific Northwest hike. Big trees. Big lake. Big glaciers. Big meadows. And big views of the whole sprawling expanse. Visible across Garibaldi Lake's vividly coloured glacial water are Guard Mountain and the Sphinx Glacier. Just above and a bit northwest of the lake are the Taylor Meadows, which you can swing through on your way to or from the lake.

After pitching your tent at the lake or meadows campground, your first dayhike should be to Panorama Ridge, high above the lake's north shore. As the name implies, this is the penultimate vantage point.

Garibaldi Lake from Panorama Ridge

So you'll need a clear sky to enjoy it fully. Here, the view expands to include the Warren Glacier on 2694-m (8837-ft) Mt. Garibaldi to the south, as well as countless other spires and patches of ice in all directions. We prefer Panorama Ridge to the Black Tusk. The Ridge is a gradual ramble that leads you closer to the big glaciers and gives you the option of forging deeper into wilderness. The Tusk overlooks Highway 99, and from the summit there's no place to go but down.

The Black Tusk is the oddest and most distinct volcanic peak in Garibaldi Park. Ascending the alpine meadows toward this striking monolith is worthwhile. But plodding over scree to its base is no joy. And reaching the summit requires serious scrambling up a chimney—it's not for everyone. Instead, we recommend heading northeast to the bizarre, fascinating, volcanic ash flats near Helm Lake. Continue at least as far as the unbridged crossing of Helm Creek to witness the bare surrealism of the black soil and voluptuous cinder cones. It's possible to hike there, explore Panorama Ridge, and approach the Black Tusk, all in a dayhike starting from Garibaldi Lake or Taylor Meadows.

Don't have a couple days to spend in the area? Fleet-footed hikers can see the highlights in a single day by hustling to Garibaldi Lake, charging up Panorama Ridge, then racing back down through Taylor Meadows. The challenge is leaving so much beauty after spending so little time in it. You really should backpack, even though you'll probably be camping with a gaggle of other admirers. Ideally, make this a more adventurous, 24-km (15-mi) shuttle trip by hiking the Helm Creek trail through a broad, subalpine valley, past the Helm Creek campground, then down into lush forest and out along the Cheakamus River. Allow at least an extra day for side trips. Experienced cross-country trekkers can escape the carnival atmosphere by picking their own route southeast from the Garibaldi Lake ranger cabin, to Mt. Price or Clinker Peak.

The campgrounds at Garibaldi Lake and Taylor Meadows are both in exquisite settings. Relaxing on the shore of the 300-meter-deep, 7-km-long lake is wonderful. So is ambling through the enormous, flower-dappled meadows. If you're lucky, you'll snag one of the choice campsites on the lakeshore, or beside Taylor Creek. The creek has the advantage of drowning out other campers' noise.

Noise. It's infuriating. You go backpacking to get away from civilization, and you find yourself lying awake, listening to other campers yuk it up. At campgrounds as big and crowded as Garibaldi Lake or Taylor Meadows, all you can do is bring earplugs and try not to be noisy yourself. After dusk, whisper, especially when passing other tents. If you speak loudly, stay in the cooking shelters. If you want peace, pitch your tent as far away from the shelters as possible. Slam the door on the pit toilet and you deserve to be locked inside the fetid contraption. At Helm Creek campground, where the sites are close together with no foliage in between, keeping quiet is even more important.

Before you commit to a one-way trip starting at the Rubble Creek trailhead and ending at the Cheakamus Lake trailhead, a warning: Muscling the cable car across the Cheakamus River might be impossible for a solo hiker. Two people can do it if they're strong, but it's still a struggle.

FACT

By Vehicle

Driving Highway 99 north from **Squamish**, continue 28 km (17.4 mi) past the turnoff for Alice Lake Provincial Park. Or, if you're driving south from **Whistler Village**, continue 13 km (8 mi) past Brandywine Falls Provincial Park.

From either approach, look for the BC Parks sign indicating where you turn east toward the Black Tusk / Garibaldi Provincial Park trailhead. Proceed 2.6 km (1.6 mi) to the parking lot above Rubble Creek. The elevation here is 595 m (1950 ft).

If you're arranging a shuttle to hike one-way and exit via the Helm Creek trail, drive Hwy 99 north 9.8 km (6.1 mi) from Brandywine Falls

Provincial Park, or 7.7 km (4.8 mi) south from the big, brown sign WELCOME TO WHISTLER. A BC Parks sign warns of the turn east onto a logging road. Near the beginning, stay right where a road forks left. At 0.4 m (0.25 mi), turn left onto dirt. Drive another 7.1 km (4.4 mi) on the good gravel road to the trailhead at road's end, 838 m (2750 ft).

Before your trip

Bring money. Park rangers collect camping fees at Garibaldi Lake and Taylor Meadows. Helm Creek campground is free of charge.

On Foot

The trail to Garibaldi Lake is posted with white and green signs indicating elevation, as well as the direction and distance to various destinations. The directions are correct on all the signs. But the elevation and distance figures are sometimes contradictory. Overall, the white signs seem to be more reliable.

Ascending east above Rubble Creek, the trail is moderately graded and wide enough to allow two people to hike abreast and talk. The trees in this ancient forest are stately Douglas fir and red cedar. Cross a bridged creek within 30 minutes. After gaining 770 m (2525 ft) in 6 km (3.7 mi), reach a **signed junction** with benches. The elevation here is 1350 m (4438 ft). Right leads to Garibaldi Lake campground in 3 km (1.9 mi). Left leads to Taylor Meadows campground in 2 km (1.2 mi).

Staying right toward the lake, the forest opens up as you approach evidence of the area's volcanic past. Garibaldi Lake was formed in the mid-1850s when a lava flow from Mt. Price hardened into a natural dam. Visible directly south, across the canyon, it's called **The Barrier**.

The trail levels, re-enters trees, passes Barrier Lake, then Lesser Garibaldi Lake, and reaches a junction. Left leads to Taylor Meadows. Stay straight for **Garibaldi Lake**. Cross Parnasus Creek on a major bridge with yellow rope railing. About 25 meters beyond is another junction and the bridge over the Garibaldi Lake outlet stream. Here, 9 km (5.6 mi) from the trailhead, the elevation is 1470 m (4822 ft).

Right (south, across the bridge) is Garibaldi Lake campground. After arriving at the lake's northwest shore, you'll see a cooking shelter and a campground map/sign.

Left (staying north of the outlet stream) ascends 105 m (344 ft) in 2.5 km (1.6 mi) to a signed junction and a pit toilet in **Black Tusk Meadows**. Turning left (southwest) there, you'll gently descend 2 km (1.2 mi) through heather meadows to the Taylor Meadows campground and cooking shelter. From **Taylor Meadows**, at 1479 m (4850 ft), you can turn left and loop southeast back to Garibaldi Lake in 2 km (1.2 mi). Or you can continue descending generally west to the Rubble Creek trailhead in 8 km (5 mi).

Luxuriant subalpine meadows

Turning right (northeast) at the Black Tusk Meadows junction, you can proceed to the Black Tusk, Panorama Ridge, Helm Lake, or the Cheakamus Lake trailhead. In 0.5 km (0.3 mi) you'll reach a fork. Left (north) leads to the Black Tusk. Straight (northeast) leads to the other points just mentioned.

On the way to the Tusk, you'll ascend through lush, marmot-mad meadows profuse with wildflowers and laced with creeklets. Within 40 minutes start crossing a boulder field. The trail switchbacks steeply toward a ridge. The south face of the Tusk glares down from above. Views of Garibaldi Lake expand. The trail then angles left (northwest). After 1 hour, at about 2.5 km (1.6 mi), you'll attain the 2012-m (6600-ft) ridge just southeast of the 2316-m (7596-ft) Tusk. Many people will be satisfied stopping here. The Fitzsimmons Range is visible northeast. South, across Garibaldi Lake, you can see Clinker Peak just right of Mt. Price. Left and farther south is the Warren Glacier on Mt. Garibaldi. Castle Towers Mountain is southeast, north of Guard Mountain and the Sphinx Glacier. To reach the summit of the Tusk, continue west under the south face, pass a few chimneys and ascend the one that's flagged.

From where the trail forked left toward the Black Tusk, if you proceed straight (northeast) you'll pass Mimulus Lake and reach another fork in 2 km (1.2 mi). Left (north) on the main trail is Helm Lake. Right (east, then south) is **Panorama Ridge**—365 m (1200 ft) higher and 3 km (1.9 mi) distant. It's a decent trail the whole way; even kids can handle it.

Turning right for Panorama Ridge, the trail initially descends and passes just east of Black Tusk Lake. It then climbs through trees and heather to the rib that leads south to the ridgecrest. Above tree-line, follow the cairns. The 2105-m (6900-ft) summit affords a 360° view: Garibaldi Lake and Mt. Garibaldi are south, the Tantalus Range southwest, the Black Tusk northwest, the Cinder Flats north, Castle Towers Mountain southeast, ice everywhere. The mesa-like mountain in front of Mt. Garibaldi was named by a genius: it's called The Table.

Experienced cross-country travelers can follow the Panorama ridgecrest east, dropping 152 m (500 ft) then ascending to Gentian Peak on the south side of Helm Glacier. With overnight gear, you can descend to Gentian Pass and ascend the northwest slopes of Polemonium Ridge, just west of Castle Towers Mountain.

Continuing northeast on the main trail, from the junction with the spur trail up Panorama Ridge, you'll descend between **Helm Lake and the Cinder Cone**. Stay on the trail through here; bootprints in the cinder are like graffiti. When you reach **unbridged Helm Creek**, however, turn right (east) off trail for a level, 400-meter walk to a view of the Helm Glacier. As for negotiating the creek, if you don't want to de-boot and wade the calf-deep water, it's possible to hop across (try downstream) on boulders and sandbars. The trail north of the creek picks up downstream from where you arrived at the south bank. Ignore footprints heading upstream on the north bank.

Heading northeast from Helm Creek, you'll easily cross two more small creeks. The trail is adequate, though much narrower than it was near Garibaldi Lake. It's again well-marked: posts with reflectors keep you on track. The view ahead is of the U-shaped, subalpine Helm Creek valley.

Helm Creek campground, in a meadow at 1555 m (5100 ft), is 8 km (5 mi) from Garibaldi Lake. It has six tent platforms and a pole for hanging your food. **Empetrum Ridge**, just west of Helm Creek, allows easy scrambling. Empetrum Peak (1950 m / 6400 ft) affords a unique view of the Black Tusk's north wall.

From the campground down to the Cheakamus Lake trailhead it's also 8 km (5 mi). Fill your waterbottles at the campground. The trail immediately drops into dense forest and pulls away from the creek. At 1.5 km (0.9 mi) before reaching the trailhead, cross to the north side of the **Cheakamus River**. You have to muscle your way across in a cable car. It can be a struggle for only two people to pull it up at the other end, but it's possible if you're both strong. Getting in or out of the car is easier if you first hook the car to the tower. Be sure to unhook it when you leave, so the car is retrievable from either side. Ascend from the river and go left to reach the trailhead in 20 minutes of easy walking.

Trip 7
Musical Bumps

Location	Garibaldi Provincial Park, near Whistler
Round trip	19 km (11.8 mi) to Singing Pass
Loop trip	27 km (16.7 mi) out Fitzsimmons Creek
Elevation gain	727 m (2385 ft) for Singing Pass; 575 m (1885 ft) one way; both gains include the 345-m (1135-ft) ascent of Whistler Mtn.
Time required	7 to 8 hours for either option
Difficulty	Easy using gondola
Available	late July through early October
Maps	ITM Whistler and Region; Whistler Hiking brochure; Whistler 92 J/2

OPINION

It really hits people up here. They're smiling. Giddy. Carefree. Blissed out. 65-year olds romping around like kids. Children staring, enraptured, like wise sages. It's as if they're all on magic mushrooms. And if you're with them, you'll be feeling euphoric too. That's the power of the supernatural mountain scenery on this sustained, high-altitude ridgewalk.

The ski-area gondola whisks you above treeline—a 1136-m (3725-ft) ascent that would normally take hardened hikers three sweat-drenched hours. A spurt of energy then propels you to the ridgecrest, where the 360° peak-and-glacier panorama will consume you. Bring at least one full roll of film. You'll be snapping photos furiously. The Cheakamus Glacier flooding off Castle Towers Mountain and Mt. Davidson is just one of the heart-stopping sights. Another is immense, intense turquoise Cheakamus Lake, far below. Keep walking (floating is what it feels like in this airy environment) southeast, and the rock-lined path leads you to vast alpine meadows like the ones that inspired Maria in *The Sound of Music*. Maybe that's the source of the fanciful names: Piccolo, Flute and Oboe Summits (nicknamed the Musical Bumps), and Singing Pass.

This combination of effortless access and surpassing beauty ensures you won't be alone. Coming mid-week helps, but not as much as it does on more remote trails; tourists flock to Whistler all summer. Don't worry about it. What would be a bothersome crowd elsewhere is

Looking toward Fissile Peak from Oboe Summit

tolerable here, even enjoyable. Everyone's ecstatic. Tripping out, just like you. Besides, they tend to disperse past Harmony Meadows.

Of course, if the weather gets nasty, this could quickly turn into a bad trip. You'll be totally exposed to whatever the sky throws at you. Wind. Rain. Hail. Lightning. Pack all the gear you think you won't need. See our *Preparation* section. And try to save this hike for a gorgeous day when the only protection necessary is sunblock, and when you won't be sorry you spent all that money on the gondola.

Although it means walking the service road, first go to the summit of Whistler Mountain for a sensational view of nearby Brandywine Mountain, the glacier-globbed Tantalus Range, and the distant, sprawling Pemberton Icefield.

On the way back from Whistler Mountain, proceed down the Burnt Stew trail described below. Although most people reach the Musical Bumps via Harmony Lakes, our recommended higher route lets you experience a wilder side of Whistler but lengthens the time to Singing Pass by no more than an hour.

Ideally, make this a one-way backpack trip over the Musical Bumps to Singing Pass, up to wild and lonely Russet Lake, then out Fitzsimmons Creek valley (see Trip 8). Most people turn around on or before Flute Summit. But farther, on the east slope of Oboe Summit, the meadows are lusher and the lupine more prolific.

To give yourself maximum time on high, be at the gondola before they fire it up—probably 10 A.M. Check prices and hours of operation by calling 604-932-3434, or 1-800-766-0449. Moderate-paced hikers should be able to reach Flute Summit and return to the gondola in time to catch the last ride down—probably 5 P.M. Even swift hikers would be pressed to reach Oboe Summit, glimpse Singing Pass, and be back to the gondola before it stops running. Your options: continue 12.5 km (7.8 mi) from Singing Pass out Fitzsimmons Creek to Whistler, or walk back down the ski hill.

FACT

By Vehicle

In **Whistler**, turn east off Highway 99, onto Village Gate Blvd. There's a traffic light here, and a large brown sign WELCOME TO WHISTLER. Continue straight through the next light at Whistler Way. Reach a T-intersection in 0.4 km (0.25 mi) and go left on Blackcomb Way. Then immediately turn right into the long dirt parking lot. Park as close as you can to the far (southwest) end. The **gondola** is a few minutes from there, across Blackcomb Way. Nearby, from the bus loop, is the dirt road that accesses the Fitzsimmons Creek trail to Singing Pass. Before hiking the Musical Bumps one-way, read Trip 8.

On Foot

Carry all the water you'll need. The entire ridge is dry.

The gondola unloads at Roundhouse Lookout. Elevation: 1837 m (6025 ft). Beyond, the trail junctions are clearly signed. Walk straight from the gondola to a signpost.

Hike the **Harmony Lakes trail** only if you want to avoid the 345-m (1135-ft) ascent to Whistler Mountain. For Harmony, go straight toward the green chairlift, then left at its top and down into the bowl. In 3.9 km (2.4 mi) the Harmony Lakes trail is joined by the Burnt Stew trail, which is what you'll descend if you follow our recommendation and first ascend Whistler Mountain. It's 4.5 km (2.8 mi) to the Burnt Stew / Harmony junction if you go over Whistler Mountain. The added distance and elevation-gain will increase your hiking time to Singing Pass by one hour, possibly less.

If you choose to start left (southeast) on the Harmony Lakes trail, take either branch at the upcoming junction. The left fork loses about 50 m (165 ft), which you'll have to regain. Either way, you'll ascend gently around the east shoulder of Whistler Mountain before descending to the junction with the Burnt Stew trail. From there, proceed southeast toward the Musical Bumps.

If you follow our recommendation and first **ascend Whistler Mountain**, walk straight from Roundhouse Lookout toward the Ridge Lookout. Ignore the trail to Whistler Glacier. Looking south from Roundhouse, you can see Little Whistler Peak above the top of the Harmony Express chairlift; that's where you're headed. Walk the service road, ascending steeply. Below to your left are the Harmony Lakes. The Spearhead Range is east across Fitzsimmons Creek valley.

Reach 2115-m (6937-ft) **Little Whistler Peak** 1.9 km (1.2 mi) from Roundhouse. This is an especially fascinating viewpoint if you've hiked in Garibaldi Park. The Black Tusk, visible southwest, is a striking landmark. Below and east of the Tusk is Helm Lake. Panorama Ridge (Trip 6) rises southeast of it.

Proceed west on the gravel service road. Pass the top station chairlift. About 15-20 minutes from Little Whistler Peak, reach 2187-m (7173-ft) Whistler Mountain. Turn around and walk back on the service road. Before you pass the top station chairlift again, turn right (east) and descend the **Burnt Stew ski trail** into a gully. The upper end of the gully can be snow-covered through August, but the grade is gentle, and you can take giant, sliding steps. Initially there might be no sign or marked route, but where the ground is bare you'll find a meter-wide path lined with stones. That's the way to the Musical Bumps. Gradually curve southeast, descending to a signed trail.

At the sign for the Crescendo ski run, curve left around the rock clump. The trail to the Musical Bumps is 0.5 km (0.3 mi) farther. In the meadowy pass below you is Burnt Stew Lake (a pond) near 1815 m (5950 ft). The Harmony Lakes trail is northeast. Piccolo Summit is above to your right (south) as you descend east. Soon reach a signed junction with the Harmony Lakes trail. Turn right and proceed southeast to the Musical Bumps. Singing Pass is 5.6 km (3.5 mi) farther.

The trail ascends the east slope of Piccolo, but doesn't go over the top. After a minor descent to a pass, enter Garibaldi Park and ascend to 1982-m (6500-ft) **Flute Summit**. Visible south, 1160 m (3805 ft) below, is Cheakamus Lake (see photo on page 162). The Castle Towers Mountains and Cheakamus Glacier on Mt. Davidson are across and above the lake canyon.

Descending southeast to the pass between Flute and Oboe summits, the trail is marked with cairns where it becomes faint across rocky, grassy terrain. Looking east from Oboe, you can see the trail to Russet Lake switchbacking up emerald slopes. The meadows are lusher on the far (east) side of **Oboe Summit**, where you descend steeply through flowers to 1640-m (5380-ft) Singing Pass. At the pass, intersect the trail that descends Fitzsimmons Creek valley (left/north) to Whistler. Right ascends 2 km (1.2 mi) generally east to Russet Lake (Trip 8).

Trip 8
Russet Lake

Location	Garibaldi Provincial Park, above Whistler
One-way exit	14.5 km (9 mi)
Elevation loss	1280 m (4200 ft)
Time required	3-hour descent completing a 10-hour or 2-day trip
Difficulty	Moderate
Maps	ITM Whistler and Region; BC Parks brochure; Whistler 92 J/2

OPINION

Hiking to Russet Lake, you can begin to fathom the icy vastness of southwest B.C. Just above the lake, on an easily-attained ridge, is the quintessential trailside vantage for witnessing the raw resplendence of Coast Mountain glaciers.

The Cheakamus Glacier, between Castle Towers Mountain and Mt. Davidson, is a jolting sight—as spellbinding as the Athabasca Glacier in Jasper National Park. The appropriately named Overlord Glacier licks the earth from behind reddish Fissile Peak. All the east-facing glaciers on the immediate coastal mountains are visible as well. So is the enormous Pemberton Icefield. The neck-craning view from far below in Whistler only hints at these tidal waves of ice. Not even the Tantalus Range glaciers near Squamish are as magnificent.

But not all the marvels of this journey are frozen. You'll walk through hugely inviting flower-knit meadows for nearly 2 km (1.2 mi), from Singing Pass to the ridge above Russet Lake. Even if the tumbling ice weren't visible, and the trail ended here, it would still be a worthwhile trip. Beneath the ridge is dazzling turquoise Cheakamus Lake, a child of the glaciers. Then there's Russet Lake, in a stark, dramatic setting, lapping at the toe of Fissile Peak. You can enjoy staring at it without having to proceed from the ridge down to the shore.

Bear in mind, however, that this trip is now more difficult than it once was. Vehicles can no longer access the former Fitzsimmons Creek valley trailhead. Unstable slopes forced officials to close the road, requiring you to hike or bike an extra 5 km (3.1 mi) each way. That lengthens the uphill plod by 1½ hours and the downhill trudge by an hour. Result: dayhiking to Russet Lake is unattractive to average hikers and unfeasible for beginners. The round trip now totals 29 km (18 mi). The elevation gain is a whopping 1360 m (4462 ft).

The Spearhead Range, from the ridge above Russet Lake

It seems nature is attempting to withhold her pleasures from all but the keenly motivated and truly devoted. If you fit that description, then this premier area warrants an overnight trip. Russet Lake's stunning setting, as well as the luxurious ancient forest and cascading creeks en route, will more than reward your effort. Just be sure to detour from Singing Pass at least as far as Flute Summit to experience the wildly scenic Musical Bumps (Trip 7).

Can you afford the Whistler Mountain gondola? If so, descend the Fitzsimmons trail as the final leg of a one-way Musical Bumps traverse. If you must, or prefer to, earn alpine grandeur rather than buy it, ascending Fitzsimmons is really rather pleasant despite the nature-mandated extension. Dispatch the road to the former trailhead and you'll enter lovely forest. The trail is wide, smooth, free of roots and mud, easy to follow, and gently graded. You'll also avoid the crowds disgorged by the gondola. Even when you detour to the Musical Bumps, you'll do so via the less visited southeast end.

FACT

By Vehicle

Follow the directions for Trip 7 (page 56), into the long dirt parking lot at Whistler's ski area. If you're dayhiking, go right—as far as possible toward Lot 1, close to the bus loop. If you're backpacking overnight, you must park in Lot 4, near where you initially turned in.

On Foot

These directions assume you're following our recommendation in Trip 7: riding the **Whistler gondola** to the ridgecrest at 1837 m (6025 ft), then hiking over the Musical Bumps to the vast meadows of 1640-m (5380-ft) **Singing Pass** at 9.5 km (5.9 mi). Directions to Russet Lake continue below the next paragraph.

If you're hiking or biking up **Fitzsimmons Creek valley**, begin at the bus loop, near Lot 1. (Garibaldi Provincial Park intends to build an information shelter here.) Follow signs to Garibaldi Park and the Singing Pass trailhead. Hiker symbols help guide you through this initial section. It's potentially confusing until you depart the resort area. You must then hike or bike 5 km (3.1 mi), gaining 335 m (1100 ft), to the former trailhead at 1037 m (3400 ft). From there, it's 2 km (1.2 mi) to the Garibaldi Provincial Park boundary, beyond which mountain bikes are prohibited. Cross Harmony, Flute, and Oboe creeks (all bridged) while ascending good trail southeast through mature forest. Reach **Singing Pass** at 12.5 km (7.8 mi). Just past the trees, the right (west) fork ascends to Oboe Summit and the Musical Bumps.

Continuing to Russet Lake, go east from the junction in Singing Pass. (If you've descended from Oboe Summit, you'll take the right fork. If you've ascended Fitzsimmons Creek valley, you'll turn left.) The moderate, switchbacking ascent from the junction, southeast to the ridge above Russet Lake, takes 40-60 minutes. After climbing 340 m (1115 ft) above the junction, you'll be at 1928 m (6500 ft) high on the open slopes of the Fitzsimmons Range, with broad views of glaciers near and far. The dominant one, Cheakamus Glacier, is south. The Pemberton Icefield is northwest, beyond the Musical Bumps ridge and Whistler Mountain. Cheakamus Lake is visible southwest, 1100 m (2821 ft) below.

As you round the ridge and head east, Russet Lake appears beneath the reddish slopes of Fissile Peak. The Overlord Glacier peeks out from behind the peak's north face. It's an 80-m (262-ft) descent to the shore of Russet Lake, 14.5 km (9 mi) from the trailhead. Campsites (no charge in 2001) are at the lake's northwest corner, near an emergency hut built by the B.C. Mountaineering Club.

If you don't want to drop to the lake, but need to refill water bottles for the return trip, you'll find deep-enough dribbles crossing the trail 10 minutes back down from the ridge. Or wait until Oboe Creek, 40 minutes down.

Trip 9
Wedgemount Lake

Location	Garibaldi Provincial Park, near Whistler
Round trip	14 km (8.7 mi)
Elevation gain	1160 m (3805 ft)
Time required	5 to 7 hours
Difficulty	Challenging
Maps	ITM Whistler and Region; BC Parks brochure; Whistler 92 J/2

OPINION

Not all violence is ugly and destructive. When nature turns violent, it can be a beautiful act of creativity resulting in a magnum opus like the glacier-gouged Wedgemount Lake cirque. Here, long ago, great masses of rock heaved so dramatically, you can still feel the impact today—with your heart. It's as moving as any trail-accessible sight in the Coast Mountains; as awesome as the scenery prevalent in the Canadian Rockies.

You might have heard rabid descriptions of the ascent to Wedgemount Lake. It is severe. But it's not insane, or dangerous. If your workouts are limited to hanging on in a moving bus, Wedgemount could be your heart-attack hill. But even occasional hikers survive it and merely wake up sore the next morning. Wedgemount requires you to climb only 300 m (1000 ft) more than the Grouse Grind, which many Vancouverites hike regularly. And, unlike the Grind, what you'll see on the way up Wedgemount is inspiring. Compared to Lake Lovely Water (Trip 4), a setting of comparable beauty, Wedgemount is less demanding, especially when backpacking. You'll gain 1100 m (3600 ft) in 6 km (3.7 mi). If you're tempted by cheesey television ads for exercise gizmos, figure about 4 hours one way. Shoot for 2¼ hours if you have buns of steel.

Climbing through forest, the trail sidles up to rowdy Wedgemount Creek—a welcome diversion. The grade eases at times, granting you a reprieve. Crossing a rockslide adds variety (see photo on page 7). Then Wedgemount Creek lifts its skirt, revealing a 300-m (980-ft) waterfall. This is among the most impressive cascades in the Coast Range.

Wedgemount Lake

Even on a dayhike, bring warm clothing, so you can hang out in the lake basin a couple hours and gawk at the phenomenal surroundings. It's a waste to hike all the way up here, then have to leave in 15 minutes when you start shivering. Wedgemount can get cold, even on a nice day. Camping in the basin will ensure you have time to explore the area. Bring your tent. There's a hut near the lake, but it's a pit. Competent scramblers hungry for more height can pick any of several routes. Attain open views north by continuing 2 hours up the talused ridge on your left when facing the lake from the cirque lip.

Trekking poles will ease your ascent. This is your opportunity to discover what a difference they make. On the descent, poles will do more than protect your knees, they'll keep you from imitating that crazed bus in the movie *Speed*. Competent pole-wielding hikers can schuss down the rocks and roots in 2 hours. Anyone less agile, or empty handed, will be waddling safely like a porcupine and take at least 3 hours.

FACT

By Vehicle

From the **Whistler Village** turnoff at Village Gate Blvd., near the sign WELCOME TO WHISTLER, drive north 11.8 km (7.3 mi) on Highway 99. Or, from the 3-way junction just outside **Pemberton**, drive southwest 20.6 km (12.8 mi) on Highway 99. From either approach, turn east at the sign (GARIBALDI) WEDGEMOUNT LAKE. Cross railroad tracks and the Green River. Hit a T-junction in 100 meters. Go left on Wedge Creek FS Road. At 0.4 km (0.25 mi) curve right at a signed fork, then left at the next. Reach the parking lot at 1.9 km (1.2 mi). The elevation here is 760 m (2493 ft).

On Foot

The trail starts at the far corner of the parking lot. It ascends moderately through a brushy area. In 15 minutes cross large planks over plummeting **Wedgemount Creek**. Enter big timber. Head generally southeast. Soon, at a break in the forest, look west to glacier-topped Rainbow Mountain and north up the Green River valley. After ascending 440 m (1443 ft), the grade relaxes for 10 minutes.

The trail is rooty—typical for these mountains—but the roots are not major obstacles. With the roaring creek on your right, climb 215 m (705 ft) higher, then enjoy another reprieve. Strong hikers will be here in about 1Z\v hours. Then cross the base of a **boulder field**. Near 1524 m (5000 ft), you can see Wedgemount Creek plunging down the cliffs of Rethel Mountain. Near 1723 m (5650 ft), cross a creeklet, just before emerging onto **alpine slopes**. By filling water bottles here, day-hikers can later forego the 70-m (230-ft) descent to the lake for water.

The **final pitch** through rocks and heather is rugged, but you'll find good footholds as the route ascends. Views west and northwest over the Coast Range are tremendous. At 1950 m (6400 ft), reach the **lip of the Wedgemount Lake** cirque and enter the mountain sanctum.

Wedgemount Glacier tests its toe in the turquoise lake. 2905-m (9527-ft) Wedge Mountain, the highest peak in Garibaldi Park, rises to the southeast, its snowfields extending to the Weart Glacier higher above. Mt. Weart is northeast.

The best view of the lake is from the knoll to the right (north) as you enter the basin. Look for a boot-beaten path on your right as you cross the cirque lip. It climbs 10 m (33 ft) through heather and lichen-splotched rocks. On **top of the knoll**, you'll be just across the lake from the spires of Rethel Mountain.

From the cirque lip, the trail leads straight to the red B.C. Mountaineering Club hut and a smaller toilet hut. There are **campsites** sheltered among boulders, left (north) of the hut, and more sites on rock slabs higher up the heather slopes. Beyond the hut, north and a bit east, a path wanders 10 minutes to a cascade at the edge of heather. This is where competent scramblers will likely begin ascending the northerly ridge.

Trip 10
Joffre Lakes

Location	Duffey Lake Road
Round trip	11 km (6.8 mi)
Elevation gain	370 m (1214 ft)
Time required	4 to 5 hours
Difficulty	Easy
Maps	ITM Garibaldi Region; Duffey Lake 92 J/8

OPINION

The Joffre Lakes are to the Coast Mountains what Robson Street is to shopping in Vancouver. All the treasures are grandly displayed within tempting reach: three teal lakes in an achingly perfect mountain setting that includes a daunting glacier and striking cliffs. It's enough to entice shopaholics out of the city. Which is why you'll see people on the trail who've never carried much more than a Gucci bag. Though you'll probably leave them behind at the first lake, you still won't be alone. The high price you'll pay here is having to tolerate a crowd. On weekends, expect to see three dozen cars at the trailhead. On a long weekend, expect 50 cars. The beauty and accessibility is exceptional, but not worth suffering a Robson Street mob. Try to come midweek, or after Labor Day.

The trailhead starts high, at Cayoosh Pass, so the scenery is immediately lavish. The first lake would be worth hiking hours to see, but it's so close you could push a shopping cart to it in 10 minutes. The Matier Glacier, visible beyond, doesn't just hint of what's to come, it screams. Fledgling hikers will get turned on to the sport here. Veterans will appreciate the reprieve from stiff ascents and long, unscenic approaches. Fit dayhikers can reach Upper Joffre Lake in 1½ hours.

Though the trail is easier than most in the range, the boulder field 30-45 minutes in can be challenging to kids and anyone accustomed to groomed paths.

Cold-blooded swimmers will love the plunge-hole where Joffre Creek flows into a deep, sandy bowl at the northwest end of Upper Joffre Lake, near the bridged crossing.

Upper Joffre Lake and the Matier Glacier

FACT

By Vehicle

From the 3-way intersection at the Petro Canada station on the edge of **Pemberton**, drive Highway 99 northeast 30.5 km (18.9 mi) to the Joffre Lakes Recreation Area pullout. From **Lillooet**, at the junction of Highways 99 and 12, drive Highway 99 southwest 69 km (42.8 mi) to the pullout, at 1220 m (4002 ft).

On Foot

At the end of the dirt parking lot, walk the pleasant, gravel path through forest. Reach the north end of **Lower Joffre Lake** in about 5 minutes. Go right to continue to Middle and Upper Joffre lakes. Soon cross bridged **Joffre Creek**, then ascend gently through beautiful trees. Devil's club and ferns thrive here. You'll soon lose sight of the first lake as you climb above its west side. Ignore older, secondary trails branching right. Stay left on the main trail. Follow the orange blazes.

In about 20 minutes, descend left. Reach a **boulder field** and, soon after, traverse a brushy area where a stream is audible. Follow the pink flagging. Watch out for deep gaps between the boulders. Behind you (north) are Cayoosh Mountain and Mt. Marriott. After negotiating boulders for about 10 minutes, you'll be back on a rooty trail through forest. Descend 20 m (66 ft) to cross **Joffre Creek**.

About 1 hour after setting out, reach **Middle Joffre Lake** at 1540 m (5050 ft). There are good tent sites at the north end, where you arrive. No fires allowed. The trail continues on the east (left) side of the lake. At the south end, cross **Joffre Creek** again on two log bridges. After ascending a small rockslide, ignore a blazed path descending right, back to Middle Lake. Bear left toward Upper Lake and views of Matier Glacier.

At 5.5 km (3.4 mi), elevation 1590 m (5215 ft), about 20 minutes beyond Middle Lake, reach the north end of **Upper Joffre Lake**. You're entering the cirque created by 2713-m (8900-ft) Joffre Peak and glacier-draped 2774-m (9100-ft) Mt. Matier (both southeast) and Slalok Mountain (south). The trail stays above the rocky shore, soon reaching high-traffic campsites next to the bridged inlet stream.

Most hikers turn left (east) here, cross the creek, and pick up one of two faint, rough routes leading to desirable picnic spots and tent sites on a sandbar at the south end of the lake, near the booming waterfall. The lake level determines how many tents can fit on the beach.

At the bridged inlet stream, your other choice is to stay on the west (right) side and proceed south. The trail soon dwindles to a cairned, blazed route. Cross a boulder field and ascend to a forested saddle. The route then angles southeast, crosses the stream at a higher point, and ends below the snout of the glacier.

Trip 11

Stein Divide

Location	Stein Wilderness, near Pemberton
Round trip	28.6 km (17.7 mi) to Tundra Lake
Elevation gain	1265 m (4150 ft), includes the trek up the 4WD road; 305 m (1000 ft) going out
Time required	3 to 4 days
Difficulty	Challenging
Maps	ITM Stein Valley Trail, Garibaldi Region; Stein Lake 92 J/1

OPINION

The Coast Range has higher mountains, bigger lakes, and more impressive glaciers elsewhere. Yet the totality of the alpine Stein moves us more deeply than anyplace else we've trekked in the B.C. Coast Mountains. Check out the photo on page 164. It was taken from Table-top Mountain, just above Iceberg Lake, looking east at the Stein Divide—where this journey leads.

Wandering the boulder-strewn benches and flower-peppered slopes between Arrowhead and Tundra lakes is a sublime alpine experience. Meltwater creeklets are omnipresent. Ponds, tarns and lakes are set just far enough apart so you continually feel the thrill of discovery. The peaks are not fierce, but they're sufficiently imposing to keep your eyes flitting across the rock and ice. Intent on no particular destination, it's easy to spend many happy hours rambling in a single exquisite basin or scrambling up just one of the smaller mountains.

Watching the sun perform its morning and evening ablutions on the cliffs and snowfields in this wide-open expanse is ethereal. In the course of a day, you can see the water surfaces shift hues like kaleido-scopes: iridescent pink and blue at dawn; brilliant turquoise in the morning, glassy mirrors reflecting the landscape in the afternoon; and finally bronze, silver and charcoal in the evening. There's one body of water that's unearthly: Tundra Lake. It's an impossibly vivid, Milk-of-Magnesia-bottle blue. See photo on page 164.

Some people, thinking they can adequately sample the area in an afternoon, turn around at Lizzie Cabin. Big mistake. The western Stein

Near Caltha Lake

begins to climax just above, at Arrowhead Lake. That's where you enter the unique, magical alpine country. Though strong dayhikers can get there or perhaps farther before turning around, it's a waste to invest all that energy and miss camping in such blissful surroundings.

One of the rewards of backpacking in a wilderness area like this is camping where you please. Find a private, idyllic site, and you're home. It's a tension-relieving joy not to be forced to huddle next to others, as in the Garibaldi Provincial Park backcountry campgrounds. Here, your destiny is your own. Your sense of adventure deepens when you can opt to camp high on a ridge (like Tabletop Mountain) or near a lonely lake. Of course, with this freedom comes the responsibility of practicing Leave No Trace camping. Don't pitch your tent on grass or heather; limit yourself to bare dirt, gravel or rock slabs. Don't wash anything near a lake or stream; do it far enough away so you won't pollute the fresh water. Don't build a fire; carry a stove for cooking. Carefully bury human waste. Pack out all trash, including toilet paper.

Hiking the alpine Stein means facing rough-hewn trails and cairned routes. They work you hard, but they enhance the wild atmosphere. Children and neophytes will struggle here. You'll climb above Lizzie Lake on a narrow, slanted, muddy, deadfall-plagued, hacked-out gash of a trail. It often requires you to lift your boots as high as your waist. Past Lizzie Cabin, the going is easier though usually sloppy in the wet meadows. To reach the first alpine lake basin, you must then negotiate a steep, challenging boulder field. Following the intriguing, small trail from Arrowhead Lake toward Tabletop Mountain is easy. Later, the traverse from Cherry Pip Pass (see photo on page 162) toward Tundra Lake is across more awkward, ankle-eating boulders.

Other negatives? Bugs, of course. The samurai warrior strain. Both flies and mosquitoes. Come prepared to do battle. Another potential enemy here is heat, despite the high elevation. Above treeline, there's no shade except your tent. Bring a lightweight, long-sleeve shirt to block out harmful rays, as well as insects. Sunglasses are essential unless cataract surgery appeals to you. Also, extended alpine terrain means exposure in severe weather. Pack storm-worthy clothing and shelter.

Though the Stein is much less crowded than Garibaldi Park, you'll still have to explore off the beaten paths if tranquility and solitude are your goals. Midweek you'll see maybe a dozen other hikers on the route described here. The vantage points you'll hit along the way will reveal possibilities for exploration. Long and Rainbow lakes, for example, are easy to reach, southwest and southeast of Arrowhead Lake. From Long Lake, you can continue cross-country to Sapphire Lake, Crystal Tarns, and other unnamed, inviting alpine ponds. Or, on your way to Caltha Lake, scope out the rough trek southeast, high above Rogers Creek canyon, to achingly beautiful Figure Eight Lake. The truly hardy venture past Tundra Lake to Elton Lake.

FACT

By Vehicle

From the 3-way junction in **Mt. Currie**—east of Pemberton—drive 10.3 km (6.4 mi) northeast on Highway 99. Or, if you're heading southwest from **Lillooet** on Highway 99, drive 13 km (8 mi) past Joffre Lakes Recreation Area. From either approach, turn southeast at the bottom of a steep hill, onto the In Shuk-ch Forest Service Road. Drive this dirt road southeast along Lillooet Lake, past several Forest Service campgrounds. At 16 km (10 mi) Lizzie Bay Recreation Site is on the right. At 16.6 km (10.3 mi) turn left onto Port Douglas—Lizzie Creek Branch FS Road. Set your trip odometer to 0 here.

Ascend the valley, now on a narrow, rough road, with Lizzie Creek on your right. At 1 km (0.6 mi), where a lesser road ascends left, bear right, staying with the creek. Fork right on the lower road at 7.4 km (4.6 mi). After 8 km (5 mi), the road gets much rougher and steeper. Most people in 2WD vehicles will want to park here, beside the road. Those

Camping near the Stein Divide

with 4WD and the confidence to negotiate a narrow, steep road with an alarming dropoff on one side can continue 3 km (1.9 mi), gaining 320 m (1050 ft) to the road's end at Lizzie Lake.

On Foot

Without a 4WD vehicle, you'll be hoofing it at least 3 km (1.9 mi) up a steep, dusty road to Lizzie Lake, where the actual trail begins. There's no shade on these lower, clearcut slopes, so start early to avoid getting broiled by the sun.

Most people will start hiking the road at about 1005 m (3300 ft). (This is just before the orange road on the topo map intersects the broken black line designating a rougher road.) In a few minutes, come to a fork. Go left. There should still be a sign here pointing the way to Lizzie Lake. There's parking space here too, in case you kept driving and now want to bail out. Where the main road veers right (southeast) and a fork heads left up a ravaged slope into the East Fork of Lizzie Creek, stay right and start ascending steeply.

Strong roadbusters will cover the 3 km (1.9 mi) to the **Lizzie Lake** parking lot in about 1 hour. The elevation here is 1326 m (4350 ft). Follow the path toward the lake and turn left (southeast) where it intersects the **lakeshore trail**. A third of the way along the lake (0.5 km / 0.3 mi), look for the tree stump cut like a throne. Take the blazed trail left (east) from there and start ascending away from the lake. Walk through dense timber with a lot of deadfall. If you need to camp now or on the way out, there's a private, lakeview campsite here. Then the trail steepens. As you ascend, the trail periodically divides for short stretches. Often the left path requires less elevation loss and gain.

The trail levels at 1585 m (5200 ft) as it enters the rocky defile of the **Gates of Shangri-La**. Before descending a huge boulder slide to the refreshing creek, you can look east and see Arrowhead Mountain, which is where you'll enter alpine country and reach the first lake. The trail drops sharply through the Gates. Watch your footing here. The creek has gorgeous pools with sandy bottoms—tempting on a hot day. You'll also find a couple bare tent sites in trees close to the creek. Then the trail resumes through forest, reaching **Lizzie Cabin** about 10 minutes past the Gates. The cabin is at 1615 m (5300 ft). It's 3 km (1.9 mi) from the Lizzie Lake trailhead. The rickety cabin has a woodstove, a loft, table, and old foamies. Treat it kindly.

Follow the trail east of the cabin and soon cross to the south side of the creek. Climb a grassy slope into a basin where the trail levels outs then forks. The minor path right (south) leads to Long Lake. Go left (southeast), aiming for the cascade visible on the rock-face above. It's pouring out of Arrowhead Lake. As you get higher, nearing the lip of Arrowhead Lake basin, you can see glaciers northwest above Lillooet Lake.

After gaining 220 m (720 ft) from Lizzie Cabin, reach **Arrowhead Lake**, just above treeline, at 1835 m (6020 ft). Jump across the outlet stream and continue hiking north along the west side of the lake. There are good tent sites here, though you're likely to have company. From the short rise just west of the lake, you can see the Coast Mountains west and northwest. From the south tip of Arrowhead Lake, where you arrived, it's an easy 30-minute hike through rock-and-heather gardens to **Heart Lake**, in a bouldery, grassy bowl at 1935 m (6350 ft).

Ascend around the west and north sides of Heart Lake. Follow the cairned path toward the meadowy saddle visible to the east. Where the lake pinches out, there's a faint junction of paths. From here, a steep route heads directly up Tabletop. Look just east of north and you might recognize the namesake table. It's best, however, to stay straight and gently traverse east toward the saddle. Cross above and north (left) of the saddle's lowest point. If you want to go to Iceberg Lake (directly below the east side of the saddle), when the route starts rising steeply, stay lower, contouring southeast to the low point of the saddle. Keep in mind, Iceberg will lose the evening light earlier than Heart or Arrowhead lakes. Immediately southwest of Iceberg Lake, Arrowhead Mountain rises sharply.

From the **saddle**, as well as higher on the slopes of Tabletop Mountain, you can look east, across Rogers Creek canyon, at massive, ice-laden Mount Skook Jim. Caltha Lake is northeast in the large, level basin. With the aid of a topo map, you can pick out the cross-country route from Caltha Lake, southeast to the hidden Figure-Eight Lake basin.

Proceed north from the saddle, over the east shoulder of **Tabletop**, staying away from the steep drop into Rogers Creek canyon. Contour at about 2043 m (6700 ft), gradually curving northwest, then northeast. If you like to camp high, this is the place to do it—in favourable weather. Water should be available in meltwater pools and trickles.

To reach Caltha Lake, work your way northeast, gradually ascending, until you're just below the northeast ridge of Tabletop Mountain. Follow cairns along the prominent, boulder-strewn benchland. You might pick up a path for a while. Reach about 2088 m (6850 ft) on the gentle slope before cairns lead you down, on the east side of the ridge, to the trail zigzagging through meadows and rocks to 1905-m (6250-ft) Cherry Pip Pass.

Arrive at the pass 1 ¼ hours after leaving the east shoulder of Tabletop. You're now at the head of Rogers Creek canyon and can look southeast down its course. From here, follow the cairned, boot-beaten path 75 m (250 ft) up the north side of the pass along the ridge. The path stays just left of a few trees as it heads east toward the base of Tundra Peak. Then gradually descend east toward the broad, gentle, Caltha Lake basin.

The angling descent to **Caltha Lake** is across an immense boulder field that requires a lot of leaping, dancing and balancing—hard work with a full pack. Occasionally you'll tag onto traces of dirt path through patches of heather, but mostly just follow the cairns. The lake is now in plain view anyway. You'll cross a few meltwater creeklets big enough to refill bottles. Looking back, you can survey the shoulder of Tabletop that you traversed. The wall of fluted cliffs southeast, off Arrowhead and Tynemouth mountains, is stunning from this vantage. About 1 hour from Cherry Pip Pass, reach good trail that descends steeply at first as you proceed toward Caltha Lake. You don't have to descend all the way to Caltha, at 1814 m (5950 ft), if you're heading to Tundra Lake. Stay north of Caltha and travel northeast, across heather.

Looking northeast, you'll see a stream flowing down from a pass, in front of stunted trees. Aim for the stream and you'll pick up a path climbing to the 1966-m (6450-ft) unnamed pass, which forms the western boundary of Stein Valley Provincial Park. **Tundra Lake** is 107 m (350 ft) directly below the northeast side of the pass. The pass is about 45 minutes from the west end of Caltha Lake and 11.3 km (7 mi) from Lizzie Lake.

Tundra Lake is an intense blue (some say purple) similar to Oregon's famous Crater Lake. Looking east beyond the lake, you can see the sharp, ragged, snowcapped peaks of the Coast Mountains dwindle into dull, dry, meadow- and glacier-less ridges.

Rounding Tundra Lake's north shore is difficult but possible. The only place near the lake that's flat enough to pitch a tent is at the far east end. To continue from there to Stein Lake, Elton Lake, or around the east side of Caltha Peak to **Figure Eight Lake**, requires a topo map, compass, and advanced cross-country skills. To ensure safety, you'd also want a couple days of bombproof blue sky.

On your return trip, descending from the shoulder of Tabletop Mountain it can take as little as 1 ½ hours to Lizzie Cabin, and another 1 ¼ hours to Lizzie Lake.

Trip 12

Southern Chilcotin/Taylor Basin

Location	Carpenter Lake / Gold Bridge
Round trip	37 km (23 mi) plus side trips
Elevation gain	1340 m (4400 ft)
Time required	3 to 4 days
Difficulty	Moderate
Maps	Lillooet FS Spruce Lake Trails; Bralorne 92 J/15, Noaxe Creek 92 O/2

OPINION

The Southern Chilcotin is just a whisker outside the Coast Mountains. It's on the east edge, where icy peaks melt into the Interior Plateau. We offer a sampling from this wondrous country, for several reasons: (1) any serious hiker in southern B.C. will want to know about the Chilcotin; (2) you'll find few long-distance, flexible-itinerary backpack trips farther south in the range; (3) the easy-to-ascend ridgecrests here are a unique vantage, where you can peer south into the snow-capped Bendor Range at the north edge of the southern Coast Mountains; (4) within a half-day drive of Vancouver, the Chilcotin is more accessible for most people than similar mountain terrain in Mt. Edziza or Spatsizi Plateau parks; (5) it's a satisfaction-guaranteed hiking destination.

This is an intriguingly inconsistent land. Dusty dry yet meadowy lush. A see-forever alpine vastness that's also forested for miles. Peaks coloured junkyard rust on one side, golf-course green on another. You'll see all these surprises and more within a day's hike. We came away fascinated, scheming to come back and trek the entire area.

The topography here is unique in southern B.C. and unlike any in the southern Canadian Rockies. You're likely to feel like a stranger in a strange land. The ridges are rounded; the peaks blunt; the slopes mauve, cinnamon, charcoal, cobalt. Many of the summits are gentle, cliffless, yet the immensity of these formations clearly defines them as mountains. We were initially confounded by the area, but it grew on us rapidly. It has a mysterious appeal, a beauty that haunts long after you've left.

Overlooking Cinnabar Basin

The meadows are bigger than some airports. Brilliant flowers, wildly prolific and varied, keep your eyes dancing across the landscape. Some of the flowers are common elsewhere: lupine, aster, arnica, fleabane, subalpine daisy. Thistle are so numerous here, their heads so big, they look like an alien invasion. Other species are more exotic. This is one place a wildflower identification book can be worth its weight. After a cool summer, flowers could still be fresh and vibrant into late August.

You might feel a lightness of being here, a sensation we associate with desert hiking in winter. It can permeate your body on a warm day. Occasional patches of sand in basins and on ridges enhance this desert atmosphere. You'll also find unusual scatterings of rock. In one respect, however, the area is typically Coast Mountain: the jumbo-jet horseflies are obnoxious.

Without a 4WD vehicle, you'll probably have to walk the initial 6 km (3.75 mi) on a mining/logging road. Don't get discouraged. Though it's not a pretty approach, views of distant red-soiled peaks will be the first few pieces of the mental puzzle you'll be building of the area.

Once you reach Taylor Basin, you'll need at least two days to explore nearby passes, ridges and basins. If you basecamp in Taylor, be sure to dayhike south over Cinnabar Pass into the flower-splattered meadows of Cinnabar Basin (see photo on page 165). If you camp higher, near the pass, pitch your tent on dirt, not on heather.

West of Cinnabar Basin, the trail is less scenic, ambling through subalpine fir, Englemann spruce and whitebark pine, before reaching the sprawling meadows of upper Eldorado Basin. It's possible to complete a 15-km (9.3-mi) loop in one day, linking all three basins—Taylor, Cinnabar and Eldorado—but you'll have to scoot, giving the scenery less attention than it deserves.

If you day trip from Taylor to Cinnabar one day, spend the next day hiking west of Taylor. From the nearby Lucky Strike mine, ascend the road to the 2110-m (6920-ft) pass between Taylor and Eldorado basins, then continue northwest to Windy Pass. From there, roam the spine rising southwest into the heavens. This is our favourite ridge in the area. It's gentle enough at both ends to allow you to make a circuit, and it gives you a great view of the jagged, snow-clad Coast Mountain peaks.

From Windy Pass, it's not far to the most popular destination in the Southern Chilcotin: Spruce Lake. Most hikers, mountain bikers and horse packers (expect to see them all) reach the lake via the Gun Creek trail, starting northwest of Gun Lake. Instead, we recommend hiking to Taylor Basin, then roller-coasting over Windy Pass to Spruce Lake. It's about 10 km (6 mi) longer than the Gun Creek approach, but you'll see the highlights of the area. The trail along Gun Creek is forested nearly all the way to the lake. From Taylor Basin, the trail to the lake is on open slopes and through showy meadows. En route, camp in lovely, wide open, upper Eldorado Basin. But if your time is limited, skip Spruce Lake and focus on Taylor, Cinnabar and Eldorado basins. Also, the side trip to Windy Pass is definitely worthwhile even if you don't continue to Spruce Lake.

FACT

Before your trip

There are so many hiking options here—on trail and cross-country—you should bring a map to supplement our description. Ask the Lillooet Forest District office (250-256-1200) to send you their *Recreation* and *Spruce Lake Trails* maps. The FS map provides enough detail for most hikers and eliminates the need to purchase topo maps.

Learn more about the Southern Chilcotin by contacting the Western Canada Wilderness Committee (WCWC): www.wildernesscommittee.org; 227 Abbott Street, Vancouver, BC V6B 2K7. Phone: (604) 683-8220. They're working to gain provincial park status for the area. It's currently unprotected from mining and logging, which threatens to destroy more of this special wilderness. Ask WCWC for their newspaper explaining the issues and featuring colour photos.

By Vehicle

There are two approach options: a 2½-hour drive from Pemberton, or a 1¾-hour drive from Lillooet. From **Pemberton**, travel north on the Hurley Road—60 km (37 mi) of dirt, rocks, washboards and potholes. It's passable but jittery in a 2WD car. From **Lillooet**, travel well-graded gravel road and long stretches of pavement northwest. If you arrive one way and leave the other, you'll complete a fascinating BC backroads tour. There are lots of forest service campgrounds along Duffey Lake and Carpenter Lake roads. Read our *Camp Free in B.C.* for details.

To reach the **Hurley Road**, set your trip odometer to 0 at the edge of Pemberton, at the 3-way intersection on Highway 99, by the Petro Canada station. Drive north into town and cross the railroad tracks. At 1 km (0.6 mile) reach a T-junction. Turn right, heading toward the Hurley River FS Rd. At 2.8 km (1.7 mi), turn left (northwest) on Pemberton Valley Road.

At 25 km (15.5 mi) there's a sign for Meager Creek, Gold Bridge and Lillooet. Turn right here onto the Hurley River / Upper Lillooet River FS Road. At 26.5 km (16.4 mi), cross the small bridge over the Lillooet River. Proceed left on the Lillooet River FS Road. At 34 km (21.1 mi) turn right and begin ascending the Hurley Road on a long switchback.

Continue on the Hurley 60 km (37 mi) to **Gold Bridge**. Cross the Bridge River to the Carpenter Lake Road and turn right (northeast). Drive 11.7 km (7.3 mi) to signed Tyax Junction, where you turn left (north) then proceed up the Tyaughton Lake Road, described below.

In **Lillooet**, set your trip odometer to zero on the west side of the Fraser River bridge (junction of Hwys 12 & 99).

0 km (0 mi)
Departing the junction of Hwys 12 & 99, drive through Lillooet.

2.9 km (1.8 mi)
Turn left onto Moha Road. Follow signs for Gold Bridge.

33.8 km (21 mi)
Stay left at the Yalakom junction.

51 km (31.6 mi)
Reach the Terzaghi Dam junction. Stay straight. Proceed along the north shore of Carpenter Lake.

69.6 km (43.2 mi)
Reach the BC Hydro campground at Bighorn Creek. The Jones Creek FS campground is 2.4 km (1.5 mi) farther northwest, just before the Marshall Lake Road.

Mauve, cinnamon, charcoal, and cobalt slopes near Cinnabar Pass

95.8 km (59.4 mi)
Arrive at Tyax Junction. Turn right (north).

Both approaches arrive at Tyax Junction. Now follow the directions below.

0 km (0 mi)
Ascending north up Tyaughton Lake Road. At the top of the climb, on your left, is Mowson Pond FS Recreation Site with 5 well-spaced campsites.

3.5 km (2.2 mi)
Continue past rough Gun Creek Road on your left. Follow signs for Tyax Lodge.

6 km (3.7 mi)
Pass a road going left. Immediately there's a fork. Curve left and descend the main road. Pass Hornal Road on your right.

8.6 km (5.3 mi)
Stay straight. About 200 meters farther, ascend left. Tyax Lodge is below to the right. Continue to a steep descent around a ridge at 13.5 km (8.4 mi).

14.2 km (8.8 mi)
Reach a Y-junction. Mud Cr-Taylor Cr FS road continues right (north).
The extreme left fork might still be signed TAYLOR CREEK. That's the
way. But you'll need a truck, or at least a low-clearance 4WD vehicle,
because the road can get very muddy and is deeply rutted in places.
The alternative is to park in the pullout at the Y-junction, then walk the
Taylor Creek road. With a capable vehicle, you can drive 6 km (3.75 mi)
until the road reaches bridged Taylor Creek.

On Foot
The Taylor Creek road starts at 1128 m (3700 ft). Ascend the road,
first a bit northwest, then north. Cross a regrowing clearcut that allows
views. The Bendor Range is south, behind you. Shulaps Peak is the
gentler, mauve-coloured peak nearby, southeast. To the west are
rounded peaks. After 45 minutes, curve left (west) on the road, where
an old road forks right. Rust-red 2448-m (8029-ft) Eldorado Mountain
is northwest. More of the mauve and cinnamon mountains are visible
northeast, across the valley.

After 1 hour, stay straight on the main road, still heading into the
valley. Ignore the side roads. After 1¼ hours, strong hikers will reach
what appears to be the **end of the road**. The elevation here is 1372 m
(4500 ft). A sign points to a steep trail ascending north through a wide,
ugly scar, to the edge of forest. Climb 60 m (200 ft), then go right, heading west onto another old road. This upper road is passable in 4WD
and can be reached by turning left on a spur before the seeming road's
end mentioned above.

At 6 km (3.7 mi), within 2 hours, cross to the north side of **bridged
Taylor Creek**. The elevation here is 1494 m (4900 ft). If you've driven
this far, park and start hiking. The bank is steep and rugged. Beyond,
the road narrows and becomes more trail-like as it moderately ascends
southwest. The scenery perks up as you enter the lower Taylor Basin.

About 2½ hours from the start of the Taylor Creek road, you can
begin to see green, rust, and mauve slopes typical of the gentle
Chilcotin peaks. After 3 hours, at 1787 m (5860 ft), you can look directly
into Taylor Basin. The views rapidly expand.

At 11 km (6.8 mi) reach the old cabin in **Taylor Basin** at 1840 m
(6040 ft). Strong backpackers can be here in 3¼ hours. Others might
take up to 4½. The cabin is just below treeline, near the creek. Anyone
can use the cabin, if it's vacant. Clean up after yourself and leave cut
firewood. You can also pitch your tent nearby. There's a fire pit and a
picnic table.

From the cabin, head straight south up the bench. In a few minutes, a road forks right (west). It's signed SPRUCE LAKE VEHICLE CLOSURE AREA JAN 1-NOV 30. That's the road you'll descend at the end of the loop we describe. It's possible to camp near here, in trees surrounded by meadows. Or head another 15 minutes south onto open slopes.

To reach Cinnabar Pass, proceed south. Pass the Lucky Strike mine on your right. The narrow trail through meadows is overgrown. Just past the mine, pick up a boot-beaten path climbing through lupine, lavender fleabane, and white mop tops. Continue ascending left (south and a bit southeast).

Arrive at 2122-m (6960-ft) **Cinnabar Pass** 2 km (1.2 mi) from the Taylor Basin cabin. Laced with streams, the meadows of Cinnabar Basin spread out below you. Looking southeast you can see the Carpenter Lake canyon and the snowcapped Bendor Range beyond.

From Cinnabar Pass the trail drops southeast through meadows into subalpine forest. At the junction with the Old Chilcotin trail, which descends the Pearson Creek drainage, turn right (west). Regain elevation via meadowed slopes to reach the 2050-m (6720-ft) **unnamed pass** above Cinnabar Basin. The pass is 4 km (2.5 mi) from the Taylor Basin cabin.

From the unnamed pass, the trail descends west into dry forest that can be dusty. After dropping 183 m (600 ft) reach a boggy spot. Horses stomping through here have made it worse. Where the indistinct trail splits, stay high (right). The trail resumes at a dip in the ridge, then drops toward Eldorado Creek.

Reach Eldorado Forks at 1750 m (5740 ft), nearly an 1 hour from the unnamed pass. The trail then curves north, heading upstream, soon entering the **vast meadows of Eldorado Basin**. Again you'll see cinnamon-coloured mountains. Where a faint trail veers left in the lower meadows, stay straight (north) on the main trail. Shortly after rockhopping across a shallow, upper fork of Eldorado Creek, ascend steeply to a junction at 1910 m (6260 ft). You've now hiked 9.5 km (6 mi) from Taylor Basin cabin. To complete the loop, go right, reaching Taylor in 5.2 km (3.25 mi).

Left ascends 2 km (1.2 mi) to 2200-m (7220-ft) **Windy Pass**. A red ridge juts northeast of the pass, separating Bonanza and Nea creek canyons. Castle Peak, Cardtable and Relay mountains are visible north. Spruce Lake is just north of west, but is blocked from view. A trail drops steeply west from the pass, through meadows then forest, to intersect the Spruce Lake trail in 5 km (3.1 mi). Turn right (north) to approach the south end of the lake in 0.5 km (0.3 mi). Bear right at the fork to proceed 2.5 km (1.5 mi) up the east side of the lake to the campground.

For more expansive views, ascend the grassy, rounded ridge southwest (left) from Windy Pass. Top out at roughly 2332 m (7650 ft), overlooking forested Gun Creek valley. Hummingbird and Trigger lakes are visible west, up the valley. The Coast Mountains are south and southwest. The nearby Leckie Range is southwest. The Shulaps Range is east. North of Relay and Cardtable mountains, the Chilcotin Range peters out into a plateau.

If you're intrigued and capable, it's possible to walk the ridgecrest southwest, then descend southeast, looping around the canyon you ascended from upper Eldorado Basin. Regain the trail at treeline and return to the junction where you previously went left to Windy Pass.

To return to Taylor Basin, head east on a narrow, old mining road. Soon pass the site of the Lucky Gem mine. Subalpine fir are on your right, red talus slopes on your left. Volcanic hoodoos line the ridges. About 3 km (1.9 mi) from the junction in upper Eldorado Basin, reach a 2110-m (6920-ft) unnamed pass. From there, the road drops northeast into Taylor Basin.

Trip 13
Cathedral Lakes

Location	Cathedral Provincial Park
Round trip	28 km (17.4 mi) to Quiniscoe Lake via the jeep road; 32 km (19.8 mi) via the Lakeview trail
Elevation gain	1200 m (3936 ft)
Time required	3 to 5 days
Difficulty	Moderate
Maps	B.C. Parks brochure; Ashnola River 92 H/1

OPINION

Above sweeping forested slopes, hidden from the valleys below, is this kingdom of piercing peaks and lovely lakes crowning a high plateau. Once you're up there, the dayhike possibilities to open ridges, granite outcroppings, and azure waters beneath serrated mountains—all connected by a generous trail network—make it an alpine playground. But playgrounds get crowded and noisy, and this one's no exception. There's a private resort on the shore of the park's central lake, Quiniscoe, and guests are shuttled in on a jeep road. So if you've always yearned to penetrate the realm of the persistent hiker, but would rather pay for it with money instead of muscle, here's your chance.

Cathedral's location between the Cascade rain forests and the arid Okanagan Highland makes it unique. So does its trail system, which offers vantages at varying altitudes, giving you a more complete picture of the geography. And Cathedral's Rim trail is uniquely rewarding, because it provides a sustained alpine experience: you don't plunge back into forest immediately after climbing above treeline, as so often happens in the Cascades.

There are several ways to storm this bastille: Lakeview Creek, Ewart Creek, Wall Creek. Since all the approaches are in trees, we recommend the shortest—either the Lakeview trail or the jeep road that parallels Lakeview Creek—so you can enjoy more time up top.

Denture Ridge

Officially, hikers aren't allowed on the road, but as long as you politely yield the right-of-way to the resort's shuttle vehicles, they don't mind. The road and the trail are both featureless endurance tests. The trail grants you a few more glimpses of the distant horizon, but you'll see it all while dayhiking above. The road is more

direct and therefore quicker than the trail, and the one or two vehicles you'll encounter aren't enough to be annoying. Both
approaches are aggressive, rocketing onto the plateau. The level
lapses are few and short, with liftoff resuming immediately.

Once you've powered your way up to Quiniscoe Lake at 2100 m
(6888 ft), you can establish your launchpad there, at nearby Lake of
the Woods, or even at Pyramid Lake. All are gorgeous, but the latter
two feel wilder and are only a 10- or 15-minute walk from Quiniscoe. Quiniscoe offers cages to keep your food safe from marauding
squirrels. Pyramid has the most dramatic view, with the cliffs of
Pyramid Mountain in your face. We prefer Lake of the Woods,
where the sites are sprinkled around the lake.

Grinding up to Quiniscoe Lake is hardly worthwhile until the
trails above it are snow-free. That's usually mid-July, possibly late
June in years of light snowfall. Keep in mind, although Cathedral is
conducive to a basecamp-and-dayhike setup, it isn't necessarily the
ideal first backpack trip of the season. You'll find the wickedly steep
approach less challenging later in the summer, after you've developed
your mountain muscles; however, that's when the area gets busy.

Although you might enjoy a week-long Cathedral trip, consider four days the minimum: one in, two for dayhiking, and one
out. Devote the second day to the Rim trail, the third day to Lakeview Mountain via Goat Lakes.

Now a few suggestions on dayhiking. If the sky is clear, burst
out of your tent and race onto the Rim trail for a spectacular, high-
elevation tour. If you see serious weather moving in, get down
quickly. At 2614 m (8573 ft) on the south end and 2551 m (8367 ft)
on the north, you'd be a red flag for a bullish lightning bolt. Low
clouds can pose a danger here, by obscuring the route and making
it impossible to follow the cairns. The loop is more rugged than the
park map indicates, especially when gaining the lip of the rim, so
don't expect the trip to go quickly. Allow a full day.

If the weather is threatening, and you don't want to venture
onto the rim, you can still enjoy descending into the upper reaches
of Lakeview Creek and visiting Goat Lakes. If you're lucky, a break
in the clouds will grant you a view of Denture Ridge taking a bite
out of the sky. They should have named it Monster Mouth.

On a clear day, think of the Goat Lakes cirque not as a destination but rather a point of interest en route to Lakeview Mountain.
Ascending its rounded slopes is easy and will afford you a tremendous view southwest to Denture Ridge, Matriarch Mountain,

On the edge of Cathedral Lakes plateau

Macabre Tower and Grimface Mountain. Even if you only scurry above the trees, it's worthwhile.

Once you attain the broad, open saddle between Lakeview Mountain and the Boxcar, you can ascend either or both. Go south to the Boxcar for a fix of rock and rubble. If you're a capable scrambler, you'll grok the way. Starting from a campsite at the core lakes near Quiniscoe Lake, experienced, fit hikers can bag the Boxcar and Lakeview Mountain in a single day—if the pleasant roaming at the saddle, amidst talus and alpine forget-me-nots, doesn't weaken your resolve to push on.

If possible, turn the ascent of Lakeview Mountain into a loop excursion. Enjoy the creek-and-meadow walk southeast to Goat Lakes. Ascend Lakeview Mountain from there. Then, if the weather holds, you have the option of traversing the mountain and picking up the Centennial trail, descending to Lakeview Creek, and looping back to the core lakes.

Finally, be sure to take in Glacier Lake before you leave the park. Surrounded by mountains on three sides, it seems wilder— higher and more remote—than the other lakes. Also, from the ridge separating Quiniscoe and Glacier lakes, you can see Lakeview Mountain southeast and the Similkameen Valley northeast. If bad weather is keeping you off the rim, it's worth checking out the views from lower ridges like this one.

FACT

Cougar, wolverine, deer, and black bear inhabit the park, but not grizzlies—they were all shot long ago by ranchers. And the black bear stay down in the valleys, because it's such paltry dining for them at higher elevations.

Before leaving home, get the B.C. Parks brochure and map of Cathedral Park by contacting the Okanagan District Manager (250-494-6500). Mountain bikes are not allowed on any trails in the park. Dogs are prohibited in this core area surrounding Quiniscoe Lake because they've harassed wildlife and people in the past.

By Vehicle

Driving Hwy 3, near the western edge of **Keremeos**, you'll see a B.C. Parks sign 24 KM CATHEDRAL LAKES PROVINCIAL PARK. Turn south onto Ashnola River Road. If you're going to pay for the shuttle up to Quiniscoe Lake, drive 22.2 km (13.8 mi) southwest to the Cathedral Lakes Resort Base parking lot. Pick-up times are 10 A.M., 2 P.M., and 4 P.M. The round trip costs CDN $75 per person in July and August; CDN $55 in June, Sept., and October. Call 1-888-255-4453, or (250) 226-7560 for reservations. Study their website (www.cathedral-lakes-lodge.com) for lodge and cabin details. If you're going to hike up, drive 1.6 km (1 mi) farther to the Lakeview Creek trailhead and campground, 900 m (2952 ft). There are walk-in tent sites here along the Ashnola River, 30 meters from the parking area.

On Foot

From the Lakeview Creek trailhead, the hike to Quiniscoe Lake is 14 km (8.7 mi) on the jeep road, or 16 km (9.9 mi) via the trail. Start by crossing the Ashnola River on a footbridge, then ascending a trail southeast to the jeep road.

For the shortest route, stay on the road. You'll initially ascend the east side of Lakeview Creek (locally referred to as Noisy Creek) then, at approximately 1.6 km (1 mi), cross a bridge to the west side for the rest of the way. You'll see the mileage posted on trees along the road. Camping is not allowed anywhere along the road. The steepest sections are at 8 km (5.1 mi) and 12.1 km (7.5 mi). The only view from the road is at 12.9 km (8 mi), where you can see the barren summit of 2628-m (8620-ft) Lakeview Mountain (southeast), the highest point in the park. Arrive in 14 km (8.7 mi) at **Quiniscoe Lake**, 2100 m (6888 ft).

If you opt to hike the trail to Quiniscoe, after ascending 1 km (0.6 mi) on trail, rejoin the road just before crossing Lakeview

Creek. At 3.5 km (2.2 mi) up, you'll see a sign where trail resumes off the road to the right (northwest). Halfway up there's a campground on the north side of Lindsey Creek. Farther southwest the trail breaks out of the trees and reaches a junction at 12.4 km (7.7 mi). Stay straight, continuing southwest on the Lakeview trail to arrive at Quiniscoe Lake in 16 km (9.9 mi).

If you take the side excursion from the 12.4-km (7.7-mi) junction, the Diamond trail goes right (northwest), circling around Scout Mountain. Stay left at junctions with the Centennial and Rim trails to rejoin the Lakeview trail 0.8 km (0.5 mi) before Quiniscoe. This route adds 3.2 km (2 mi) to the total trip. Check in at the ranger cabin at Quiniscoe Lake and get the park map showing all the trails. There's a $3-a-night fee to camp at Quiniscoe.

Radiating from the core lakes, all the Cathedral trails are well maintained, clearly signed, and marked on the park map. The Rim and Lakeview Mountain trails, however, are actually routes, not trails, and are marked by cairns, not signs. Beginning at Quiniscoe Lake, these are the approximate distances and elevation gains for the possible dayhikes:

Lake of the Woods—1.3 km (0.8 mi) one way, level; Glacier Lake—1.5 km (0.9 mi) one way, 125 m (410 ft); Ladyslipper Lake—3 km (1.9 mi) one way, 150 m (490 ft); Goat Lakes—5 km (3.1 mi) one way, 150 m (490 ft); Lakeview Mountain—13-km (8-mi) loop, 600 m (1970 ft); Rim trail, south end—11.3-km (7-mi) loop, 540 m (1770 ft); Rim trail, north end—9.7-km (6-mi) loop, 480 m (1570 ft).

To reach **Goat Lakes**, head southeast from the east end of Quiniscoe, toward Pyramid Lake. Just past Pyramid, come to a junction. Go left (east), descending about 15 minutes to another junction. Then turn right (south), staying west of Goat Creek. (If the weather allows a traverse of Lakeview Mountain, this junction is where you'll loop back on the Centennial trail.) There are no more junctions south to Goat Lake.

The routes up **Lakeview Mountain and the Boxcar** begin near the rocky, tussocky Goat Lakes outlet. Look for a sign and cairns indicating where to hop across the stream. Then go east, following orange blazes on trees. At the trailer-size boulders, turn left onto a narrow route. It's steep and lacks switchbacks, but it's short—only about 15 minutes to the saddle. From there, turn right (south) to scramble up the Boxcar, left (north) to reach the summit of Lakeview Mountain. The route down the north side of Lakeview Mountain joins the Centennial trail to loop back to the core lakes.

The Rim trail offers three choices. You can hike it end-to-end: from Stone City in the south, to Red Mountain in the north. Or you can start by ascending above Glacier Lake, then hiking just the south or north end of the rim.

To hike the rim end-to-end, first walk from Quiniscoe Lake southeast to Pyramid Lake. Just past it, stay right at the junction and ascend south to Ladyslipper Lake. Before the final drop into the Ladyslipper basin, there's a view south of Goat Lakes and Denture Ridge, and southeast to the saddle between Lakeview Mountain and the Boxcar. From Ladyslipper's southeast side, cross the outlet stream and follow the trail climbing steeply southwest through rock piles. When the ascent eases and you attain the rim, keep following the cairns. To see the rock formations called **Smokey the Bear** and the **Giant Cleft**, detour left (southeast) before continuing north along the rim.

To hike either end of the rim, first walk along the south side of Quiniscoe Lake. Go through the campground and ascend southwest on the ridge separating Quiniscoe Lake from Glacier Lake. This trail will meet the trail coming up from Glacier Lake. Continue climbing the talus slope above **Glacier Lake** to the south end of a saddle.

To hike the south end of the rim, when you reach the saddle above Glacier Lake turn left (southeast). You'll swing around **Pyramid Mountain**, skirting the unusual geologic features called Devil's Woodpile and Stone City. Just after Stone City, you'll see a trail descending left to Ladyslipper Lake. To visit Smokey the Bear and the Giant Cleft, detour straight (southeast), then return to the junction, drop to Ladyslipper and follow the well-defined trail back to Quiniscoe.

To hike the north end of the rim, when you reach the saddle above Glacier Lake, turn right (north). Following cairns, pick your way through scree, boulders, and meadows. This **King-of-the-Mountain route** will lead you over 2551-m (8367-ft) Quiniscoe and 2469-m (8098-ft) Red mountains. From a northeast arm of Red Mountain, the Rim trail descends southeast to a junction with the Centennial trail. Descend right to the Lakeview trail, then go right again to head south to Quiniscoe Lake.

Trip 14
Gwillim Lakes

Location	Valhalla Provincial Park
Round trip	11.6 km (7.2 mi), plus exploring
Elevation change	701-m (2300-ft) gain; 146-m (480-ft) loss
Time required	2 days
Difficulty	Easy
Maps	Burton 82 F/13; BC Parks brochure; Valhalla Society 1:125,000 Visitor's Guide to Valhalla Provincial Park

OPINION

Wilderness is precious no matter how people appraise its appearance. A wilderness that nobody ever visits, or even wants to, still contributes ecologically, socially and spiritually to life on earth. So the wilderness of Valhalla Provincial Park has meaning and value regardless that few people venture here, and despite that well-traveled hikers enthusiastically recommend just one of the five trails that penetrate the park.

That trail leads to Gwillim Lakes, in the park's southwest corner. It's short enough for a moderate dayhike, but a surfeit of comfortable campgrounds begs you to enjoy a couple days of exceptionally easy backpacking. Every step is a scenic joy. The lakes basin is an exquisite sight and an entertaining destination. (See photo on page 165.)

The access road is long, but it's broad, brush free, reasonably smooth, suitable for the average 2WD car. Shortly before the road ends, it curves east. Here your eyes will widen and your heart quicken as you gaze up to where you're headed. This is the park's impressive southwest edge. Beyond the trailhead, enticements multiply and expand.

You'll climb through cool, mature forest, then cross a bouldery headwall to reach Drinnon Lake, between Gregorio and Drinnon peaks. Resuming the ascent, soon cross subalpine Drinnon Pass and enter the park. Small campgrounds at both Drinnon Lake and Pass are attractive, but the superior campground at Gwillim Lakes isn't much farther. From the pass, you'll descend back into forest,

Dazzling August day in the Valhallas

cross a bridged creek, and begin the final ascent. Views expand. The trail itself engages your attention as it dances along a rock rib and steep slabs.

Gwillim Lakes basin is a broad, bi-level shelf tucked at about treeline into a rugged, mountainous amphitheatre. Though the campground is large, the tent pads are scattered in a meadow, so you can see in all directions, and you won't be cheek-by-jowl with your neighbours. The separate cooking area has a wastewater drain and metal food cache. On a hot day, plunging into the gorgeous lakes is irresistible. The surrounding alpine slopes invite a full day's exploration: easy wandering or full-on scrambling. The *On Foot* directions explain how to surmount Lucifer Pass and attain a view north into the recesses of the park.

Speedy hikers can reach Gwillim Lakes in a mere two hours. So unless you're probing deeper into the park (it's strictly mountaineering beyond Lucifer Pass) consider dayhiking. It will significantly reduce your impact on the land, as well as your pack's impact on your body. Doughty dayhikers can scramble past the smaller lakes in Gwillim's upper basin, tag Lucifer Pass, and return to the trailhead within 10 hours.

FACT

By Vehicle
The access is long, but easily doable in 2WD. To reach Gwillim Lakes trailhead, drive south from New Denver, or north from Playmor Junction (between Nelson and Castlegar). Below are separate directions for each approach.

From New Denver
Start at the Petro Canada station at the junction of Hwys 6 and 31A in New Denver. Drive Hwy 6 south, along Slocan Lake's east shore, 32.5 km (20.2 mi) to the village of Slocan. (Near the village, ignore the signed turnoff for Drinnon Pass.) Turn right (west) onto Gravel Pit Road. Reset your trip odometer to 0.

0 km (0 mi)
Starting west on Gravel Pit Road. Proceed straight and cross the bridge over Slocan River.

0.8 km (0.5 mi)
Stay left on Slocan West FS road.

1.2 km (0.7 mi)
Cross a bridge over Gwillim Creek.

2.3 km (1.4 mi)
Go right on Little Slocan FS road.

13.2 km (8.1 mi)
Reach a junction. Bear left (southwest) on the main road for Gwillim Lakes. Right onto Bannock Burn FS road leads to Gimli Ridge / Mulvey Basin trailhead.

20.3 km (12.6 mi)
Reach a junction. Turn right (southwest) onto Hoder Creek FS road for Gwillim Lakes. Reset your trip odometer to 0. Directions continue at the bottom of page 92. Bear left to reach Little Slocan Lakes FS campground entry road in just 200 meters (220 yards).

From Nelson or Castlegar
Drive Hwy 3A to Playmor Junction, midway between Nelson and Castlegar. Then follow Hwy 6 north 15.4 km (9.5 mi). Across from a power station, turn left (northwest) onto Passmore Upper Road. Reset your trip odometer to 0.

0 km (0 mi)
Starting northwest on Passmore Upper Road.

0.3 km (0.2 mi)
Cross a bridge over Slocan River. Go left to follow Little Slocan River upstream along its north bank. Gradually curve north.

3.3 km (2 mi)
Pavement ends.

3.7 km (2.3 mi)
Bear left on Little Slocan FS road.

5.3 km (3.3 mi)
Bear right.

7.5 km (4.7 mi)
Proceed straight on the main road.

9 km (5.6 mi)
Stay right.

13.3 km (8.2 mi)
Proceed straight where Koch Creek FS road forks left.

16.1 km (10 mi) and 23 km (14.3 mi)
Proceed straight.

25 km (15.5 mi)
Proceed straight (northeast) for Gwillim Lakes. Turn right and descend to reach Little Slocan Lakes campground in 200 meters (220 yards).

25.2 km (15.6 mi)
Reach a junction. For Gwillim Lakes turn left (southwest) onto Hoder Creek FS road. Reset your trip odometer to 0 and continue following the directions below. For Gimli Ridge / Mulvey Basin proceed straight (northeast) 7.1 km (4.4 mi), turn left onto Bannock Burn FS road, and proceed 13 km (8.1mi).

0 km (0 mi)
Starting southwest on Hoder Creek FS road.

6.5 km (4 mi) and 10.3 km (6.4 mi)
Bear right.

Ascending to Lucifer Pass, from Gwillim Lakes basin

10.6 km (6.6 mi)
Bear right and descend. Notice the huge cedar just before a granite wall.

18.5 km (11.5 mi)
Fork left. Do not ascend right.

18.8 km (11.7 mi)
Fork right. Impressive granite mountains are soon visible.

21.3 km (13.2 mi)
Reach Gwillim Lakes trailhead and road's end at 1615 m (5300 ft).

Upon leaving Gwillim Lakes trailhead, when you reach the junction of Hoder Creek and Little Slocan FS roads, you can (1) turn right to continue retracing your approach, or (2) turn left for the village of Slocan on Hwy 6, as described here.

0 km (0 mi)
Turning left (northeast) from Hoder Creek FS road onto Little Slocan FS road.

7.1 km (4.4 mi)
Reach a junction. For the village of Slocan on Hwy 6, proceed straight (northeast) and continue following the directions below.

18 km (11.2 mi)
Bear left.

19.1 km (11.8 mi)
Cross a bridge over Gwillim Creek.

19.4 km (12 mi)
Go right and cross the bridge over Slocan River.

20.3 km (12.6 mi)
Reach the village of Slocan and intersect Hwy 6. Turn left (north) for New Denver. Turn right (south) to reach Hwy 3A at Playmor Junction, between Nelson and Castlegar.

On Foot
Directly north of the trailhead is Gregorio Peak. (The outhouse window offers a perfectly-framed view of it.) Gwillim Lakes basin is directly north of Gregorio. But to reach the basin, the trail initially heads east toward Drinnon Peak. The ascent is moderate, steepening as you curve north and cross a boulder slide. The trail is well defined and easy to follow all the way to Gwillim.

Within 1 hour, reach **Drinnon Lake** at 2 km (1.2 mi), 1950 m (6400 ft), beneath granite-walled Drinnon Peak. Just above the lake's south shore is a small campground. You'll find an outhouse, several tent pads, and a metal food cache.

Cross the lake's outlet stream on a sturdy bridge. The trail ascends through open forest, northwest then north, gaining 116 m (380 ft) to a tiny lake in **Drinnon Pass** at 3.5 km (2.2 mi), 2225 m (6780 ft). There's another small campground here: outhouse, several tent pads, metal food cache. So far, you've been hiking through a "Scenic Forest Corridor." Enter Valhalla Provincial Park at the pass.

Proceeding north of the pass, descend 146 m (480 ft) to cross a headwater tributary of **Gwillim Creek** at 1921 m (6300 ft). Figure about 1¾ hours to this point. Soon begin the final 250-m (820-ft) ascent generally northwest to the lakes basin.

Part way up, at about 2043 m (6700 ft), the trail is on a rock rib above a steep cliff allowing an aerial perspective of Gwillim Creek valley. North is Gwillim Creek, cascading down from the lakes basin. Northeast are the craggy Devils Range peaks forming the north wall of the valley. East, beyond Slocan Lake, is Kokanee Glacier Provincial Park.

Premier camping in Gwillim Lakes basin

After the valley overlook, traverse a narrow rockslide beneath steep rock slabs. Just above, the trail levels, entering **Gwillim Lakes basin** at 5.8 km (3.6 mi), 2171 m (7120 ft). Total hiking time: about 2½ hours.

The first of the two main lakes is a few minutes straight ahead (north). On the way, you'll pass a couple campsites, a metal food cache, and a communal cooking area with a wastewater drain. The **campground** has 8 tent pads, mostly scattered to your right (east) in the boulder-strewn alpine meadow. That's also where the outhouse is perched on a platform.

The second main lake is nearby, northwest of the first lake, at the same elevation. A smaller third lake is a bit farther northwest and about 250 feet higher. The two upper basin lakes are north of the first lake and 134 m (440 ft) higher—an easy, off-trail ramble en route to Lucifer Pass, described on the next page.

LUCIFER PASS

Round trip 3 km (1.9 mi) from Gwillim Lakes campground
Elevation gain 415 m (1360 ft)
Time required 3 hours
Difficulty Easy to upper lakes basin, challenging to the pass

Looking north from Gwillim Lakes campground, you can see Lucifer Pass, a narrow arete between an unnamed peak on the left and Lucifer Peak on the right. The pass grants you a view of Rocky Lakes basin (north) and one of the Hird Lakes (farther north).

Between Gwillim Lakes campground and Lucifer Pass is upper Gwillim Lakes basin with two lakes: one small, one long and thin. No established trail continues into the upper basin. Sections of boot-beaten tread are helpful but unnecessary. The one moderately steep, rocky slope is easily overcome.

Continuing beyond the upper basin to Lucifer Pass requires strenuous scrambling. The terrain steepens, and huge, awkward boulders force you to stop and plan your route. But there's no exposure, nothing technical.

From the campground, follow the path around the southeast side of the first main lake, then curve north. Ascend the **green chute**, right of an escarpment and waterfall. Work your way up the rocky slope to enter the upper basin—134 m (440 ft) above the main basin. The lakes are surrounded by soft, grassy tussocks and scattered boulders. Where you first reached the upper basin, at its south edge, you can survey the entire Gwillim area and scope out other possible explorations.

Aiming for Lucifer? Stay right (east) of the upper lakes. Climb northeast then north to the obvious **2585-m (8480-ft) pass**. From there you an see it's an arduous, precipitous scramble north down to the Rocky Lakes and across the valley headwall to the Hird Lakes. Left of and above the Rocky Lakes is Mt. Bor. Right of and beyond Hird Lakes is Urd Peak. Blocked from view, farther down valley, is Evans Lake, the park's largest.

Trip 15
Glory Basin

Location	Kokanee Glacier Prov. Park, Selkirks
Circuit	24 km (15 mi)
Elevation gain	823 m (2700 ft)
Time required	2-day backpack, 10-hour dayhike
Difficulty	Moderate backpack, Challenging dayhike
Maps	Kokanee Peak 82 F/11, Slocan 82 F/14; BC Parks brochure; Valhalla Society 1:125,000 Visitor's Guide to Valhalla Provincial Park

OPINION

Some hikers rate a trip's difficulty in terms of the fuel require-ment—expressed in Power Bar consumption. For example, the vast majority of visitors to Kokanee Glacier Provincial Park go for a one-Power Bar dayhike. Their destination is a string of lovely subalpine lakes in the park's popular core area. Robust, resolute dayhikers prefer the challenge of a two-Power Bar circuit. They zoom past the core-area lakes, rocket into alpine meadows, jet past Sapphire Lakes and Glory Basin, then blast down the Outlook Creek exit route. Slow-is-beautiful disciples who abstain from speed and espouse the virtues of a full pack (stuffed with Power Bars galore, cooking gear, wine-filled Platypus, freeze-dried Santa Fe chili dinners, and upside-down pineapple-cake desserts), opt to backpack the circuit. They break it into a leisurely, palate-pleasing two days, pitching their tent at Kaslo Lake campground.

Even the one-Power Bar dayhike will reward you with premier scenery. The two-Power Bar dayhike circuit just offers more of it, as well as a look at the park's wilder side beyond the core area, plus a heightened sense of adventure and accomplishment. The multi-Power Bar backpack trip offers all the above, without risk of caloric deficit.

Kaslo Lake and Kokanee Glacier, from near Enterprise Pass

From Gibson Lake trailhead, a pedestrian highway ascends to Kokanee Lake: brilliant cobalt water, in an austere, sharp-sided notch. The trail traverses a steep slope above the west shore.

Next you'll enter the subalpine basin that cradles Keen, Garland and Kaslo lakes. This is the park's core. Some consider it the apex of pastoral mountain beauty in the West Kootenays. The idyllic atmosphere is often shattered, however, by a steady stream of hikers. Even if you're here when others are not, you'll witness man's heavy hand. An elaborate infrastructure (broad trails, frequent oversized signs, extensive drainage ditches, numerous bridges, deluxe campgrounds) softens visitor impact but is itself highly impactful. The wilderness has been corseted, doused with cosmetics, and exiled to charm school. Anyone accustomed to the savage West Kootenay backcountry will feel coddled. Those who rarely hike, especially if they have city-soft visitors in tow, will feel secure. But even if you resent the urbane atmosphere, you'll have to concede that despite the "improvements," maybe even because of them, the gentle scenery remains enchanting.

Escape the park's core by pressing on toward Sapphire Lakes and Glory Basin. The pedestrian highway dwindles to a trail as it climbs into meadows that roll along near treeline. The two Sapphire Lakes are small—mere ponds, really—but their delicate, poetic charm deeply affects sensitive souls. Glory Basin is an ascetic's delight, a minimalist alpine landscape consisting of slabs, boulders, tarns, trickles, moss gardens, and the occasional, tenacious wildflower. It's the ideal place to practice the zen of hiking.

Though there's a tiny campground at lower Sapphire Lake, recommending it would be irresponsible. If you arrive when it's full, you'll be forced onto the meadows, which cannot survive repeated crushing. Please pitch your tent at Kaslo Lake campground, then dayhike to Sapphire and Glory. Another overnight option, slightly out of the way, is Kalmia campground near Slocan Chief cabin.

Considering the Outlook Creek descent? It's a route, not a defined trail. The gorge is steep and rocky. If you're an experienced cross-country rambler, seize this opportunity to add a little zing to your day, while shortening the trip by at least an hour. If you've rarely strayed from established trails, don't start experimenting here—particularly if you're wobbling under the weight of a full pack. It's safest to return the way you came.

FACT

Before your trip

In 2001, the per-person, per-night fees in Kokanee Glacier Park were $5 for tenting in a campground, $15 for bunking in a backcountry cabin. Bring sufficient cash. A ranger might stop by to collect. Fires are not allowed in the park, so campers who intend to cook need a stove. Dogs and bikes are also prohibited. It's first come, first served at Kokanee Park cabins, so pack a tent in case you're unlucky. Slocan Chief cabin sleeps twelve and is furnished with propane stoves and lights, as well as foam mattresses.

By Vehicle

In **Nelson**, from the middle of the orange bridge over the West Arm of Kootenay Lake, drive Highway 3A northeast 18.5 km (11.5 mi). Or, in **Balfour**, from the turnoff to the Kootenay Lake ferry terminal, drive Highway 3A southwest 11.8 km (7.3 mi). From either approach, turn northeast at the sign for Kokanee Glacier Provincial Park and reset your trip odometer to 0.

0 km (0 mi)
Starting northeast on Kokanee Glacier Park Road.

2.2 km (1.4 mi)
Bear right on the main road.

Descending Outlook Creek route to Garland Lake

2.4 km (1.5 mi)
Bear left.

7.3 km (4.5 mi)
Stay straight.

11.5 km (7.1 mi)
Pass the Cedar Grove trailhead on your left.

16 km (10 mi)
Bear right and arrive at road's end. There's a spacious parking lot here, next to Gibson Lake. Elevation: 1536 m (5040 ft). There's a day-use shelter here, as well as picnic tables, outhouses, and a trailhead kiosk with park maps. You'll also notice chicken wire strewn about. If you're staying overnight in the park, wrap the wire around your vehicle and secure it with rocks and pieces of wood. It will prevent porcupines from munching the tires, hoses and fan belts. Seriously. You don't want to hitchhike down the mountain to call a tow truck.

On Foot
Distances posted on the trailhead sign differ from those published in the park brochure. We considered both, as well as data from other sources, when calculating the distances stated here.

The trail to Kokanee Lake is initially an old road. It begins right of the kiosk, at the northeast corner of the parking lot. Ignore the trail starting near the day-use shelter; it merely circles Gibson Lake.

The road/trail ascends moderately. In 15 minutes, before a creek culvert, turn left onto a signposted trail. The road continues straight. Within another 5 minutes, the trail curves left to rejoin the old road. Your general direction of travel is northwest.

After gaining 95 m (310 ft) in about 25 minutes of brisk hiking, turn left onto trail. The signpost here states it's 2.5 km farther to Kokanee Lake. Streams tumbling down the valley walls are audible. Impressive cliffs appear. Soon enter the subalpine zone. Gibson Lake is visible south.

At 3.3 km (2 mi), within 1 hour of the trailhead, pass through a narrow draw. A signpost here states it's 1.2 km farther to Kokanee Lake. Just beyond, look up to your right (north/northeast) to see where The Keyhole pierces the high valley wall. About 150 meters (165 yards) farther, the unsigned **Keyhole trail** forks right and ascends 2 km (1.2 mi) over rugged, rocky terrain to Kokanee Glacier. Proceed straight (northwest) on the main trail, gaining little elevation for the next 0.75 km (0.5 mi). Reach the south end of **Kokanee Lake** at 4.5 km (2.8 mi), 1975 m (6480 ft), about 1½ hours from the trailhead. Contouring about 24 m (80 ft) above the lake's west shore, cross an enormous rockslide beneath the northeast flank of Outlook Mtn.

North of Kokanee Lake, cruise through meadows to reach 2035-m (6675-ft) **Kokanee Pass**. Then descend along beautiful moss-hugged creeklets, reaching small **Keen Lake** at 5.8 km (3.6 mi), 1721 m (6540 ft). Still heading northwest, the trail stays east of Keen Lake and, soon after, small **Garland Lake**. (If you're hiking the Glory Basin circuit, pause here and take note. Southwest is the Outlook Creek gorge—the recommended descent route from Sapphire Lakes. It follows the creek downstream to the west shore of Garland Lake, then skirts the north shore to rejoin the main trail near where you now stand.)

A few minutes past Garland Lake, reach larger **Kaslo Lake** at 7.5 km (4.7 mi), 1973 m (6470 ft). The campground here has 10 tent pads, an outhouse, metal food cache, and wastewater drain. Most dayhikers, not intending to complete the Glory Basin circuit, turn around at Kaslo Lake.

To continue the Glory Basin circuit, follow the trail along the east shore to a **junction** at the northeast corner of Kaslo Lake, and turn left (northwest). Right heads east, then northeast, gaining 100 m (328 ft) in 1.4 km (0.9 mi) to historic Slocan Chief cabin, where the edge of Kokanee Glacier is visible. From there, the trail proceeds northeast to Kalmia campground and Helen Deane Lakes before descending to Joker Millsite trailhead at the head of Keen Creek valley.

Turning left (northwest) at the Kaslo Lake junction, a 10-minute ascent leads to **Enterprise Pass** and another junction, at 8.2 km (5.1 mi), 2027 m (6650 ft). The three lakes you recently passed are now visible below, south/southeast. From here, the Enterprise Creek trail descends right (northwest). It's signed for Tanal Lake, 1.8 km (1.1 mi) distant. Resuming the Glory Basin circuit, turn left (southwest) following the sign for Sapphire Lakes via Griffin Lake. Another hour of moderate-paced hiking should get you to Sapphire Lakes. Glory Basin is farther and higher.

Ascending the Griffin Creek drainage southwest toward Griffin Lake, the trail narrows and becomes rougher. Experienced hikers will appreciate this, feeling relieved to depart the manicured, monitored park core and enter wilder country. You can now glimpse Kokanee Glacier southeast, and see stark, dry Sawtooth Ridge northeast. About 10 minutes above the pass, a tiny gap (right / northwest) grants a view of Tanal Lake far below in Enterprise Creek valley.

SPIRIT OF
BRITISH COLUMBIA

u're above and east of shal-
annel courses through it—
ids south now, ascending
st of Mt. Giegerich. From
1, subalpine **Lemon Pass**.
oward a stand of subalpine
:ampground with room for
inds, a metal food cache,
:t. Just beyond and slightly
below the campground is **lower Sapphire Lake**, at 2238 m (7340 ft).
You've now hiked 10 km (6.2 mi) from Gibson Lake trailhead.

Lower Sapphire Lake is perched on the south edge of Lemon
Pass, between Mt. Giegerich (northwest) and Sunset Mtn (south).
From the campground, round the lake on either shore to peer
southwest into Lemon Creek valley. Though the trail continues in
that direction, the scenery quickly diminishes, and the descent is
long, steep and rough—worthwhile only if a vehicle awaits you at
Lemon Creek trailhead.

Upper Sapphire Lake is a couple minutes southeast of the
campground. Drop to the shore of the lower lake, angle left and
hike over a short rise. Jump the stream linking the two lakes. Turn
left, pass a small cascade-fed pool, and rock hop up to the lake.
Beyond is **Glory Basin**.

To explore Glory Basin, follow the west shore of upper Sapphire Lake, then head southeast. As you ascend, gradually curve south, between Sunset Mtn (west) and Outlook Mtn (east). No trail penetrates this alpine sanctuary, but the terrain is open and gentle, allowing easy cross-country travel. Wander past tarns, beside creeklets, over rock slabs, and around mossy gardens, as far as the **unnamed pass** to the south. Here, at 2400 m (7870 m), 2.3 km (1.4 mi) from upper Sapphire Lake, you can gaze southwest into Nilsik Creek valley.

To return to Gibson Lake trailhead you can, of course, retrace your approach via Griffin Lake and Enterprise Pass. But the circuit route described here is shorter and more interesting. Starting at the campground near lower Sapphire Lake, descend northeast. Drop through the open, grassy, lower reaches of Lemon Pass. Do not ascend north to the saddle over which you originally entered the pass.

Follow sections of bootbeaten path. Watch for an occasional cairn. Initially you'll be on the north side of **Outlook Creek**, but you'll cross it farther down. Precise directions are unnecessary. Just follow the creek and keep descending; you'll eventually reach Garland Lake and the main trail just beyond. In general, stay more right than left. Then, as you approach Garland Lake, go left, off the last boulder field and descend the final 23 m (75 ft) through forest. There might still be a few cairns in this jumbled area. Cross the meadow between Kaslo and Garland lakes to intersect the main trail.

From the campground near lower Sapphire Lake, you'll descend 274 m (900 ft) in about 1.6 km (1 mi) to Garland Lake, where you're on familiar ground. Turn left on the main trail to return to Kaslo Lake campground. Turn right for Gibson Lake trailhead via Kokanee Lake.

Trip 16
Lyle Creek Basin / Mt. Brennan

Location	South edge of Goat Range Provincial Park
Round trip	14.6 km (9 mi)
Elevation gain	1463 m (4800 ft)
Time required	7 to 10 hours
Difficulty	Challenging
Maps	Rosebery 82 K/3; Valhalla Society Guide to the White Grizzly Wilderness

OPINION

Though Kootenay Lake is girded by the peaky Selkirks and Purcells, the lake valley is so deep and narrow that views from the water's edge are generally limited to rounded, forested slopes. One exception is just north of Riondel on the east shore. Standing on the rocky beach, facing northwest up the lake, much of the year you'll see a white crack in the otherwise green panorama. That crack is the snow-laden immensity of Mt. Brennan, 35 km (22 mi) distant, looming above Kaslo River canyon. Late summer through fall, the white fades to steel gray. It's an invitation. The mountain is saying to adventurous hikers: "Come on up!"

Do it. Brennan is a friendly giant. You can walk up his shoulder and dance on his head. No climbing skills required. Once the snow is gone, it's just a steep hike. A good trail leads 3.1 km (1.9 mi) into the upper cirque of Lyle Creek basin. This upper cirque is so ravishing you could be seduced into abandoning the ascent. Resist the temptation to stop and plop. Though the cascade, lakelets, meadows and steep walls make this an exceptionally beautiful enclave, it's not the scenic climax of the trip. You're less than half way. Proceed up the trail, then continue following the cairned route. An astonishing sight awaits you on the mountaintop.

Brennan affords one of the grandest views of any hiker-accessible perch in the West Kootenays. The summit panorama is studded with significant landmarks, including Four Squatters Glacier, the Bugaboo Spires, Kootenay Lake, Macbeth Icefield, glaciers near Jumbo Pass, even the Rocky Mountains. On subsequent West

Whitewater Mtn and glacier from summit of Mt. Brennan

Kootenay hikes, Brennan will be one of the landmarks you seek on the horizon. Spotting it will be gratifying, like meeting an old friend in a crowd.

If the cairns between the upper cirque and the summit are no longer in place, don't worry. The route is easy, with lots of leeway and no technical difficulties. Experienced off-trail hikers won't need directions; they'll find the ascent logical, straightforward. Everyone else can rely on our *On Foot* description. It's sufficiently detailed so you don't have to bounce off every cairn like a human pinball. Just don't attempt to surmount Brennan before late July. Wait until most of the snowpack has melted. The route we suggest will be recognizable then. And a slip-and-slide injury will be less likely.

Grizzly-bear sightings are common between the trailhead and the upper cirque. Be alert and make noise. The rocky environs above that provide little or no bear food, so you can relax your guard somewhat on the rest of the ascent.

FACT

Before your trip

Reaching the Mt. Brennan trailhead might be a problem. The entire area, just south of Goat Range Provincial Park, is riddled with mining claims. The vehicle access described here is the traditional route, which crosses private land. The owner blocked the road in 1998. It has been open sporadically since then, but might not be now. The Forest Service is attempting to negotiate alternative access. Before your trip, call the Kootenay Lake district office: (250) 825-1100. Ask the recreation officer about the current status of the Mt. Brennan trailhead access road. It's worth walking the road to the trailhead, if necessary.

If the traditional access described here is open, it will require you to drive 5 km (3.1 mi) of rough, brushy, steep dirt road to reach the trailhead. When dry, it can be passable but challenging in 2WD. A high clearance vehicle is preferable. If muddy, 4WD might be necessary.

By Vehicle

From the junction of Hwys 6 and 31A in **New Denver,** drive east 19.7 km (12.2 mi) on Hwy 31A. Or, from the junction of Washington and "A" streets in **Kaslo,** drive west 26 km (16.1 mi) on Hwy 31A. From either approach, upon arrival at the former mining townsite of Retallack, turn north onto the dirt road between the old abandoned buildings. Proceed 100 meters (110 yards) into a clearing beyond the buildings. It's easiest to turn right, then curve left. Set your trip odometer to 0 before this left curve at the east end of the clearing.

0 km (0 mi)
Starting at the east end of the clearing. The road ascends north.

350 meters (0.2 mi)
Turn right.

1.2 km (0.7 mi)
Stay left, on the higher road.

1.4 km (0.9 mi)
Turn right, onto the lower road. Left leads to Whitewater Canyon.

1.7 km (1.1 mi)
Cross the bridge over Whitewater Creek.

3.5 km (2.2 mi)
Turn right.

3.6 km (2.25 mi)
Bear left.

5 km (3.1 mi)
Reach the signed trailhead at road's end. Elevation: 1433 m (4700 ft).
Parking space is severely limited; try to leave room for other vehicles.
A beautiful cascade graces the headwall of this lower basin.

On Foot

The trail starts next to the sign at the far end of the parking
area. Initially your general direction of travel is northwest. Don't set
out on the barricaded old mining road. Despite switchbacks, the
ascent is instantly steep. Brush, however, is minimal. Soon rejoin
the old mining road for a short distance, then resume on trail. Cross
a rockslide and traverse the headwall directly north of the trailhead.
Then curve north, climbing through subalpine forest and huckleberry bushes.

About 1 hour of hiking grants you an expanded view. Southwest is the prominent ridge culminating at Idaho Lookout. Beyond
it, to the right, is New Denver Glacier in Valhalla Provincial Park.
South, across Kaslo Creek valley, is the Kokanee Range.

After gaining 579 m (1900 ft) in 3.1 km (1.9 mi)—a task that takes
strong hikers a little more than an hour—enter the **upper cirque of
Lyle Creek Basin** at 2012 m (6600 ft). A dramatic cascade leaps off
the headwall to feed a chain of three small lakes. Surrounding them
are meadows and subalpine forest. To assess the rest of the journey,
angle right, rockhop across the outlet stream, and proceed until
more of Mt. Brennan is visible northwest. To resume the ascent,
angle left from where you first entered the upper cirque. The trail
climbs across a rockslide. From here on, you're out of the trees,
hiking mostly on rock, occasionally on grass or heather.

Switchbacking up the southwest side of a creek gorge, you can
soon see Mt. Loki and Kootenay Lake, both southeast. Near the
head of the gorge, turn left (south) onto rockier terrain. The trail is
cairned, still discernible here, but disappears just above, near the
abandoned **mining shafts along a mineral seam.**

Go left (southwest) along the mineral seam for a couple minutes,
then ascend northwest toward a narrow, shallow gap in the chunky,
white rocks. That gap leads to a **tarn** clutched in a rocky declivity.
Following cairns, ascend the small ridge right of the tarn. At 2271 m
(7450 ft), about 30 minutes from the upper cirque, the ice-splattered
peaks of Kokanee Provincial Park are visible south. Your goal, the
summit of Mt. Brennan, reveals most of its bulk northwest.

From the small ridge above the tarn, ascend north. Cross a
creeklet, angle right (northeast) and attain the next ridge. Go left

(northwest) for a few minutes, then proceed through a cleft in the ridge and follow that draw north. The ascent eases now.

Head toward the first big, **year-round snowfield.** Ascend steeply right of it. The ascent eases again just above. A wide, vertical **vein of white and brown rocks** provides a natural pathway toward the summit. Follow it. Go left around the next, even **bigger snowfield.** The top of Mt. Brennan is obvious now. Take aim and work your way up the bouldery slope to the summit cairn: 2896 m (9500 ft). Strong hikers will be high-fiving each other 1¾ hours from the upper cirque, or within 3 hours of departing the trailhead. Total elevation gain: 1463 m (4800 ft).

Given a clear day, the 360° horizon is crowded with prominent, recognizable features. These are a few of the highlights. North/northeast is Four Squatters Glacier; beyond are the Bugaboo Spires. Northeast is Kootenay Lake; beyond is Macbeth Icefield; farther yet are glaciers in the upper Glacier Creek valley north of Jumbo Pass; and way beyond are the Rocky Mountain peaks of Kootenay National Park. East/southeast are domino-like spires in the Purcell Wilderness Conservancy. South are glaciers in Kokanee Glacier Provincial Park. Below, southwest, is Whitewater Creek canyon. Directly west is Whitewater Mtn, with a small glacier on its face and a tarn below. Distant north/northwest are the Monashees. Below, north, are cascades at the headwaters of South Cooper Creek canyon.

Ascending Mt. Brennan from upper Lyle Creek basin

Trip 17
Keystone and Standard Basins

Location	Columbia Mountains, north of Revelstoke
Round trip	14.6 to 22 km (9 to 13.6 mi)
Elevation gain	400 m (1312 ft) to 608 m (1994 ft)
Time required	5 to 10 hours
Difficulty	Easy
Maps	Downie Creek 82 M/8; Columbia Forest District trail map

OPINION

Up here you get the impression the world is nothing but mountains and glaciers. Because that's what you see in every direction. It's an inspiring illusion for a hiker. And it begins at the trailhead: so high above Lake Revelstoke that you're at eye level with the icy Monashee Mountains rising sharply from the far shore. Twenty minutes up the trail, after surmounting a low ridge, the view expands to 360°. From there on, as you easily contour open slopes, the horizon is sharply serrated and thickly frosted.

You can adequately sample the area on a four-hour dayhike, turning around at Mars Creek in Keystone Basin. Ideally, allow at least five hours, turning around at the highpoint on an outlier of Keystone Peak. Beyond, the trail drops into forest en route to Standard Cabin. Want a longer, even more fulfilling day? Scramble 390 m (1280 ft) above the trail, to the top of Keystone Peak. Or wander the alplands at the head of Standard Basin. (See photo on page 166.)

Standard Cabin is more attractive than its setting. And once the trail begins descending to it, you'll see little but trees. It's a small, sturdy, tidy shelter beside a subalpine pond. It has a woodstove, accommodates about six people, and is free of charge—available first come, first served. Beyond the cabin, a route ascends 428 m (1403 ft) in 7.5 km (4.7 mi) to the summit of Standard Peak. Bagging the peak on a dayhike is a grueling marathon. Instead, backpack to the cabin, then launch your assault the next morning.

Beware: the Keystone / Standard trailhead is horsefly infested. Thousands of the hideous, thimble-sized insects will swarm your vehicle, a la Alfred Hitchcock. And they give a painful nip if

Keystone Basin

allowed to linger on bare skin. You'll elude all but the most persistent fiend while hiking, but before mid-September expect to be harassed every time you stop.

FACT

By Vehicle

From Trans-Canada Hwy 1 at Revelstoke, drive paved Hwy 23 north 50 km (31 mi) along the east shore of Lake Revelstoke. Turn right (east) onto the dirt road (signed for the trail) and set your trip odometer to 0.

0 km (0 mi)
Starting east, ascending moderately steep Keystone Creek FS road. All junctions are signed.

2 km (1.2 mi)
Go left.

3.4 km (2.1 mi)
Go right.

5.7 km (3.5 mi)
The road levels after curving south.

6.5 km (4 mi)
Go left. The glacier-capped Monashee Mountains are soon visible west.

8.4 km (5.2 mi)
Proceed straight.

9.4 km (5.8 mi), 9.7 km (6 mi), and 10.8 km (6.7 mi)
Bear right.

16.3 km (10.1 mi)
Reach the road's end trailhead in a cutblock at 1692 m (5550 ft).

On Foot

The trail rises northeast through the cutblock. Soon enter forest. In 20 minutes, at 1.75 km (1.1 mi), after gaining 150 m (492 ft), enter rolling subalpine meadows. Keystone Peak is visible northeast. Mt. Revelstoke National Park is south. The Selkirk Mountains, climaxing in Glacier National Park, are southeast.

Shortly beyond the 3-km (1.9-mi) sign, descend briefly into trees, then gently ascend, entering **Keystone Basin** at 5 km (3.1 mi). Strong hikers can veer north and ascend grassy slopes to the 2372-m (7784-ft) summit of Keystone Peak. To continue following the trail, rockhop across the headwaters of **Mars Creek**.

Just past 6 km (3.7 mi), high on a steep slope, at 1951 m (6400 ft), the trail curves south. It soon turns east again, traversing the southward-jutting outlier of Keystone Peak to enter **Standard Basin**. Glacier-laden Carnes Peak is visible southeast. Beyond it is Durrand Glacier. The imposing summits and vast icefields of the Sir Sanford Range are northeast. The Monashees, rising abruptly from Lake Revelstoke canyon, are west and southwest.

Having hiked 7.3 km (4.5 mi) and gained 400 m (1312 ft), you're now on the outlier's 2073-m (6800-ft) crest, which divides Keystone and Standard basins. Most hikers turn around here. But if you have more energy and curiosity, and you're not spending the night at Standard Cabin, don't stop. But neither should you keep following the trail, which descends into forest. Abandon it for a couple-hour cross-country ramble north into Standard Basin.

If the cabin is your goal, carry on. Occasional flagging helps you stay on the path. Upon reaching a subalpine pond, you'll find the **cabin** on the south shore, at 11 km (6.8 mi), 1884 m (6180 ft).

The Monashees, from just above Keystone / Standard trailhead

Departing the cabin for the trailhead, you'll gain 188 m (617 ft) before again topping out on the outlier. Swift hikers can be back at the trailhead in 3 hours.

From the cabin, a route leads east briefly, then south up Standard Creek drainage toward Standard Peak. It's discernible for about 2 km (1.2 mi), then you must navigate your way south. At the head of the drainage, bend east about a kilometer before ascending the slopes of 2312-m (7583-ft) Standard Peak.

Trip 18
Glacier Crest

Location	Glacier National Park, Selkirks
Round trip	10.4 km (6.4 mi)
Elevation gain	1005 m (3296 ft)
Time required	5 to 6 hours
Difficulty	Moderate
Maps	Environment Canada Mount Revelstoke and Glacier National Parks 1:70,000; The Adventure Map Rogers Pass 1:50,000

OPINION

Glacier National Park harbours a distinguished ensemble of trails. All are short. Most are spectacular. None disappoints. Four are included in this book. Hike as many as time permits. But if you can devote only a single day to the park, hike Glacier Crest. It starts in luxuriant ancient forest. Follows a raucous stream. Surges up a precipitous canyon wall. Climbs into the realm of exalted peaks. And climaxes on a narrow ridge with a 360° panorama. Below you, on either side, are two of the park's namesake glaciers—stubborn, ice-age monuments doing their damnedest to hang on for another century.

Even if you stay a couple days in the park, Glacier Crest should be your first hike, because it allows you to see and assess other trails. Abbott Ridge is visible nearby northwest. Avalanche Crest is the long slope rising just southeast of the park visitor centre, farther from peaks and glaciers. Northwest, across the highway, is the Cougar Brook / Balu Pass trail, which curves behind a mountain that obscures views. East, on the other side of Illecillewaet Glacier, is the trail to Perley Rock. Many say it affords the most impressive perspective of the park. It's worth debating. We tend to favour Glacier Crest, because in addition to granting an equally striking view of Illecillewaet Glacier, it acquaints you more fully with Asulkan Glacier. But hike both trails if possible, then decide for yourself.

Illecillewaet Glacier from Glacier Crest

All the park's trails, including Glacier Crest, are degraded by the Trans-Canada Highway. The valley is so narrow and steep-sided that the pavement is often visible to hikers. Even when it's not, speeding vehicles are audible. A true wilderness experience is attainable here only by climbers capable of continuing beyond trail's end. At least the first leg of the Glacier Crest trail is deep in forest, where the swish of Asulkan Brook is pervasive. Later, the trail is far enough from the highway that you can ignore it, choosing instead to merge with the tumultuous rock-and-ice spectacle surrounding you.

Despite an inescapable highway, the trails in this awesome little park are a national treasure. So, here's a quick history lesson to deepen your appreciation for the area. Climbers the world over were drawn to the Selkirk Mountains as early as 1888. Canadian Pacific Railway laid track through Rogers Pass in 1885. They later built a 90-room hotel just south of where Illecillewaet campground is today. It operated from 1887 to 1925. CPR also built the hiking trails to provide access for climbers. In 1916 the railway bypassed the hotel, which closed in 1925. The Trans-Canada Highway came blaring through Rogers Pass in 1962. The area was granted national-park status in 1886.

FACT

Before your trip

Has it rained in the park recently? If so, consider that the trail degenerates—briefly but dramatically—on the final push to the ridgecrest. This short section is little more than a dirt scar tilted sky-ward at perhaps 45°. It poses no danger when dry. But it's precarious when slick. No acrophobe would dare attempt it. If you recoil from such obstacles, choose another trail—one you're confident you can complete.

By Vehicle

If you're driving west on Trans-Canada Hwy 1, after entering Glacier National Park, continue 3.7 km (2.3 mi) beyond the Rogers Pass Visitor Centre and turn left at the signed entrance for Illecille-waet campground.

If you're driving east on Trans-Canada Hwy 1, after entering Glacier National Park, turn right at the signed entrance for Illecille-waet campground. It's 66.5 km (41.3 mi) from the controlled inter-section (where the Chevron, Petro Canada and Shell stations are located) in Revelstoke.

From either approach, drive southeast on the Illecillewaet road. (Glacier Crest is now visible. It's the forested ridge between the two glaciers at the head of the valley. The trail ascends the spine.) Proceed 1.1 km (0.7 mi) to the trailhead parking lot at road's end. Elevation: 1250 m (4100 ft).

On Foot

At the upper end of the paved parking lot, the road forks. Right enters the campground. Follow the dirt road straight ahead and uphill. In 100 meters (110 yards) pass the Alpine Club of Canada (ACC) hut on your left and confront two trail signs that appear to be quibbling over distances. No matter. Turn right and cross a berm over the Illecillewaet River.

About 200 meters (220 yards) farther, reach Glacier House Monument at 0.4 km (0.25 mi). Turn left (south) for Glacier Crest. In another 150 meters (165 yards), stay left where the Abbott Ridge trail forks right. A couple minutes farther, bear right at another signed fork. The good, gravel trail flows through a mossy forest of mature hemlocks and spruce. The goliath boulders you'll encounter crashed to their current resting place long ago, after a cataclysm ejected them from above. The boisterous Asulkan Brook (really a robust creek) is nearby, left. Elevation gain is still minimal as you continue generally south.

Reach a junction at 1.2 km (0.75 mi), 1295 m (4250 ft). The Great Glacier trail veers left, dropping to cross the brook. Proceed straight. Soon you can see east into Illecillewaet valley, which the Perley Rock trail probes. Cross a bridge to the east side of Asulkan Brook. A few minutes beyond, turn left at a signed fork where the Asulkan trail resumes straight.

Now begins the ascent of Glacier Crest. From here on, you're heading generally southeast. Where a rough trail forks left, stay on the main trail curving right. As you climb, glaciers up-valley as well as north of the Trans-Canada are increasingly visible.

You're assaulting the ridge that separates Illecillewaet valley (east) from Asulkan valley (southwest). Both were once filled by their respective glaciers, which have since melted furiously and are today greatly diminished though still impressive. East is 3277-m (10,750-ft) Mt. Sir Donald. North of the Trans-Canada, rising above the visitor centre, is the Hermit Range. It bears numerous glaciers, but most are tiny compared to those here on the south side of the highway. Northwest the densely forested lower slopes of Abbott Ridge career down to the highway. The roaring Illecillewaet River, far below, is now audible.

After switchbacking up toward the north end of the ridge, the trail stays on the west-facing slope and steepens. The forest opens and berry bushes are prevalent as you enter the subalpine zone, near 1820 m (5970 ft). Fast hikers will be here in 1½ hours. The trail gradually narrows above but remains evident.

At 1980 m (6500 ft) you've surpassed treeline and are ascending along the rocky west face of the ridge. But you're still below the crest. Asulkan Glacier is visible southwest. Beneath it you can see the Asulkan trail ascending the moraine. Across the upper valley, 610-m (2000-ft) meltwater plumes grace the cliffs.

The ascent eases through the base of a rockslide. Even here, a trail has been cleared through the boulders. About 2¼ hours of marching at a drill sergeant's pace will bring you to 2135 m (7000 ft), where the trail appears to divide at the end of the rockslide. Turn left (east) and climb skyward. This heathery, 65-m (215-ft) slope tilts nearly 45° and takes 10 to 15 minutes to surmount. Catch your breath on the ridge, then turn right. Follow the rocky, trailless, gently-ascending crest southeast for the final 0.4 km (0.25 mi).

A large cairn marks the end of the route at 5 km (3.1 mi), 2255 m (7396 ft). Just beyond and below is an arete, a narrow ridge gnawed away on both sides by glaciers. Northeast, beneath you, is the Ille-cillewaet Glacier. Across it, a bit higher than your perch, is the dark hump of Perley Rock (Trip 19). Scrutinize the slope left of and below it; you can see the switchbacking scrape of the trail. It's steep, but not as forbidding as it appears. South/southwest is Asulkan Ridge. Southwest is 3107-m (10,191-ft) Mt. Bonney.

Trip 19
Perley Rock

Location	Glacier National Park, Selkirks
Round trip	11.4 km (7.1 mi)
Elevation gain	1162 m (3810 ft)
Time required	5 to 6 hours
Difficulty	Challenging
Maps	Environment Canada Mount Revelstoke and Glacier National Parks 1:70,000; The Adventure Map Rogers Pass 1:50,000

OPINION

When the Glacier House Hotel was flourishing, manager H.A. Perley had perhaps the best job in Canada. This hike lets you experience one of the many perks he enjoyed: a thrilling trail right out the back door, allowing a quick ascent of alpine slopes to wondrous glacier views. He and his guests also enjoyed, on the house, all they could drink of an extraordinary, invigorating elixir: glacial air.

If you're reasonably fit, and not acrophobic, the Perley Rock trail can be highly motivating. Each vantage point, more astounding than the last, inspires upward progress, until you finally top out on the rocky knob that bears the lucky hotel manager's name. The terrain is vertiginous, but the path was smartly engineered, with long switchbacks across heathery slopes and through rock gardens. And, like all the park's trails, this one continues to be well maintained. If you reconnoiter the Perley Rock trail from Glacier Crest (Trip 18), don't be alarmed. The shoulder that juts southwest between Mt. Sir Donald and Terminal Peak appears insanely steep. It's actually not. The ascent poses no problem.

Here, in the heart of glacier country, you'll enjoy a more intimate encounter with ice than is possible on most western Canadian mountain trails. Compared to Glacier Crest—on the other side of the canyon, just across Illecillewaet Glacier—the Perley Rock trail enables you to see more of the glacier plus all the polished bedrock below the glacier's receding tongue. Glacier Crest, however, affords a more impressive perspective of the glacier's vertical length. Remember: proceeding onto the ice is dangerous unless you're experienced at glacier travel and properly equipped.

Ascending to Perley Rock

After surmounting Perley Rock and quaffing the intoxicating view, a rare treat awaits you: a sensational descent. On this trail, you can actually appreciate the scenery better on the way down. The glacier's fractured tongue and the scoured bedrock beneath it are in constant view. And the roar of myriad meltwater cascades grows louder.

FACT

By Vehicle
Follow the directions for Glacier Crest (Trip 18) to the road's end trailhead parking lot at 1250 m (4100 ft).

On Foot
At the upper end of the paved parking lot, the road forks. Right enters the campground. Follow the dirt road straight ahead and uphill. In 100 meters (110 yards) pass the Alpine Club of Canada (ACC) hut on your left and confront two trail signs that appear to be quibbling over distances.

Continue straight, descend toward the Illecillewaet River, and head upstream on the trail above its east bank. Within 10 minutes stay straight at a signed junction. Your general direction of travel will be southeast all the way to Perley Rock.

The trail ascends moderately through a mature forest of hemlock, spruce and cedar. Within 30 minutes, at 1357 m (4450 ft), an open stretch grants views. Left (east) is 3277-m (10,750-ft) Mt. Sir Donald and the small Vaux Glacier. Right (southwest) is Glacier Crest, separating Illecillewaet and Asulkan valleys. Cross open avalanche slopes broken by stands of trees. Ahead (southeast) is Illecillewaet Glacier.

Within 45 minutes, near 2 km (1.2 mi), 1700 m (5576 ft), the trail steepens. Cross a bridged creek, ascend a small moraine, then cross the bridge over Vaux Glacier's meltwater stream. Mt Sir Donald towers above you. The grade becomes extreme. Tight switchbacks climb through krummholz and berry bushes. Re-enter forest on the now rocky, rooty trail.

At 2.5 km (1.6 mi), 1850 m (6068 ft), reach a signed junction. A climbers' route forks left, aiming for the base of Mt. Sir Donald. Bear right, still ascending steeply through forest. You're nearing Illecillewaet Glacier. Southwest, Asulkan Glacier peeks over Glacier Crest. Above treeline, continue switchbacking upward on the open, heathery slope.

Proceed onto a boulder field and enter a gorge near 4 km (2.5 mi), 2317 m (7600 ft). You've hiked about 2¼ hours and gained 1067 m (3500 ft) so far. Much of Illecillewaet and Asulkan glaciers are now visible. Perley Rock is the knoll to your right (south), just across the gorge.

The trail, little more than a route from here on, curves beneath a sheer rockband at the head of the gorge. Completing that curve takes only a few minutes but can be dicey. When snow-filled, the gorge can be impassable. If it's bare, warily cross the steep talus chute on an eroded, inches-wide path. Then work your way over boulders as you follow cairns up through a gap.

Finally, you're on level ground. About 250 meters (270 yards) ahead (south) is a turquoise meltwater pool at the edge of the glacier. Immediately right (west) is 2412-m (7910-ft) Perley Rock, quickly and easily surmounted.

Perley Rock overlooks the tongue of Illecillewaet Glacier, which has receded 1 km (0.6 mi) since the early 1920s. The bare rock slabs you see below were polished by the ice that once covered them. Visible south are two summits bursting through the Illecillewaet Neve. Asulkan Ridge and 3107-m (10,191-ft) Mt. Bonney are south-west. The Hermit Range is north of the Trans-Canada.

Trip 20
Hermit Basin

Location	Glacier National Park, Selkirks
Round trip	5.6 km (3.5 mi)
Elevation gain	770 m (2525 ft)
Time required	5 hours
Difficulty	Moderate
Maps	Environment Canada Mount Revelstoke and Glacier National Parks 1:70,000; The Adventure Map Rogers Pass 1:50,000; Glacier 82 N/5

OPINION

Forged as a direct route to boost climbers into the alpine zone where they can grapple with serrated peaks, this trail is dastardly steep. But it's well maintained. And it quickly conveys hikers to a walloping view from a tiny alpine shelf on the edge of the Hermit Range, beneath the Swiss and Tupper glaciers. What you'll see is the skyscraping south side of Glacier National Park and the turbulent terrain of two other hikes in this book: Perley Rock (Trip 19) and Glacier Crest (Trip 18). Enhance the experience by bringing a park map to help you interpret what you see.

Earplugs might also help. The trail starts on the Trans-Canada and is essentially vertical, so the highway is always below you. Ascending far enough to escape the noise takes most hikers a full hour. Mountain goats can do it in 40 minutes and attain the basin in 1½ hours.

You'll hike through an ancient forest of cedar, mountain hemlock and alpine fir. Creeks soften the sound of the highway. About an hour up, a rock rib offers seating and a view of the Sir Donald Range, the top of Illecillewaet Glacier, Asulkan Glacier backed by blocky peaks, and Bonney Glacier. Near the top, you'll clamber through short rocky gulleys but without exposure to cliffs.

Exploring much beyond trail's end necessitates climbing. But even a hiker can enjoy camping here and simply settling into mountain time. (See photo on page 166.) Parents ready to initiate their young children on a short backpack trip will find this an ideal

Glacier Crest (left) and Abbott Ridge (right) from Hermit basin

destination—if the kids can manage the stiff ascent. Youthful imaginations recognize a jumble of boulders and creeks for what it is: a wild playground.

FACT

Before your trip

If you want to backpack, call Glacier National Park's Visitor Centre (250-837-7500 to reserve a tentsite. The fee is $6 per adult per night in 2001.

By Vehicle

Drive Trans-Canada Hwy 1 to Rogers Pass Visitors Centre in Glacier National Park. The signed trailhead parking lot is 1.4 km (0.9 mi) northeast. It's on the left (northwest) side of the highway, at 1287 m (4220 ft).

On Foot

Your general direction of travel will be north the entire way. There are no junctions. Stay on the main trail.

About 20 minutes from the trailhead, a roaring creek briefly overwhelms the highway noise. About 30 minutes up, at 1600 m (5250 ft), Abbott Ridge and Bonney Glacier are visible southwest. Ten minutes later, at 1670 m (5480 ft), the forest opens, allowing views. Even if your motivation is waning, don't turn around yet. You'll soon reach a rock rib where you can comfortably sit, rest, and congratulate yourself for surmounting 405 m (1330 ft).

After hiking about an hour, reach a level viewpoint at 1800 m (5900 ft). Beyond, the trail wiggles up a walled creek gully. You might need your hands to ascend it.

Reach your destination, a tiny alpine shelf, at 2.8 km (1.7 mi), 2067 m (6780 ft). The camping area has four tent pads, a pit toilet (green plastic throne). Natural gravel beds serve as additional tentsites.

The 2667-m (8748-ft) peak called The Hermit looms above. It's backed by Tupper Glacier. Northwest is Rogers Glacier on 2941-m (9646-ft) Mt. Sifton.

Hermit Basin

Trip 21
Bald Mountain

Location	Glacier National Park, Purcells
Round trip	35.2 km (21.8 mi)
Elevation gain	1354 m (4440 ft)
Time required	3 days
Difficulty	Moderate
Maps	Blaeberry 82 N/6; Environment Canada Mount Revelstoke and Glacier National Parks 1:70,000; The Adventure Map Rogers Pass 1:50,000

OPINION

Staying out of step with the majority of people makes life more interesting. Adventurous hikes are a good way to swerve out of the parade. Set your own quirky pace by backpacking lonely trails to uncommon destinations like Bald Mountain.

The name Bald Mountain refers only to the absence of forest. The mountain isn't totally bald, just buzzcut, with a little Bozo-esque fringe of trees. It's covered with grass-and-heather meadows. In summer, it's dappled with wildflowers. And it's not a mountain in the classical sense. It's a broad, rolling, 8-km (5-mi) long, alpine ridge. Wandering here is as effortless and relaxing as high-elevation travel gets. As for the scenery, wear sunglasses to keep your eyes from popping out and dangling on the ends of their springs. The massif that bolsters Glacier National Park's sprawling neves (granular icefields) is in full view, just across the valley. Bald Mountain parallels this rigid tsunami of peaks.

So why is this trail lonely and the destination uncommon? Several reasons. (1) On a map it looks like a trail to nowhere. Though within Glacier National Park, the trail starts outside the popular core, wanders into an obscure valley, then halts abruptly at Copperstain Pass, on the park boundary. People assume that the end of the park denotes the end of great scenery. (2) All the park's trails, except this one, are short, steep, stellar daytrips. With a wealth of long trails available in the nearby Rockies, few people think of backpacking in Glacier National Park. (3) You must slog all day, uphill, through viewless forest before the effort pays off.

But WOW, it pays generously. Complete the ascent, and the work's done. You can leave your backpack at your tent and go roaming with nothing more than a lumbar pack. The approach is viewless, but the forest is ancient. Cedars, mountain hemlocks and larches are comely, amicable, and patient listeners—better company than a lot of people. Though the trail is long, it's well maintained and comfortably graded.

Camping on Bald Mountain can be a celestial experience. Pitch your tent near the mountain's north end, within reach of a tarn or stream. But refer to a map and stay south and east of the park boundary, where there are no fees or restrictions. Observe *Leave No Trace* guidelines, of course. You'll likely be alone. Given a sunny day, you'll be padding barefoot on the grass, admiring the meadows, ogling the summit-studded horizon, and thinking how lucky you are. (See photo on page 167.) A storm, however, would clobber you; trees are too scarce and small to block wind. If weather's a concern, pitch your tent in the treed campground at trail's end, below the crest, just inside the national park boundary. Camping there has other advantages. It's less impactful on the environment and offers the security of a bear-proof food-hanging cable. But you'll be a half-hour below the mountaintop, so views are nil. And you'll be subject to national park regulations, which means reserving a site and paying for it in advance ($6 per adult per night in 2001). Call Rogers Pass Visitor Centre (250-837-7500) for details.

Before setting out for Bald Mountain, understand that these vast meadows are prime grizzly-bear habitat. We encountered bears each day we were here in early September, 2000. If you come, expect to see a griz and know how to respond. Read our *Bears* section. Listen to the audio cassette *Bears Beware*, described in the back of this book. And, if you intend to camp atop the mountain, carry your food in a bear-resistant container, because hanging stuffsacks in a stunted tree is ludicrously unsafe.

Bald Mountain has one blemish: trails have recently been cut here by Purcell Lodge. The lodge itself is acceptably unobtrusive, below the crest, on the mountain's east slope, away from the premier scenery. Because it offers heli-hiking in summer, you might see lodge guests. That can be upsetting (read Trip 29). But far worse is seeing these absurd trails. They're extensive, permanent scars. They serve only to degrade the wilderness. Trails are utterly unnecessary in such a vast treeless expanse, where getting lost is improbable. Instead of civilizing the mountain for pampered guests, and

Mt. Sir Donald, Selkirk Range, from Bald Mountain meadows

severely marring it in the process, the lodge should protect the integrity of the land and provide a more authentic wilderness experience. Why aren't they teaching guests how to hike through meadows? It's simple: spread out and don't retrace your steps. By staying widely abreast of each other, rather than following single-file, hikers diffuse and decrease the damage they inflict on fragile alpine vegetation. Purposely not repeating a cross-country route helps prevent bootbeaten paths from developing.

FACT

By Vehicle

From Glacier National Park's northeast entrance, drive south 11.5 km (7.1 mi) on Trans-Canada Hwy 1. At the sign BEAVER VALLEY – COPPERSTAIN, get in the right lane and slow down to make a safe turn left (east) across the highway, onto the dirt road

From Rogers Pass Visitor Centre in Glacier National Park, drive northeast 11 km (6.8 mi) on Trans-Canada Hwy 1. At the sign BEAVER VALLEY – COPPERSTAIN, turn right (south) onto the dirt road.

From either approach, proceed on the dirt road. Go left at 1.2 km (0.7 mi). Reach the trailhead parking lot at 1.4 km (0.8 mi), 878 m (2880 ft).

On Foot

The trail starts at the far (south) end of the parking lot. Jog right (west), then follow the top of an embankment south. Continue the gentle ascent south/southeast on a pleasant old road for about 3 km (1.9 mi)—45 minutes—through beautiful forest of cedar and western hemlock. Highway noise is audible. About 1 hour in, enter **Beaver River Canyon**. The slopes of Mt. MacDonald now block highway noise. A glacier is visible southwest.

At 4 km (2.5 mi), 976 m (3200 ft), after hiking about 1¼ hours, reach a **junction**. Fork left (southeast), following the sign for Copperstain. Soon curve east, then northeast to ascend Grizzly Creek canyon. Right continues southeast along forested Beaver River. It goes 38 km (23.5 mi) upstream, deep in Glacier National Park, to the park boundary near Cariboo Pass.

At 6.4 km (4 mi), 1088 m (3570 ft), reach **Grizzly Cabin** beside the creek. The historic warden cabin is not an overnight shelter. There are tent pads outside. But stop here only to rest. Just beyond the cabin, cross a sturdy plank bridge to Grizzly Creek's south bank. A long, moderate ascent east ensues.

After several switchbacks, cross a lush avalanche path. Proceed through cool forest of cedar, balsam fir, and western hemlock. Devil's club and thimbleberry are profuse. The trail curves southeast, leaving Grizzly Creek canyon and entering Copperstain Creek canyon. It climbs the west slope, well above the creek. The trail crosses small cascades, however, so water remains available.

Near 12 km (7.4 mi), 1692 m (5550 ft), enter a burn—the result of a 1975 forest fire. The surrounding blunt mountains are now visible. At 12.3 km (7.6 mi), 1860 m (6100 ft) pass a **ranger cabin**. Cross a bridged tributary stream. At 13 km (8.1 mi) enter a beautiful, heather meadow at the headwaters of Copperstain Creek. Proceed southeast, on the west side of the dwindling creek. The ascent has eased dramatically. At 15 km (9.3 mi) reach **Copperstain Pass campground**, in subalpine fir at the edge of the long meadow. It has a fire pit, benches, four tent pads, and a bear pole for food storage.

Follow the trail south until it peters out in 2048-m (6717-ft) **Copperstain Pass** at 16 km (10 mi). There's a map/sign here, indicating your location and the boundaries of Glacier National Park and Columbia Forest Service District. The west slope of 2606-m (8548-ft) **Copperstain Mountain** is left (east). Should you choose to hike up it from your basecamp, begin ascending here; you'll tag onto a trail part way up. But first continue to Bald Mountain, where

Crossing Grizzly Creek

you can assess the route up Copperstain Mountain and decide if it merits your time.

The crest of **Bald Mountain** is just 1.6 km (1 mi) distant—less than a 30-minute cross-country hike up the gentle, alpine slopes right (west). Pass several large tarns en route. Top out at 2232 m (7320-ft). The panorama is unobstructed. West/southwest, across Beaver River valley, is the Sir Donald Range. The highest peak is 3277-m (10,750-ft) Mt. Sir Donald. From north to south, the glaciers are Eagle, Uto, and Sir Donald, followed by several unnamed ones. Illecillewaet Neve is hidden, on the other side of the range. The Purcell Mountains fill the eastern horizon. A stream meanders down Bald Mountain's west slope, draining the tarns above. If you camp up here, remember that the national park boundary follows the height of land south. Pitch your tent east of it, where there are no restrictions.

Your first morning on Bald Mountain, weather permitting, hike through the rolling meadows that extend south/southeast along the crest. Atop the **first bump** (2266 m / 7432 ft), Purcell Lodge is visible left (southeast). It's perched in the upper reaches of Spillimacheen River valley. A trail departs the lodge, descending 244 m (800 ft) in 2 km (1.2 mi) to a junction. It's another 10.5 km (6.5 mi) southeast to the nearest road. From there, it's a rough 60-km (37-mi) drive to Hwy 95. Definitely not a quick exit.

The Purcells, east of Bald Mountain

Continuing south/southeast along the crest, you'll cross trails scarring the once pristine meadows. The lodge is responsible for this mutilation. Follow or avoid the trails, as you wish. If you avoid them, minimize your damage to the meadows. Hike abreast of your partners, rather than single file.

Wander south/southeast over **three more bumps**. Each is about 2300 m (7544 ft) high, with troughs about 60 m (200 ft) deep between them. Turn around before the long descent to the pass below Caribou Mtn.

Trip 22
Earl Grey Pass

Location	Purcell Wilderness Conservancy
One-way trip	61 km (37.8 mi)
Elevation gain	1525 m (5000 ft)
Time required	3 to 5 days
Difficulty	Challenging
Maps	Lardeau 82 K/2, Duncan Lake 82 K/7, Toby Creek 82 K/8; BC Parks brochure

OPINION

Trekking across the Purcell range, you'll experience the West Kootenay's greatest gift to the outdoor adventurer: solitude. It's possible you'll encounter no other hikers in the three-to-five days it takes to complete the west-to-east journey up Hamill Creek, over Earl Grey Pass, then down Toby Creek. But if you surmount Slate Peak (a no-worries, one-hour scramble north of the pass) the summit-cairn register will give you a glimpse of your predecessors, including a 5-year-old kid, a 12-year-old dog, and mountaineering clubs from across the continent. The register was established in August, 1968. It contains about 30 scribbled entries. Many are powerfully enticing:

"I will never be the same," effusively declared one hiker. Another, from Nelson, B.C., marveled that "Heaven is so close to home." "England will never be the same," said a Canadian wannabe. "May the loggers drool," wrote a BC Parks employee, rejoicing that Hamill Creek's giant-cedar forest was saved when the Purcell Wilderness was granted Class A status.

The reason climbers penned so many of these comments is that Slate Peak's easily-attained 360° view comprises numerous 3050-m (10,000-ft) summits (including Quibble, Squabble, Tranquility, Ochre, Toby, Hamill, and Red Top) and is therefore invaluable for reconnaissance. But even if your goal is simply to cross the pass, you'll be inexorably drawn off trail to Slate Peak. That's because your initial delight and physical relief upon attaining the pass will fade rapidly when you realize you're still below treeline, straddling the ridge in what is just a tiny notch with severely restricted views. Don't despair. Your effort was not wasted. Invest a little more. Bag Slate Peak. You'll be enraptured by a panorama of Purcell-range grandeur: gnarly summits, ornery ridges, sprawling glaciers, alpine bowls, and 750-m (2460-ft) cascades. (See photo on page 168.) Both the Hamill and Toby valleys are visible from Slate Peak, as are the glacial headwaters of the two creeks. This vista rivals premier scenery in the southern B.C. Coast Mountains, the Canadian Rockies, and the North Cascades. The difference is that backpacking to Earl Grey Pass and nipping up to Slate Peak takes much longer than hiking to comparable vantage points in other ranges.

Want to shorten the trip? Swift, tireless dayhikers can tag Earl Grey Pass via the shorter, eastern approach along Toby Creek. But they risk not having sufficient time to attain the journey's scenic climax atop Slate Peak. Another reason to make this a multi-day backpack trip via the western approach along Hamill Creek is to revel in a vast, ancient forest of mammoth cedars. You'll spend at least an entire day hiking through it—a mystical experience. The Toby Creek trail offers enticing, up-valley views earlier and more frequently, but the predominantly spruce forest on this drier, eastern side is underwhelming, and too often the path itself is a muddy, horse-tromped morass. (Horse packers are ruining the experience here for hikers. Write to BC Parks. Ask them to ban horses from the Toby Creek trail.) The Hamill Creek route swings back and forth across roaring whitewater, so equestrians are precluded and the trail is better preserved. Yet if all the Hamill Creek cable cars and footlogs are intact (call BC Parks before you depart), hikers are spared any dangerous fords.

Starting at the west trailhead near the village of Argenta, above the north end of Kootenay Lake, the trail soon drops 230 m (750 ft) to Hamill Creek. It then gains 610 m (2000 ft) in the next 14 km (8.7 mi)—an ascent so gentle it's rarely noticeable. You'll be constantly awed by glorious cedars and often entertained by the rambunctious creek. Wrestling with your pack at all the cable-car crossings is a hassle, but pulling yourself to the opposite bank is fun, and not having to ford is a luxury. Near the upper end of Hamill Creek valley, at about 17 km (10.5 mi), the challenge begins. The trail diminishes in more rugged terrain. Expect to thrash through brush and bogs. At about 32.5 km (20.2 mi), you face a taxing 823 m (2700 ft) ascent in the final 8.5 km (5.3 mi) to the pass. The trail then descends Toby Creek valley to the east trailhead. Though downhill, it's no cakewalk. Unbridged tributary crossings (not threatening, just a

Hamill Creek cedar grove

nuisance), overgrown avalanche paths, and the aforementioned horse-induced mud demand fortitude. But if you occasionally look backward, you'll enjoy grand views of the high country you just traversed.

Now, bear with us for two more minutes. We admit the following warnings are elaborate enough to rival those of the most nervous, lecture-prone parent. But we offer them knowing they'll increase your safety and enjoyment and help you maintain the pristine quality of this wilderness stronghold.

The Earl Grey Pass trail is always distinct, so navigation shouldn't be a concern. Still, this is an arduous trip, not for wimps or novices. At the midpoint, help will be at least a long day's travel away, perhaps more. A well-stocked first-aid kit is essential. Much of the way is rooty, rocky, muddy, or brushy. Avalanche paths are frequent; if they haven't been recently cleared, you'll often wade through dense, scratchy greenery. Most of the trail is forested; if the deadfall hasn't been recently removed, you'll encounter numerous obstacles that can be gymnastically challenging. Though you'll find a cable car or footlog at all major creek crossings, a couple of the logs can be unnerving, especially when wet. Several minor stream crossings in Toby Creek valley necessitate wading, unless low water-levels allow you to rockhop. Grizzly and black bears are plentiful in these remote valleys; an encounter is possible at any time.

From Rock Creek (a tributary of Hamill), all the way over the pass and down Toby Creek, campsites are few and far between. That means you must be a strong, disciplined hiker. Except at the campsites listed in the route description below, you'll find almost no bare ground level enough for a comfortable night in a tent. Plan on reaching one of the established sites every evening. And hope the one you've chosen isn't occupied, because all are tiny. Each has space for only a couple tents. So your group should comprise no more than about four people. Larger groups would be too impactful here anyway. There are no outhouses at any of the campsites. Even the smallest groups must be fastidious while cooking and cleaning, and especially diligent about disposing human waste. Leave no trace of your stay. And if you camp at the pass, be sure to haul up plenty of water. You'll find none there, except perhaps in a seasonal creeklet about 100 m (330 ft) below the west side.

Have all those admonishments doused the flame of adventure flickering in your soul? Don't want to backpack the entire distance? Consider dayhiking up Hamill Creek to enjoy the walloping white-water and see the mother of West Kootenay cedar groves. From the west trailhead, round-trip distance to Big Bar is 24 km (15 mi), but you can turn around earlier and feel satisfied. Even a short dayhike, however, will require you to ascend 230 m (750 ft) on the way out. In shoulder season, when alpine destinations are inaccessible, Hamill Creek is a premier dayhike. It's also a cool choice on a scorching hot summer day, because the deep canyon is shady.

FACT

By Vehicle

West Approach

If you're following the *On Foot* directions below, you'll be hiking west to east. Follow the directions for Jumbo Pass (Trip 24) to Kaslo, then north 34.5 km (21.4 mi) to Argenta Road.

0 km (0 mi)
Starting east on Argenta Road, toward the Purcell Wilderness.

0.5 km (0.3 mi)
Cross the Lardeau River. Pavement ends.

1.2 km (0.7 mi)
Reach a 3-way junction. Turn right, gradually curve south, and follow Kootenay Lake's northeast shore toward Argenta and the Earl Grey Pass trailhead. (Straight leads to MacBeth Icefield and Jumbo Pass trailheads — Trips 23 and 24.)

4 km (2.5 mi)
Soon after the Argenta incorporation sign, the road starts ascending gently.

5.2 km (3.2 mi)
At the junction, go sharply left for the Earl Grey Pass trailhead and Purcell Wilderness Conservancy. Fry Creek Canyon is right.

6.2 km (3.8 mi)
Pass the Argenta community hall and post office.

7.2 km (4.5 mi)
Stay left on the main road where Press Road cuts back right.

10.2 km (6.3 mi)
Earl Grey Pass trailhead is on the left at a curve. Elevation: 875 m (2870 ft).

East Approach

Use these directions if you're picking up hikers at the east trailhead, or if you're approaching from Invermere and don't plan to hike the whole way through.

Drive Hwy 95 south from Radium, or north from Cranbrook, then turn west toward **Invermere**. Go through town, toward Panorama Ski Area. Set your trip odometer to 0 at the bridge where

Heading east through upper Hamill Creek valley, to Earl Grey Pass

left leads to Panorama. Proceed straight on Toby Creek FS road. At 19 km (11.8 mi), where the road curves right and continues toward Jumbo Pass, look for a signed, overgrown, left spur. Hikers will arrive via that spur. The elevation here is 1174 m (3850 ft).

On Foot

At the BC Parks kiosk, the trail begins on the twin ruts of a grassy old road. Follow it north. In 15 minutes, reach a sign: EARL GREY PASS RECREATION TRAIL, PURCELL WILDERNESS. About 30 minutes from the trailhead, reach a trail register at 805 m (2640 ft) and attain a view west over Hamill Creek canyon.

The trail then descends 140 m (460 ft) via steep switchbacks to a small, not-very-level campsite near the south bank of Hamill Creek. (Signpost #3) Just beyond the campsite is a bridged crossing of Clint Creek, a major tributary of Hamill. (Signpost #1) Following Hamill Creek upstream, your general direction of travel will remain east-northeast for the next 30 km (18.6 mi), and the rate of ascent will be relatively painless.

An especially captivating section of the trip begins about an hour from the trailhead, in a sheer-sided, rock-walled gorge where the path hugs the bank of the rip-snorting creek. Reach the **first cable-car crossing** at 3 km (1.9 mi), 700 m (2300 ft). On the north bank, pass an abandoned mining operation at 3.8 km (2.4 mi), about

1½ hours from the trailhead. (Signpost #9) You'll see a Pelloton compressor here. Level campsites are nearby. Shortly beyond, pass **McLaughlin Cabin** in a cedar grove at 753 m (2470 ft). Reach the **second cable-car crossing** just after the cabin. On the south bank, at 800 m (2624 ft), soon pass a yellow metal blaze indicating that you've a hiked a total of 5 km (3.1 mi).

After a gradual ascent to 884 m (2900 ft), the trail descends slightly. In an avalanche path thick with cow's parsnip and thimbleberry, attain a view of the valley you're hiking through. Soon enter a lush tributary drainage, rockhop across the stream, then resume through cedar and hemlock forest. At 8 km (5 mi), 910 m (2980 ft), about 3 hours from the trailhead, a yellow metal blaze marks a left spur descending to the creekside **Garnet Beach campsite**.

At 9 km (5.6 mi) cross an avalanche path affording an impressive view of cliffs and snowfields. The trail is interrupted here by a deep, rough, steep-sided **washout**. If a trail crew has preceded you, they might have brushed out a spur through the greenery. Look for it before the washout; follow it right, then left. It will lead to the easiest place to cross the washout. If no spur is evident, continue on the main trail to the edge of the washout, then ascend right, looking for a place to safely descend to the tributary stream. Rockhop across, climb the far wall, then pick up the trail on the other side. It immediately drops back into forest.

Reach **Big Bar campsite** at 12 km (7.4 mi), 966 m (3170 ft), beneath hemlocks and cedars. It can accommodate two tents, but is best suited to just one. A waterfall is visible on the north side of the valley. Dayhikers who turn around here should be pleased with their accomplishment.

At 13 km (8.1 mi), about 5½ hours from the trailhead, cross a huge log spanning Crazy Creek. About 30 minutes farther, at 1009 m (3310 ft), reach the **third cable-car crossing**. Then, on the north bank, the trail forges through several avalanche paths.

Reach **Boy Scout Camp** at 15.5 km (9.6 mi), 1067 m (3500 ft). Total elevation gain: 402 m (1320 ft). Including time to negotiate the three previous cable-car crossings, backpackers can be here in about 6 hours. Strong dayhikers might make it in 5 hours, which means they should now head for home. There's room here for a couple tents beneath gargantuan cedars, beside a silent creeklet. Hamill Creek is about 20 meters (yards) distant, so the roar is audible but not overwhelming.

Reach the **fourth cable-car crossing** about ten minutes past Boy Scout Camp. Just beyond, on the south bank, cross a bridged tributary beneath a cascade. Near a yellow metal blaze indicating that you've a hiked a total of 17 km (10.5 mi), a short stretch of trail is submerged. Cross this knee-deep swamp on a slender, slippery log, or circumvent it by thrashing through brush and over deadfall.

At 19.5 km (12.1 mi), above where Hamill Creek cascades steeply, reach the **fifth cable-car crossing**. On the north bank, begin a noticeable ascent. Proceed among more giant cedars. About 2.5 hours from Boy Scout Camp, reach **Rock Creek Camp** at 23.5 km (14.6 mi), 1311 m (4300 ft). Immediately before the main trail crosses the log spanning Rock Creek, look for a descending right spur. It quickly leads to two tentsites beside the confluence of Rock and Hamill creeks. The view is north to an alpine cascade.

Giant cedars have now given way to smaller spruce, but as you probe the broader, upper valley, expanded views will help compensate. Near 26.5 km (16.4 mi) a huge avalanche path is on the left, and a grassy, marshy, willowy area is on the right. You're entering prime bear habitat, so make plenty of noise.

At 27.4 km (17 mi), 1381 m (4530 ft), pass a small, unappealing but level campsite just before reaching the **sixth creek crossing**. No more luxurious cable cars. Just a long, skinny footlog resembling a horizontal flag pole. It requires the nerve and balance of a tightrope walker. A fall is unlikely to be disastrous, however, because Hamill Creek is a slow-moving pool here, not a whitewater torrent. But if you think you'll end up swimming, do it on purpose: dive in (a few quick strokes will propel you to the far bank) then line your party's packs across. This requires at least 10 m (33 ft) of rope, which you should carry anyway, in case the footlog washes away before you arrive.

On the south bank, work your way through about 80 meters (87 yards) of muck. The trail then drifts toward the right (south) side of the grassy, willowy, upper valley. Cairns should help guide you through this rough, rooty, sloppy stretch.

Pass a small lake and see an alpine cascade on the valley's north wall. An hour beyond the lake, reach the **seventh creek crossing**. A footlog spans the first of two Hamill Creek channels. A footlog with a hand cable spans the second. Glacier encrusted peaks are visible from the north bank.

Quickly reach Hamill Creek's smaller but still formidable **north forks** at about 35 km (21.7 mi), 1433 m (4700 ft). All are spanned by footlogs. At one crossing, however, where the footlog was extremely wet and slick, we opted for a dry, fallen tree 30 meters

Hamill Creek cable-car crossing

(yards) downstream. Between the last two crossings, there might still be a small, level clearing sufficient for a single tent. Proceed beyond here only if you're confident you can reach the pass (2½ to 3 hours distant for strong hikers) before nightfall. Once the ensuing climb begins, you'll find no level tentsites until near the pass. And fill your waterbottles now The pass is dry. Water is not always available en route—a good reason to hike this stretch in early morning, before the hot summer sun reaches it. A seasonal creeklet 100 m (328 ft) below the west side of the pass might be flowing, but it's not a certainty.

The trail now begins a startling, merciless ascent north—an abrupt initiation to what will be a steady, 823-m (2700-ft) climb in the remaining 8.5 km (5.3 mi) to the pass. Within about 30 minutes, enjoy a brief reprieve before the skyward tilt resumes. The trail now curves southeast—your general direction until a final, short, eastward vault into the pass.

At 1750 m (5740 ft) attain the first truly exhilarating view of the trip. Southwest, across Hamill Creek valley's upper reaches, the opposite 1067-m (3500-ft) wall is festooned with glaciers and spangled with waterfalls. Glimpse more cliffs and glaciers as you ascend. The steep grade eases occasionally, but the trail surface slumps downhill and fails to provide comfortable footing. Alpine larches appear at 2067 m (6780 ft)—visible assurance that you're nearing your goal. The trail bends eastward into the subalpine zone before cresting **Earl Grey Pass** at 44 km (27.3 mi), 2280 m (7480 ft).

Earl Grey Pass is just a small, grassy gap below treeline. Views are limited. Maneuvering among the trees will enable you to glimpse upper Hamill and Toby creek valleys. Glacier-chested Mt. Hamill is southwest. Northwest of it is 3121-m (10,237-ft) Mt. Lady Grey. East-southeast is 2961-m (9712-ft) Hyak Mtn. Toby Glacier is partially visible south-southeast. But after trekking this far, it's cruel and unusual punishment not to see more. So make the short side-trip to Slate Peak and feast your soul on the awesome panorama that Earl Grey Pass denies you.

Camping at the pass is not ideal—for you, or the fragile alpine environment. The ground is lumpy and slanted. Disposing of human waste is difficult in the shallow soil. (But it *is* necessary. Bury it 12 cm / 5.5 inches deep. Pack out used toilet paper with all other trash.) Campfires are too impactful at this elevation. (They leave ugly scars that last years. Look around, you'll see several. Dead wood is scarce and should be left untouched as part of the scenery.) There's no convenient water source. If the previously-described seasonal creeklet below the west side is not flowing, your other options are to melt snow or descend east 136 m (446 ft) to a small cascade that crosses the trail. Still intend to camp at the pass? Pitch your tent on a worn area, rather than begin killing yet another patch of grass. Look for worn tentsites up slope, north of the trail. Others are in and just beyond the band of larches along the east edge of the pass.

Heading north from Earl Grey Pass, able, agile hikers can summit Slate Peak in about 1½ hours. Start by ascending the boot-beaten path on the right (east) side of the pass. Where the grass stops, work your way up the loose, chunky boulders. Attain the first knob at 2482 m (8140 ft). Then drop 43 m (140 ft) over more unstable, awkward boulders before resuming the ascent through krummholz (stunted, gnarled, tightly-clumped trees) and over slabby slopes to 2695-m (8841-ft) **Slate Peak**. En route, look for lavender Sky Pilot (resembling tiny bottlebrushes), and magenta moss campion.

On a clear day, you'll see countless summits, glaciers, ridges and valleys from Slate Peak. A topo map is necessary if you want to begin interpreting the thrillingly vast geological chaos that surrounds you. The following are but a few of the most obvious features. Northwest is 3060-m (10,050-ft) Blockhead Mtn. Left (west) of it is 3200-m (10,500-ft) Caldron Peak, backed by 3110-m

Looking north from Slate Peak, above Earl Grey Pass

(10,200-ft) Mt. Quibble—identified by a snow cornice along its left ridge. Farther northwest is 3080-m (10,100-ft) Ochre Peak. Beyond these summits, just out of sight, is the impressive Horseshoe Glacier, which is visible from Jumbo Pass (Trip 24). On your side of these summits is Hamill Creek valley, with which you're now intimately acquainted. Northeast is Toby Creek valley. Streaking its forested walls are bright-green avalanche paths, with which you'll soon be intimately acquainted. Some 80 km (50 mi) beyond Toby Creek valley is Mt. Assiniboine and its satellite peaks, Mounts Aye and Eon, in the Canadian Rockies. Southeast is massive Toby Glacier. South is 3212-m (10,538-ft) Mt. Toby.

It takes turbocharged backpackers about six hours to hike the 17 km (10.5 mi) from Earl Grey Pass to the east trailhead. If you depart the pass after 4 p.m., you'll be shaded from hot summer sun. Compared to the trail ascending the west side of the pass, the initial 3 km (1.9 mi) descending east are in better condition and more gently graded. After several switchbacks, the trail traverses northeast—your general direction the rest of the way. Hop over a small cascade at 2150 m (7050 ft). Try not to step on the toads! We counted 16 between the pass and about the 8-km (5-mi) point. This must be their pilgrimage route to Toad Peak.

About 30 minutes below the pass, enter dense forest near 1982 m (6500 ft). Soon cross a large avalanche path adorned with yellow columbine, larkspur, white valerian, paintbrush, and swirling green Indian hellebore. About 45 minutes below the pass, near 2.5 km (1.6 mi), an unsigned spur descends right to a **campground above Toby Falls**.

At 1747 m (5730 ft), about an hour below the pass, cross a small bench-meadow beside a cascade. It has an expansive view, and ample, level ground for a couple tents. Visible north is the pointy summit of 3078-m (10,095-ft) Red Top.

At 1670 m (5480 ft), about an hour and twenty minutes below the pass, reach an unbridged creek crossing. Depending on the water level and the springiness of your legs, you might have to wade. About 30 minutes beyond, reach another unbridged creek. This one is larger (knee to thigh deep), swifter, and requires fording but is not dangerous. Then proceed through an oppressive spruce forest before descending steeply through flowery meadows to Toby Creek.

At 7.7 km (4.8 mi), 1470 m (4820 ft), about 2½ hours below the pass, the trail re-enters forest. Immediately after, near an old fence, pass a spur on the right. Stay on the main trail. The spur quickly leads to the Toby Creek horse ford en route to the creek's south fork. About 10 minutes past the spur, traverse an avalanche path lined with aspen. Listen for the roar of McKay's Falls. You'll see it after crossing yet another slide path.

Pass **McKay's Falls** at 8 km (5 mi), 1410 m (4625 ft), about 3½ hours below the pass. A bit farther (about 8 minutes after the trail grazes Toby Creek), a faint right spur leads to a **campsite** with room for several tents on a **creekside gravel flat**. Look for it where there's a swampy pond and a small stand of aspen on the opposite (left) side of the main trail. Visible southwest, just above and beyond Earl Grey Pass, is Mt. Toby. Right (north) of the pass is Slate Peak. About five mintues past the gravel-flat campsite is a lone tentsite among trees and horsetails beside the creek. The east trailhead is now about 2½ hours distant.

About 4½ hours below the pass, reach an unbridged, major tributary. The ford is knee to thigh deep but poses no serious risk. About 30 minutes beyond, you must ford another unbridged creek. Shortly after, rockhop across a small stream. The trail proceeds through forest, occasionally broken by more brushy avalanche paths. The openings grant views of the peaks above. While gently descending through a meadow at 15 km (9.3 mi), look left (northwest) toward the forest edge for **Earl Grey cabin**.

Toby Creek valley, from near Earl Grey Pass

Earl Grey was Canada's Governor General from 1904 to 1911. In 1908 he crossed the Purcell Range via the pass that now bears his name. The cabin was built for his family's vacation in 1909.

At 16 km (9.9 mi), 1220 m (4000 ft), about 15 minutes past Earl Grey cabin, cross the **park boundary** and arrive at the east trailhead register. Keep going. The trail quickly reaches a small clearing accessed by an old road. Bush-beater 4WD vehicles can get this far, but all other vehicles will be stopped 1 km (0.6 mi) short of here. The road makes a hairpin turn beside the clearing. Don't descend right. Ascend left and pass an abandoned mine. Then descend the rough, narrow, tightly overgrown road. Reach the signed, **Jumbo Pass FS road** where it curves left uphill. Right (downhill) leads to the highway. There's a small, brown, EARL GREY PASS TRAIL sign here, at 17 km (10.5 mi), 1174 m (3850 ft). If you've arranged a shuttle, this is where you want to be picked up. If you've parked your vehicle here, it should be near the horse corral, on a spur road just below and west of the trail sign.

Trip 23
Macbeth Icefield

Location	Glacier Creek valley, Purcell Mtns.
Round trip	12 km (7.4 mi) from the 4WD-accessible trailhead, 15.6 km (9.7 mi) from Glacier Creek Road
Elevation gain	874 m (2867 ft) from the 4WD-accessible trailhead, 1082 m (3550 ft) from Glacier Creek Road
Time required	9 to 10 hours
Difficulty	Challenging
Map	Duncan Lake 82 K/7

OPINION

Isn't this an amazing planet? That's the sentiment behind all the enthusiastic exclamations of wonder that hikers blurt out when they emerge above treeline and see the double waterfall pouring off Macbeth Icefield. The entire setting is powerfully wild; so recently glaciated that it bears the still-fresh fingerprints of creation.

The hike begins beside a creek whose thundering roar hints at the magnitude of the marvels you've come to witness. Then, like a hypnotist regressing you to a past life, the trail guides you into a quiet, dark, moist, leafy-green middle world—a hanging basin, above the valley floor, beneath the icefield. At times of peak runoff, hiking here can be a soggy ordeal.

The ascent out of the basin is arduous. It climbs a wickedly steep slope, through the chaos of a forest choking on its own deadfall. A network of staircases—some built out of milled lumber, others chopped into fallen trees—assists your upward progress. Thank the Forest Service for their fine work. Seriously. Write to the Kootenay Lake Forest District (see *Information Sources*). Tell them how much you appreciate this masterful section of trail. And ask what it will take to initiate other equally necessary maintenance and construction projects elsewhere in the West Kootenay backcountry. With a groundswell of support, progress is possible.

Macbeth Icefield

After wringing a water bottle's worth of sweat out of your system, the trail finally boots you into the alpine zone. And there it is: the vaunted double waterfall, dramatic evidence that Macbeth Icefield is melting furiously. From here on, you'll follow a route too sketchy to be called a trail. Ascending moderately, you'll work around and over several rock ribs, then follow the crest of a moraine, all the while admiring spectacles near and far.

The most impactful sight of all—the icefield itself—asks a bit more effort of you. A quick descent into a shallow gorge, then a few minutes of light scrambling will place you atop the ledge that the falls leap off. Here, you can gaze at a vast sea of ice and appreciate just how trivial an experience watching an IMAX movie really is.

FACT

By Vehicle

Follow the Jumbo Pass (Trip 24) directions to the fork at 22.2 km (13.8 mi) on **Glacier Creek Road.** Left is the steep, rough, overgrown spur leading to Macbeth Icefield trailhead. Straight (east) leads to Jumbo Pass.

Turning left onto the spur, it's only 1.8 km (1.1 mi) farther to Macbeth Icefield trailhead. Attempt it only in a 4WD vehicle you don't mind scratching. Otherwise park on Glacier Creek Road at 1052 m (3450 ft) and hoof it. Keep right at the fork about 10 minutes up. Strong hikers can dispatch the 208-m (683-ft) ascent to the trailhead in 20 minutes. It's signed on the right, at 1260 m (4133 ft), just before the final descent to the small parking area at road's end.

On Foot

Begin a long, ascending traverse northeast on a slumping, brushy slope. In about 15 minutes, pass a trail register at 1345 m (4410 ft) and enter a stand of timber. The trail steepens but is now better defined. Beyond the trees, sidehill through more brush above convulsing, glacier-fed Birnam Creek. Proceed into forest. At 1455 m (4770 ft), about 40 minutes from the trailhead, the trail turns left and drops to where a log bridge used to span the creek. It was blown out by a torrent in the intensely hot summer of 1998 when the glacier melted furiously and the creek raged for months. If the bridge has been replaced, **cross to the far bank** and follow the trail right (northeast).

If the bridge is still missing when you arrive, turn right and follow a boot-beaten path upstream about 100 meters (110 yards) to where a huge fallen log (possibly still flagged) should convey you to the far bank. Pick up the trail heading generally northeast. For the next 1.6 km (1 mi) you'll be on a **level basin floor** that can be inundated in spring and summer. Snowmelt from above often courses down the trail. It's not an obstacle, just annoying. Footlogs help in places but are too few to ensure dry boots.

Soon attain your first view north/northeast of waterfalls spilling off Macbeth Icefield. The trail then ascends moderately through an exquisite, mossy, virgin forest. At 1494 m (4900 ft), about 1¼ hours from the trailhead, cross a substantial bridge over a tributary stream. Giant cedars are numerous here.

Steel yourself for a long, steep climb through snarly terrain. Marvelous trailbuilding courtesy of the Forest Service makes it hikeable. **Log staircases** transport you over cliffs. Tight switchbacks dodge through chaotic deadfall. Many days of chainsaw work were necessary to tame this forbidding 45° slope. Though the trees are smaller here than in the forest below, you'll appreciate their shade on a hot day. A roaring waterfall is audible to your right.

Two hours of nonstop, determined hiking from the trailhead will bring you to a **bridged creek** crossing at 1860 m (6100 ft) where the worst of the ascent is a fait accompli. Refill waterbottles and rest in this cool, shady nook, because you'll soon be at treeline. The stunted, subalpine fir and spruce just above provide no shade.

From the creek crossing, ascend a steep rock rib. The trail now dwindles to a winding, rolling route. Head generally northeast, following cairns and short paths between **rock ribs**. About 15 minutes from the creek crossing, crest an escarpment. Graymalkin Lake, a silty tarn at 1890 m (6200 ft), is visible below. It's fed by dramatic Birnam Falls pouring off a huge cliff. Above and beyond the cliff is Macbeth Icefield, which you can fully appreciate only by resuming the ascent.

Angle left (north/northwest). Following a few cairns, ramp your way up bands of rock. Duncan Lake and icy-shouldered Mt. Brennan are visible southwest. The massive Horseshoe Glacier is southeast, way across Glacier Creek valley. Pass a wall of krummholz and look for flagging that will guide you up a very steep pitch to the **crest of a moraine**. Proceed north, ascending moderately along the trail-width crest. About 15 minutes of this easy, very scenic hiking (at least 3 hours total from the trailhead), and you'll be near 2134 m (7000 ft), across the gorge from and just past the waterfalls.

If you ascend another 15 minutes, to about 2250 m (7380 ft), you'll see a glacier tongue squeezed between two pyramidal, talusy peaks: Mt. Banquo (north/northwest) and Mt. Fleance (north).

View southeast across Glacier Creek valley

You'll also see a larger tarn in a barren talus bowl above and southeast of Graymalkin.

But you'll see much more (photo on page 145) by dropping into the gorge and scrambling northeast onto the escarpment over which the waterfalls pour. There, at about 2150 m (7052 ft), you'll witness a great expanse of **Macbeth Icefield.** Descend southeast on glacier-scoured rock slabs to peer down at the meltwater stream splitting into two waterfalls. Mountain goats roam the slopes beyond the falls.

Don't venture onto the ice without the knowledge and equipment to do it safely.

Trip 24
Jumbo Pass

Location	Purcell Mountains
Round trip	8.4 km (5.2 mi)
Elevation gain	686 m (2250 ft)
Time required	6 to 7 hours
Difficulty	Moderate
Map	Duncan Lake 82 K/7

OPINION

Pluck the Jumbo Pass trail from the West Kootenays, drop it into Banff National Park or Washington's North Cascades National Park, and it would still be a premier destination. The scenery's that good. The Jumbo Pass environs offer an exciting look at the peaks and glaciers comprising the northern Purcell Range.

The joy of a Jumbo trip begins well before arrival at the trailhead. Driving the western approach, you'll travel the entire Glacier Creek valley, occasionally glimpsing the namesake glaciers and passing through a grand mountain-hemlock forest. Hemlocks possess heart-rending grace. You'll recognize them by their colossal height (40 m / 120 ft), drooping leaders (tops), long, swooping branches, and deeply furrowed bark. It's worth driving here just to see these regal trees. Afterward, write to the Kootenay Lake Forest District (see *Information Sources*) and request that this scenic wonder be saved from the saw. Do it now, before the inevitable logging controversy begins. By then it could be too late.

The trail to Jumbo is in forest. Views are limited. You'll glimpse just enough of the massif clutching Horseshoe Glacier to inspire your upward progress. Not until the final approach to the pass, where the trail emerges into the subalpine zone, does the scenery begin to explode. To see all that you can see, turn north at the pass and continue ascending the ridge behind the hut. If spending a night in this small, cozy alpine refuge appeals to you, read the *Fact* section for details.

Admiring Horseshoe Glacier, from near Jumbo Pass

Ever see a *Save Jumbo Pass* bumper sticker? Construction of a year-round alpine resort in upper Jumbo Creek valley, on the east side of Jumbo Pass, was proposed in 1990. The plans call for a 30-hectare (75-acre) village that could ultimately have double the overnight-accommodation capacity of Lake Louise. The ski lifts, draped over the mountains visible from Jumbo Pass, could potentially serve 10,000 skiers per day. The phase-one lift would transport skiers to the top of Glacier Dome. Vancouver-based Glacier Resorts Ltd., a consortium of investors from Canada, Japan, the U.S., and Europe, is still pursuing approval of the $200-million project as of this writing. Opposition is fierce among residents of the West and East Kootenays, hence the bumper stickers beseeching your support. Arguments against the proposal are convincing. Learn more about why you should, and how you can, help save Jumbo Pass. Act quickly; decision time is near. Contact the Jumbo Conservation Society (Bob at 250-342-3147).

FACT

Before your trip

If you want to stay in the Jumbo Pass hut, reserve in advance by phoning the Invermere Forest District: (250) 342-4200. The recently-built hut is clean and comfortable but small, with room for about eight people. It's equipped with foamies, a couple propane stoves, propane tanks, cooking pots, dishes and utensils. When making reservations, ask what extra supplies or equipment you might need.

By Vehicle

West Approach, via Glacier Creek

Drive Hwy 31 to the village of **Kaslo**, on the northwest shore of Kootenay Lake. It's 40 minutes north of the Balfour-Kootenay Bay ferry terminal. Set your trip odometer to 0 at the junction of Hwys 31A and 31N. That's the intersection of "A" Avenue and North Marine Drive, just west of and uphill from downtown. Head north on 31N and pass the village of Lardeau at 28.4 km (17.6 mi). A BC Parks sign warns of the turn you'll be taking toward the Purcell Mountains and Fry Canyon. At 34.5 km (21.4 mi) from Kaslo, turn right (east) onto Argenta Road.

0 km (0 mi)
Starting east on Argenta Road.

0.5 km (0.3 mi)
Cross the Lardeau River. Pavement ends.

1.2 km (0.7 mi)
Reach a 3-way junction. Go straight for MacBeth Icefield and Jumbo Pass trailheads. You'll drive north along Duncan Lake's southeast shore. Right goes south toward Argenta and the Earl Grey Pass trailhead (Trip 22). A minor road forks left here.

11.3 km (7 mi)
Proceed straight. Left leads to the free Glacier Creek campground in 0.4 km (0.25 mi).

11.8 km (7.3 mi)
After crossing a creek, turn right (northeast) and ascend Duncan-Glacier Creek FS road.

15 km (9.3 mi)
The road is now near creek level in the upper valley.

15.8 km (9.8 mi)
MacBeth Icefield is visible ahead.

16.3 km (10.1 mi)
Slow down as you proceed through Rainbow's End Ranch. Watch out for free-ranging animals.

22.2 km (13.8 mi)
Reach a fork. For Jumbo Pass proceed straight (east). Left is the steep, rough, overgbrown spur leading to MacBeth Icefield trailhead (Trip 23).

23.6 km (14.6 mi)
Cross a bridge over Glacier Creek, near the KM 22 sign.

35.7 km (22.1 mi)
Immediately after another bridged creek crossing, reach a signed junction. Turn right (east) for Jumbo Pass.

36.1 km (22.4 mi)
Bear right, following a small sign depicting a hiker. The road is level and not too brushy.

38.7 km (24 mi)
Reach Jumbo Pass trailhead and the end of passable road at 1585 m (5200 ft). The parking area is small. Park efficiently to leave room for others.

East Approach, via Jumbo Creek
Drive Hwy 95 south from Radium, or north from Cranbrook, then turn west toward **Invermere**. Go through town, toward Panorama Ski Area. Set your trip odometer to 0 at the bridge where left leads to Panorama.

0 km (0 mi)
Across from the Panorama turnoff, proceeding straight on Toby Creek FS road.

19 km (11.8 mi)
Curve right (northwest) on Jumbo Creek FS road. Left leads to the Earl Grey Pass trailhead. Stay on the main road, paralleling the creek.

20.5 km (12.7 mi)
Go left.

25 km (15.5 mi)
Stay left and cross a bridge to the south side of Jumbo Creek. Fork right just after the bridge.

32.2 km (20 mi)
Cross back to the north side of Jumbo Creek at Leona Creek bridge.

34 km (21.1 mi)
Just before another bridge over Jumbo Creek, a skid road forks left near the 16-KM sign. Park here beside the road at 1665 m (5460 ft).

On Foot, via West Approach

The Save Jumbo Pass effort, contesting the proposed ski area, has made this a celebrity among trails. Increased public attention has resulted in plenty of maintenance. So the trail is in good condition the entire distance. It's steep the whole way too, but long switchbacks ease the ascent. Expect to be in forest until you approach the pass.

The trailhead sign is at a fork in the road. The overgrown right branch continues toward a moraine of Horseshoe Glacier. Ascend left. In a few minutes this road narrows to trail. Soon cross a creeklet and begin ascending steeply. In about 15 minutes, enter standing timber near 1677 m (5500 ft).

Visible southwest is the sprawling Horseshoe Glacier, pierced by various summits including several with an intriguing name theme: Quibble and Squabble peaks, Truce, Covenant and Tranquillity mountains. Occasionally glimpse glacier-adorned Mt. Lady MacBeth back northwest.

After gaining 305 m (1000 ft)—a 45-minute task for swift hikers—the grade relents. At about the one-hour point (2045 m / 6700 ft) huckleberry bushes are profuse. The trail then curves east for the final approach to the pass. Moderately steep pitches are broken by short, level respites.

About 1½ hours from the trailhead, ascend a gentle, meadowy draw followed by steep switchbacks. Soon enter subalpine meadows laced with larch trees at 2195 m (7200 ft).

Attain 2270-m (7450-ft) **Jumbo Pass** after a 1¾-hour ascent. Clearcuts mar the view northeast, but there's abundant beauty to distract your gaze. Soaring above the logged slopes are twin peaks. The jagged one on the right is Jumbo Mtn. Left is Karnak Mtn. A glacier oozes between them on the south side. The dull, talusy peak south of Jumbo is unnamed.

Karnak and Jumbo mountains from Jumbo Pass

The trail splits at Jumbo Pass. Right ascends briefly southeast toward the grey talus slopes of Bastille Mtn before dropping past a tarn and continuing down to the Jumbo Creek logging road east of the pass. The road provides access to Jumbo Pass from Panorama Ski Area and, farther down valley, Invermere.

The signed left fork at Jumbo Pass leads to the **hut**. You'll be there in 10 minutes, after gaining only another 45 m (150 ft). East of and just below the hut is a tarn. From the hut, you can better survey the peaks southeast of the pass. Redtop Mtn bears a small hanging glacier. Just left of it is Mt. Earl Grey.

To ascend the **ridge north of the hut,** start behind the outhouse and proceed directly north. This side trip (0.8 km / 0.5 mi one way) takes only about 20 minutes but will greatly enhance your appreciation of the Jumbo Pass environs. As you climb, waterfalls crashing off Horseshoe Glacier at the south end of Glacier Creek valley become more audible. A bootbeaten path leads most of the way up the first 2470-m (8100-ft) bump. From there, you can see Glacier Dome north and the Lieutenants standing at attention northeast. Obscured behind them is Lake of the Hanging Glacier (Trip 25), accessed from Radium Hot Springs via Horsethief Creek Road. Northwest, across upper Glacier Creek Valley, is the massif comprising Mounts Macduff, Macbeth and Lady Macbeth. Obscured behind them is the sprawling Macbeth Icefield. Southwest, the tarn beneath Horseshoe Glacier is now within view, as is the overgrown road leading to the moraine. Glacier-trussed Blockhead Mtn is partially visible south of Bastille Mtn.

The next couple bumps on the ridgecrest are easily attainable, but the scenery doesn't improve sufficiently to justify the elevation loss and gain. Go only for the going's sake. Experienced scramblers can forge north along the ridgecrest about 3 km (1.9 mi) before it gets seriously narrow and rugged.

On Foot, via East Approach

Begin hiking on the skid road. Soon rockhop across the creek and resume on the skid road. At 0.5 km (0.3 mi), after crossing another stream, fork left onto a flagged trail that departs the cutblock. The trail ascends through forest to reach Jumbo Pass at 3.8 km (2.4 mi), 2270 m (7450 ft).

Trip 25

Lake of the Hanging Glacier

Location	Central Purcell Mountains
Round trip	16 km (10 mi)
Elevation gain	700 m (2296 ft)
Time required	6 to 7 hours; 2 more for Glacier Dome
Difficulty	Moderate
Maps	Duncan Lake 82 K/7; Invermere FS District brochure

OPINION

New Age seminars, workshops and retreats promising to "change your life!" have been spewed at North American society as if from a fire hose. And a lot of suckers are getting soaked. Sure, there are genuinely wise teachers illuminating the path of self-knowledge. But there are a lot of quacks taking advantage of those too insecure to realize how far down the path you can go on your own. You want enlightenment? Start walking. Devote yourself to it as a spiritual practice. You want a life shift? Walk to a glorious cathedral, like the one concealing Lake of the Hanging Glacier.

After a decade-and-a-half of exploring the Canadian Rockies, we're still astounded by this 2.5-km (1.6-mi) long lake and its rock-and-ice cirque. Thick with glacial sediment, the water is opaque turquoise. Bergy bits punctuate the surface. (That's actually the glaciological term for small icebergs.) Soaring skyward from the shore is a ring of lofty peaks. Their bold names—Commander, Jumbo, The Lieutenants—are justified by their sensational appearance. The tongue of Jumbo Glacier, for which the lake is named, hangs precariously above the lake's far shore.

Though smaller, the environs of Lake of the Hanging Glacier are comparable in beauty to Amethyst Lake and the Ramparts in Jasper National Park, or Marvel Lake and Mt. Assiniboine. But here, the approach is shorter and the crowds are slimmer. The optimal time to visit? Whenever you can get here. But in September you'll encounter even fewer hikers, and you'll see larches flaunting their golden regalia.

Lake of the Hanging Glacier

Blessed with a sunny, warm day, you can relax at the lake and gaze upward in awe. It's easy to imagine the venerable Mt. Commander has ordered his Lieutenants to whip these Purcells into shape for a battle with the renowned Rockies across the Trench. Your other option is to keep moving. Attain a superior lake-and-glacier vantage by ascending above treeline on the steep slope west of the shore. (See cover photo.) Rocky terraces enable you to keep roaming up toward Glacier Dome.

FACT

Before your trip

En route to the lake, you'll cross Hell Roaring Creek. In previous years, the bridge was washed out by torrential spring runoff. So the BC Forest Service installed a sturdy metal bridge. But it's only in place July through September; they remove it each fall. Attempting this trip when the bridge is out necessitates a potentially perilous ford.

By Vehicle

Don't be discouraged by the following directions. They're not complicated; it's just a long way to the trailhead. The road is good, suitable for 2WD cars. Just slow down near 41 km (25 mi) where deep waterbars (drainage ditches) cross the road.

From Invermere, drive out through Wilmer onto the Westside Road. Stay on the main road to a 4-way junction at 10 km. Turn left (west) onto Horsethief Creek FS road, and set your trip odometer to 0.

From Radium Hot Springs at the junction of Hwys 93 and 95, drive west onto Forsters Landing Road next to the Prestige Inn. In 1.4 km (0.9 mi) reach a junction just before the Slocan Group mill. Continue west on dirt Horsethief Creek FS road. Stay left on the main road at 4.3 km (2.7 mi) and proceed straight on the main road until you reach a junction at 10.6 km (6.6 mi) with Westside Road coming from Invermere. Set your trip odometer to 0

0 km (0 mi)
Heading west on Horsethief Creek FS road, from its junction with Westside Road. West is signed for Hanging Glacier.

4.3 km (2.7 mi)
Go left.

12.3 km (7.6 mi)
Enter the valley bottom and continue beside the creek.

14 km (8.7 mi)
Curve left and cross to the creek's south side.

26.8 km (16.6 mi)
Stay right. The left fork heads south up McDonald Creek.

30.3 km (18.8 mi)
Pass a spur on the right, signed for Stockdale Creek BCFS Recreation Site. The campground is unscenic and small—just 2 or 3 sites—but the creek is audible. If you see the KM 39 signpost, you've gone slightly too far.

31.8 km (19.7 mi)
Slow down before hitting a deep waterbar. The road narrows and gets rougher. The mountains are now more visible.

33.4 km (20.7 mi)
Cross a narrow wooden bridge. On your right, the creek funnels through a slot canyon.

37.2 km (23.1 mi)
Cross a waterbar here and again 1 km farther. Starbird Glacier is visible southwest.

38.3 km (23.7 mi)
Pass the signed Farnham Creek trailhead on the left. The hike
begins with a bridged crossing of Horsethief Creek.

40.7 km (25.2 mi)
The road is now very narrow and rough. It has been blocked by a
landslide here. Road's end and the trailhead parking lot are 200
meters farther, at 1460 m (4790 ft).

On Foot

Begin by detouring around a short, washed-out section of old
road. Ascend the trail right of the trailhead sign. Surmount a bluff,
then drop back to the road, which serves as your trail for a mostly
level 2.2 km (1.4 mi). You're heading generally southwest, following
Horsethief Creek upstream through an old clearcut in a dramatic
valley.

In about 20 minutes, a glacier is visible southeast clinging to a
ridge on Granite Peak. Also visible across the valley is a plummeting waterfall. The road/trail now begins a gradual climb. It curves
left, broadens, and enters a stand of mature forest. It then narrows
to trail width and resumes through alder.

Cross bridged Hell Roaring Creek at 2.5 km (1.6 mi), 1637 m
(5370 ft). A few minutes later, enter beautiful forest. Ascend briefly,
then descend to a signed junction at 3 km (1.8 mi), 1662 m (5450 ft).
Turn left on the foot trail. A horse trail forks right.

Just below the junction, a left spur leads to a lookout above
Horsethief Falls. Take the easier middle path down to a substantial
metal bridge spanning Horsethief Creek at 3.1 km (1.9 mi), 1631 m
(5350 ft). On the east bank, the trail stays nearly level along the
creek, curving south for the next 1 km (0.6 mi) through a lush,
stately, moss-laden hemlock forest. Up-valley (southwest) you can
see glacier-draped Mt. Monica.

At 4.5 km (2.8 mi), begin climbing southeast on a long series of
switchbacks through forest. Gain 396 m (1300 ft) in the next 2.3 km
(1.4 mi). Water music (the hard-rock variety) accompanies your
deep breathing, because Lake of the Hanging Glacier's outlet
stream is nearby for about half the ascent. It speeds through a gorge
and crashes over boulders. Near the top of the cascades, bear left
on a rough, steep, up-and-down route skirting a section of washed-
out trail.

After crossing avalanche paths, encounter larch trees (vibrant gold in late September) near 6.5 km (4 mi). Cross a tributary on a footbridge, negotiate slide debris, and pass several large spruce trees. Heading south now, the gradient eases in subalpine meadows near 2058 m (6750 ft). There's a small campsite and outhouse on the right at 7.4 km (4.6 mi) and another campsite just beyond. The lake is 0.6 km (0.4 mi) farther, above a broad outlet-stream cascade. Reach trail's end, on the rocky, driftwood-scattered north shore, at 8 km (5 mi), 2160 m (7080 ft).

East/northeast is Granite Peak. Southeast is Mt. Maye. The lake reaches 2.5 km (1.6 mi) southeast to Jumbo and Commander glaciers, flowing from high on Commander Mtn. (Jumbo is the lower, smaller one.) South are the 3170-m (10,400-ft) Lieutenants. Southwest is Glacier Dome.

For a superior lake-and-glacier vantage, climb above treeline on the steep slope west of where you arrived at the lake. Start by rock-hopping across the outlet stream. Then ascend northeast for a few minutes before turning west again.

Continue upward through krummholz and open larch forest. The terraced, grassy benches grant level respites between short, steep, rocky pitches. Gradually curve southwest. Gain 305 m (1000 ft) in about 1 km (0.6 mi) to attain an aerial view southwest over the lake to Jumbo Glacier. You can even roam higher on the rocky terrain to approach Glacier Dome. When you descend, be aware that the slant of the terraces will pull you farther north than where you departed the lake. It is, however, easy to rockhop across the outlet stream below the broad cascade, then regain the trail above.

South end of The Rockwall rising from Floe Lake (Trip 42)

Atop Flute Summit (Trip 7)

From Cherry Pip Pass to Caltha Lake (Trip 11)

Helmet Falls (Trip 42)

On Tabletop Mountain, near the Stein Divide (Trip 11)

Tundra Lake (Trip 11)

Gwillim Lakes basin (Trip 14)

Southern Chilcotin, near Eldorado Pass (Trip 12)

Standard Basin (Trip 17)

Hermit Basin (Trip 20)

Mount Sir Donald, from Bald Mountain (Trip 21)

Kokanee Glacier Provincial Park

Mt. Hamill, from just north of Earl Grey Pass (Trip 22)

Crossing one of many meltwater streams on the way to Thunderwater Lake (Trip 26)

Bugaboo Spires from Chalice Ridge (Trip 27)

Hargreaves Lake and Mt. Robson (Trip 30)

Ascending Pinnacle Creek canyon to Diana Lake (Trip 31)

Limestone Lakes basin (Trip 33)

Marvel Pass and Cabin Lake (Trip 35)

Mt. Aosta reflected in Lower Elk Lake (Trip 36)

Petain Creek waterfall, just before steep ascent to upper basin (Trip 36)

Goodsir Towers (Trip 39)

Alpine larch near Floe Lake (Trip 42)

The Rockwall, near Wolverine Pass (Trip 42)

The Prairie on Hudson Bay Mountain (Trip 43)

Western Wood lilies are rare but present in the Kootenays and the western Rockies

Indian Paintbrush

Lupine

Trip 26

Thunderwater Lake

Location	Purcell Mountains
Round trip	12 km (7.4 mi)
Elevation gain	455 m (1492 ft)
Time required	8 hours
Difficulty	Challenging
Map	Howser Creek 82 K/10

OPINION

The water does indeed thunder. It rages down from Catamount glacier, then crashes across moraines to feed the vast, luxuriant meadows of Forster Creek valley. En route to Thunderwater Lake, which is hidden above the headwall, you'll navigate cross-country through the valley. It's exceptionally beautiful and—if you're here during peak summer runoff—extremely wet.

Try to delay this trip until autumn. The moisture laden valley will be less buggy. And the meltwater should be less thunderous and therefore not such an obstacle. Still, expect to ford. If you're lucky, you can vault over the streams using trekking poles. (See photo on page 169.) Then it's on to the headwall and the final, scrambling ascent to 1.2-km (0.75-mi) long, turquoise Thunderwater Lake between Whirlpool Glacier and Taurus Mountain's eastern outlier. Just beyond is smaller Whirlpool Lake, frozen most of the year. A bit farther is Forster Pass. All around are spectacular, raw alplands.

Fervent dayhikers can tag both lakes. But this is a primo backpack destination. The 2-km (1.2-mi) long lakes basin is attained with little elevation gain, but affords lots of exploratory wandering. Camping is comfortable and scenic on the moraine in Forster Creek valley, or above near Thunderwater Lake.

Bear in mind that routefinding skill is necessary on this trip. You'll follow trail and/or old road for just 2.2 km (1.4 mi). After entering Forster Creek valley, you'll have only our directions, plus your topo map and compass, to guide you through the rough-and-tumble terrain. Also, any ford can be treacherous. At their highest level, the streams here might be impassable. If you doubt your ability to cross safely, turn back. Your trip won't be wasted. Just experiencing Forster Creek valley is worthwhile.

Finally, after you turn off the highway, before you begin the access road, stop. Take a deep breath. Understand that a cautious driver needs 1½ hours to reach the trailhead. The approach isn't difficult; just long. Accept the fact. Enjoy the journey. It's an opportunity to get better acquainted with the Purcell Mountains.

FACT

By Vehicle

From **Invermere**, drive through Wilmer onto Westside Road. Follow it to a 4-way junction at 10 km (6.2 mi). Turn left (west) onto Horsethief Creek FS road and reset your trip odometer to 0.

From **Radium Hot Springs**, at the junction of Hwys 93 and 95, drive west onto Forsters Landing Road next to Prestige Inn. Reach a junction at 1.4 km (0.9 mi), just before the Slocan Group mill. Continue west on Horsethief Creek FS road. Stay left on the main road at 4.3 km (2.7 mi). Follow it to a 4-way junction at 10.6 km (6.6 mi). Left on Westside Road leads to Invermere. Reset your trip odometer to 0 and proceed on Horsethief Creek FS road.

0 km (0 mi)
Starting west on Horsethief Creek FS road, from the junction with Westside Road.

4 km (2.5 mi)
Go right onto Horsethief-Forster Creek FS road.

8.8 km (5.5 mi)
Cross a bridge at the watershed sign.

9.8 km (6.1 mi)
Go left on Horsethief-Forster Creek FS road. Right is Horsethief-Dogleg road.

26.8 km (16.6 mi)
Pass the narrow, 4WD road that ascends left to Welsh Lakes trailhead. (Excluded from this book, because it's not a premier hike.) Proceed straight. A moderate ascent begins. From here to the Thunderwater Lakes trailhead, the road gains 213 m (700 ft).

Scramble up the headwall of upper Forster Creek valley to reach Thunderwater Lake.

28.7 km (17.8 mi)
Pass Forster Falls on the right. The road remains passable in 2WD, but expect narrow sections and loose rock.

32 km (19.8 mi)
Reach Thunderwater Lake trailhead at road's end. Elevation: 1725 m (5658 ft). The parking area has room for about 4 vehicles.

On Foot
Immediately cross a bridge to Forster Creek's south bank. Ascend the overgrown road west—your general direction of travel into the valley ahead. In a few minutes, where the gravelly road curves left (south), follow a short bit of trail. Continue on the road. Cross a washout at 0.5 km (0.3 mi). Within 15 minutes of leaving the trailhead, attain a **knoll-top view** west, up Forster Creek valley. Thunderwater Lake is not visible; it's beyond and left of the far end of the valley.

Enter forest. About 30 minutes from the trailhead, arrive at feisty **Scotch Creek**. It's fed by North Star Glacier, far above to the south. Logs might be in place to aid your crossing of the two channels.

Follow the road another 200 meters (210 yards) to a private, heli-skiing **cabin** at 2.2 km (1.4 mi), 1866 m (6120 ft). Directly behind the cabin, a faint trail leads northwest through forest to a slow, narrow stream at the edge of **boggy meadows**. From here on, there are no bridges, roads or trails; you're navigating cross-country. Head generally northwest, favouring the south side of Forster Creek valley.

Pick whatever seems the best way along the left side of the wet meadows. Stay near the slope. Expect to cross and perhaps re-cross the stream's narrow channel; it's easy to hop over. Proceed through heather and clumpy grass. This soggy area takes about 15 minutes to negotiate. The going is then easier on rocky moraine.

Don't ascend yet. Watch for orange flagging. Continue generally northwest, staying left (south) of mid-valley. You're now hiking over rocks, around granite boulders, through open forest of alpine larch and Englemann spruce. Soon reach **gravel flats** where possible campsites abound. Tall, magenta-flowered willow herb, and fuschia Indian paintbrush add tiny bursts of colour to the predominantly white and grey moraine.

On the left (south) valley wall, near 2.5 km (1.6 mi), a **raging stream**—meltwater from Catamount Glacier—is visible and audible. At times of heavy runoff, the stream is an obstacle to hikers. Above, where it's a single stream, the current is dangerously swift and deep. On the flats, it's braided, slower and shallower. Fording (or vaulting, if you're lucky) should be easy and safe here. Right (north), near Forster Creek, the braided stream-channels merge and the water again deepens.

Beyond the stream, stay in the center of the valley, but south of Forster Creek. Your general direction of travel is west. Aim for the cascades on the valley headwall. After two more creek crossings, go far right of steep slopes. Several **rock ramps** ascend left here on the slopes of Taurus Mtn. See the prominent cascade and large ramp? Ascend the ramp left of it. Scramble into the alpine zone just north of the headwall. Then let the easiest topography guide you west, then briefly south, to the east end of **Thunderwater Lake**. Reach the shore at 6 km (3.7 mi), 2130 m (7000 ft).

Proceed west, along the lake's north shore, then ascend 60 m (200 ft) to reach **Whirlpool Lake**. Continue around Whirlpool's north shore, then angle southwest to enter 2274-m (7460-ft) **Forster Pass**. The pass, about 1½ hours from Thunderwater Lake, affords views south to the Tricorn Peaks and Edouard Lake, and west down Howser Creek to Four Squatters Glacier and The Virgin (horn shaped). Taurus Mtn is immediately north of the pass.

Trip 27
Bugaboo Spires

Location	Bugaboo Provincial Park, Purcells
Round trip	10 km (6.2 mi)
Elevation gain	660 m (2165 ft)
Time required	2 to 4 hours
Difficulty	Moderate
Maps	Howser Creek 82 K/10; BC Parks brochure

OPINION

A *bugaboo* is an imaginary object of fear. These Bugaboos look both imaginary and frightening. Actually they're solid granite monoliths shooting thousands of feet out of a glacial sea. The were volcanically injected upward. After they cooled and solidified, the surrounding land eroded and left them standing naked. But geologists didn't call them Bugaboos. Climbers did, because they grapple with fear as much as with rock. The first to summit what is now known as Bugaboo Spire was Conrad Kain, sort of the Captain Cook of the Canadian Alps. He and his climbing buddies thought one of the fantastic spires blocked their intended route. Recognizing that it imposed not just a physical obstacle, but a psychological one, they called it "a veritable bugaboo."

An excellent trail allows you to follow in the daring Kain's path, if only to the base of the spires. For a hiker, that's far enough. You'll be awed by these outrageous formations. And you'll partake in the atmosphere of pilgrimage they inspire. Climbers the world over revere the Bugs and arrive in a continual flow. That makes solitude unlikely. But the thrill you'll experience just being here, and the vivid memory you'll retain afterward, will more than compensate.

Smash the spires and you'd still be left with Bugaboo and Crescent glaciers, themselves an overpowering sight, well worth hiking to see. For that matter, you don't even have to hike. The glacier view from near the trailhead justifies the long approach via logging road. Hiking, however, reveals yet another Bugs attraction: the trail itself. It's very short, but wow, what a joy. It winds through pristine, fragrant, creek-laced forest, with footlogs placed at botanical-garden frequency. On an avalanche slope overgrown with hateful slide alder, the trail broadens like Moses parting the seas, sparing you an invective-inducing thrash. Above, it clings to ledges, climbing airy rock slabs, giving hikers a safe adrenaline rush and acrophobes serious pause. There's even a fixed ladder to help you up a short vertical pitch that would otherwise be an exposed scramble. Cables also help ensure your safety.

Most dayhikers stop at the hut. But you really should continue above and beyond. Everywhere are scoured boulders inviting gymnastic play. Most years you can hike here from late June through early October.

FACT

Before your trip

Be aware that park regulations prohibit dogs and horses. A horse would need wings to reach Conrad Kain hut anyway.

For overnighting up top, you have three options: stay at Conrad Kain Hut (open June 1 through September 30), or pitch your tent at Boulder or Applebee Dome campgrounds. In 2001, the per-person per-night fees were $18 at the hut, $5 for camping. Campers pay at the hut. Up to 40 people can bed down in the hut, but that would be sardine-can conditions. Each campground accommodates about 12 tents. You'll have fewer neighbours before July or after mid-September. At the hut, you'll need a sleeping bag and pad. Also bring cooking pots, plates and utensils. BC Parks supplies stoves, propane, and some sleeping pads. If you want to stay in the hut, check the current price and make reservations with the Alpine Club of Canada. The contact numbers are listed under *Information Sources* in the back of this book.

By Vehicle

Follow the directions for Cobalt Lake (Trip 28). Continue to the spacious trailhead parking lot at road's end. Elevation: 1510 m (4953 ft). Also read the porcupine warning in Trip 29's *Before your trip*.

Exultant hiker among the Bugaboo Spires

Luxuriating in Bugaboo brilliance

On Foot

Though steep, the trail is well maintained and easy to follow—southwest, then west—all the way to Conrad Kain Hut. It starts left of the kiosk, at the southwest end of the parking lot.

Soon cross to the south side of the creek. Numerous footlogs keep hikers from straying off trail through the wet forest. The initial 20 minutes are virtually level. Gentle ups and downs ensue. At 1.6 km (1 mi) ascend through boulders then return to forest.

The work begins where the trail assaults a steep **lateral moraine**. There's a creek in the gorge on your right. The sprinkling of larch trees here is especially evident in September when the leaves turn golden. Left, far below, is roaring Bugaboo Creek; across its canyon is a vast avalanche path on Frenchman Mountain. Ahead, the famous spires lure you higher and deeper into the realm of rock and snow.

After a brief level reprieve near 1646 m (5400 ft)—about 30 minutes from the trailhead—the trail appears to end at a **boulder pile** but actually veers sharply left. Continue ascending behind the moraine, then across an avalanche path overgrown with slide alder, and into the subalpine zone. Ice fangs (seracs) on the tongue of nearby Bugaboo Glacier are visible left (southwest). The hut is also in sight, though it's still high above to your right (west). Climb a fixed ladder at 3.5 km (2.2 mi), 1920 m (6298 ft). Cables further aid your progress on the steep rock as you near your goal.

Reach the hut at 5 km (3 mi), 2170 m (7118 ft). If your boot soles are smoking, you got here in about 1¼ hours. Most dayhikers arrive in less than 2 hours. Surrounding the impressively perched hut is a world of vertical granite and deep ice. Snowpatch Spire (3063 m / 10,047 ft) is west/southwest, Bugaboo Spire (3176 m / 10,417 ft) is northwest, Crescent Spire (2843 m / 9325 ft) is (north/northwest), Eastpost Spire (2697 m / 8846 ft) is north. Bugaboo Glacier is south and southwest. Crescent Glacier is west.

A sign near the hut directs you onto the short trail to **Boulder Camp**. Descend 75 m (246 ft) to the level tent sites, outhouse, and rodent-proof food storage racks. **Applebee Dome campground** is northwest, above the hut, atop a large rock knob, reached via trail in about 1 hour. It too has level tent sites and an outhouse.

To fully appreciate this supernatural setting and find your own private rock balcony, roam above the hut. Scamper toward Crescent Glacier. Continue up to Applebee Dome even if you're not camping. Where there's no defined tread, the scoured boulders allow easy, enjoyable cross-country travel.

If you're looking at BC Parks' brochure and map, unless you're an experienced, equipped climber, don't venture onto the dotted route heading north/northeast from the hut: past Eastpost Spire, over to Cobalt Lake. The route demands routefinding skills and glacier-travel savvy. It's too dangerous for hikers.

Trip 28

Cobalt Lake

Location	Bugaboo Provincial Park
Round trip	17.4 km (10.4 mi)
Elevation gain	930 m (3047 ft)
Time required	6 to 8 hours
Difficulty	Moderate
Maps	Bugaboo Creek 82 K/15; BC Parks brochure

OPINION

Cobalt Lake is often referred to as Blue Lake. Neither name is accurate. The lake is a silty, opaque teal. But it matters no more than a single daub of paint on a Monet. Lovely though the lake is, upon over-coming the headwall where Cobalt is first visible, you'll find much more to gaze upon. In every direction, swaggering, boastful moun-tains vie for attention—like musclemen flexing and posing. The Buga-boos seem to have stabbed and ripped their way through the fabric of the earth. The Septet Range leaps and shouts, forcing you to acknowl-edge it too. Even the very distant southern horizon is a compelling sight, fangy as a shark's mouth, ice-caked as an old freezer.

Presumably, the goal of this hike is to set foot on the shore of Cobalt Lake. Many hikers abandon it upon attaining the aforemen-tioned headwall. They're discouraged to see a canyon between them and the lake. So they're drawn northward along Grizzly Ridge, where they can see that the hiking is effortless and the stir-ring panorama continues. It's a decision nobody loses sleep over. Blessed with a calm, sunny day, wandering this tame, alpine ridge could well end up among the cherished images that flash before your eyes during your final moment on earth.

The only way to improve upon this hike is to do it on a multi-day Bugaboo adventure in which you devote another two days to exploring Chalice Ridge (Trip 29) and Bugaboo Spires (Trip 27). If you have time, also include a day of blobbing-out at one of the many isolated, forested, lakeside, FS campgrounds in the area. *Camp Free in B.C.* gives precise directions. It's described in the back of this book.

Cobalt Lake, among the Bugaboo Spires

Now, having heard our thunderous applause for the Cobalt Lake hike, your expectations will be soaring. Keep in mind that the steep trail demands a couple hours of sweaty grunt-work during which the scenic reward is modest. Reality won't begin to catch up with your imagination until you enter the basin beneath the head-wall. Even there, you'll face another precipitous pitch before the horizons explode. Just keep plugging. It's worth it.

FACT

Before your trip
Be aware that park regulations prohibit dogs and horses. Also, camping is not allowed at Cobalt Lake. But neither is it necessary. You can fully appreciate the area on a dayhike.

By Vehicle
From **Radium Hot Springs**, at the junction of Hwys 93 and 95, drive Hwy 95 northwest 28.5 km (17.7 mi) to Brisco. Or, from **Golden**, at the junction of Hwys 1 and 95, drive Hwy 95 southeast 77.3 km (48 mi) to Brisco. From either approach, you'll see BC Parks signs announcing Bugaboo Glacier Provincial Park. Turn west onto Brisco Road. Don't be discouraged by the following directions. They're not complicated; it's just a long way to the trailhead.

0 km (0 mi)
Turn west onto Brisco Road. At 0.5 km (0.3 mi), before the mill, turn right along the railroad tracks. Cross two bridged channels of the Columbia River.

3.5 km (2.2 mi)
Turn right at the signed junction.

4.9 km (3 mi)
Reach a junction and trail info sign. Turn left. Ascend steeply for 1.5 km (0.9 mi).

6.4 km (4 mi)
Turn right on Bugaboo Creek FS road. Most of the elevation gain from the Columbia Valley floor is now behind you. The road improves.

7 km (4.3 mi)
Reach a Y-junction. Bear right on the better road.

7.1 km (4.4 mi)
Stay on Bugaboo Creek FS road—the one in the middle.

8.5 km (5.3 mi) and 9.6 km (6.0 mi)
Proceed straight on the main road.

18.6 km (11.5 mi)
Bear right, passing Bugaboo-Cartwright FS road on the left.

20.9 km (13 mi)
Cross a bridged creek.

21.2 km (13.1 mi)
Stay straight.

23.4 km (14.5 mi) and 23.8 km (14.8 mi)
Stay left, along the creek.

40.2 km (24.9 mi)
Reach Bugaboo Falls—worth stopping to see.

43.3 km (26.8 mi)
Turn right onto the fork signed for Conrad Kain Hut and Cobalt Lake.

To camp at **Bugaboo-Septet FS campground**, turn left here. Turn left again in 0.7 km (0.4 mi). After crossing the Bugaboo Creek bridge, turn left and continue 200 meters (220 yards) to the signed campground spur on the left.

44.6 km (27.7 mi)
Reach the signed Cobalt Lake trailhead on the right, at 1510 m (4953 ft). Below to the left is Bugaboo Lodge. There's no parking lot here, so continue to road's end. Then walk back to begin the hike.

44.8 km (27.8 mi)
Enter Bugaboo Glacier Provincial Park. The famous granite spires and gleaming glaciers are visible ahead.

46.3 km (28.7 mi)
Reach the spacious, road's end parking lot, at 1510 m (4953 ft). This is the trailhead for Bugaboo Spires. There are outhouses here, and a trailhead kiosk with park maps. You'll also notice chicken wire strewn about. If you're staying overnight in the park, wrap the wire around your vehicle and secure it with rocks and pieces of wood. It will prevent porcupines from munching the tires, hoses and fan belts. Seriously.

On Foot
From the Bugaboo Spires trailhead, walk the road northeast 1.7 km (1 mi) back to the signed Cobalt Lake trailhead, on the left. The trail leads generally northwest, until near the signed Walter Lake fork.

Pass the trail register and begin an excruciatingly steep climb. The broad, well-maintained path switchbacks up through an old burn overgrowing with alder. On a clear summer day, be prepared for a hot hike on this shadeless, sunblasted slope. Views are initially minimal. Chalice Ridge is east, beyond the immediate ridge. Impressive Bugaboo Lodge is visible just below the trailhead. You'll also hear the roar of its huge generators—not exactly the call of the wild, but perhaps an incentive to ignite your after burners and escape uphill.

Within 30 minutes of sweaty hiking, the ascent eases, heading north. Enter trees and cross a creeklet. The reprieve is brief. Steep switchbacks soon resume: in and out of trees and through the overgrown burn. Your general direction of travel remains northwest. It feels like you're leaving the Bugaboo area, going down-valley, which would be discouraging if you didn't know otherwise.

The switchbacks are still steep after an hour of hiking. Most of Chalice Ridge is visible southeast. Beyond is the Septet Range. Enter a forest of spruce, larch, and subalpine fir. At 2110 m (6921 ft), the trail levels heading southwest. In a few minutes, arrive at a **signed fork**: Walter Lake left, Cobalt Lake right. You've hiked 5.4 km (3.2 mi) and gained 600 m (1968 ft). Aspiring Eco-challengers will be here in 1¼ hours. Figure 1¾ to 2 hours at a moderate pace. Walter is just a small tarn, visible from above. Turning right (west), a gentle ascent eases you into a pretty, larch-filled **basin**. Directly west is the basin headwall on top of which you'll see Cobalt Lake.

About 15 minutes from the signed fork, cross a creeklet in the lower half of the basin. Comfortable boulders and a pleasing view invite you to rest. Beyond, the trail switchbacks skyward on the basin's grassy, alpine headwall. Upward effort is compensated by inspiring scenery east: more of Chalice Ridge and the Septet Range. Walter Lake is below, on the south side of the basin.

After 1¾ hours of fast striding (2½ hours at a moderate pace) top out on the **headwall** at 6.7 km (4 mi), 2363 m (7750 ft). Having gained 853 m (2798 ft) from the parking lot, your chores are done. It's time to play. Cobalt Lake is west, below you. The famous peaks, spires and glaciers of the Bugaboos huddle around the lake and crowd the western horizon from northwest to southwest. Way south is more of the mighty Purcell Range. East, below you is Bugaboo Creek valley. Farther east is the Septet Range. Distant northeast are the Rockies.

Atop the headwall, you have a choice: proceed directly to Cobalt Lake, or turn (right) north onto Grizzly Ridge where you can later opt to visit the lake. Either way you'll be travelling cross-country. To complete a circuit, go to the lake first, then return via Grizzly Ridge; it's less taxing that way, and routefinding is simpler. Don't care about a circuit, but want to visit the lake? Go out and back via the ridge; it's a bit longer, but easier and more panoramic. If you hike the ridge first, the endless vista might persuade you it's unnecessary to descend to the lake.

The **direct route** from the headwall to Cobalt Lake is short, a mere 1 km (0.6 mi). It requires a sharp, rugged, descent of 137 m (450 ft). If you're comfortable on steep, trailless slopes (got your trekking poles?), and determined to tag the lake, go for it. But realize that much of the scenery you're appreciating from atop the headwall will vanish as you descend. Before proceeding, scope out the terrain you must negotiate. Drop about 15 m (50 ft) while wading through krummholz, then angle right (northwest).

Crash through more krummholz en route to the canyon bottom. Staying right of Cobalt Lake's outlet stream, ascend through open larch forest. Turn left (southwest) toward the outlet falls. Ramp up through grass, heather and rock to the east shore. Elevation: 2330 m (7642 ft). Total distance from the parking lot: 7.7 km (4.6 mi).

Via the **Grizzly Ridge route**, north of where you crested the headwall, it's another 2 km (1.2 mi) to Cobalt Lake. Though slightly longer than the direct route, it's gentler and more scenic. Resuming along the ridge, climb the still defined trail. It fades in a couple minutes where the ridge levels and hikers spread out to lessen impact. Contour north through grass and heather. More of the surrounding tumultuous topography is now visible, including the Taurus Group (south), the Vowells (northwest), and Malachite and Horsemen spires (north). Even the distant southern horizon looms larger. An ideal place to chew on the view, and maybe your tofu sandwich, is about 20 minutes north of where you crested the headwall. There you'll find a knob on a rocky, southwest-jutting rib. It commands a perfect aerial perspective of Cobalt Lake. Spires are visible above and beyond the lake basin. If they're not snagging clouds, you're lucky. Mountaineers climb the glacier behind the lake, then traverse several high cols to arrive at Conrad Kain Hut.

To reach Cobalt Lake via Grizzly Ridge, follow the ridge north about 1 km (0.6 mi) from where you crested the headwall. You'll be farther north than the lake. Your highpoint on the ridge will be about 2439 m (8000 ft). You'll have gained 930 m (3047 ft) from the parking lot. Where the slope left (west) is less severe, descend to a pass—headwaters of Vowell Creek. Then drop south below Cobalt Lake. Turn right (southwest) toward the outlet falls. Ramp up through grass, heather and rock to the east shore. Elevation: 2330 m (7642 ft). Total distance from the parking lot: 8.7 km (5.2 mi).

From where you first crested the headwall, it's possible to return to the trailhead in 1¼ hours. Allow 2 hours at a moderate pace.

Trip 29
Chalice Ridge

Location	Purcell Mountains, just east of Bugaboo Provincial Park
Round trip	13 km (8.1 mi) to Chalice Saddle, longer for ridge
Elevation gain	650 m (2130 ft) to the saddle, more for ridge
Time required	8 hours, includes 4 hours on ridge
Difficulty	Moderate
Maps	Howser Creek 82 K/10; Invermere FS District brochure

OPINION

Not all premier trails offer a premier experience immediately. This one takes longer than most to loft your emotions. The first hour is an uninspiring tramp on an old logging road. After climbing through an ugly clearcut, the road turns to trail and enters nondescript forest. You'll have to be satisfied with a view of the Bugaboos early on, and later a glimpse of Chalice Creek headwaters valley. That's it for the first two hours, until you reach Chalice Saddle. And with so little to distract you from the physical chore of hiking, it feels like work. But then, suddenly: rapture. Can you achieve kundalini through hiking? Maybe. Follow your bliss north or south along Chalice Ridge. Splendid vistas unfold in both directions.

Chalice Ridge allows you to cruise at high elevation with little effort. So dayhikers should start early. You've squandered a rare opportunity if you turn around at the saddle. From there on, your constant companions will be the bold Bugaboo Spires and hulking Septet Range. Though the mostly alpine ridge is trailless, hiking it in either direction is easy. If you head south, which we recommend, your eyes can also clamber into the greater Purcell Range. Late September through early October, the mountains will even be decorated in honor of your visit: every treed slope ablaze with larches turned traffic-light amber.

For dayhikers, the ridge begins to climax 1 km (0.6 mi) south of the saddle. There, the eastern half of the panorama comprises the broad groove of Septet Pass and the tarn-dotted alpine slopes of

The Septet Range from Chalice Ridge

Lead Queen Mtn—rewarding terrain for backpackers. It's all visible, so you can confidently choose your goal and plan your route before resuming a cross-country, overnight adventure.

Because Chalice Ridge is a natural grandstand for admiring the justly famous Bugaboos (see photo on page 170), and because nearby Bugaboo Lodge offers heli-hiking, your reverie here might be shattered by noise and crowds. In the wilds, the whop-whop-whop of a helicopter can be maddening. When one lands and disgorges a gaggle of hikers nearby, it's infuriating. You assume that (1) if they had to rely on muscle instead of money, they'd stay home; (2) they're oblivious to the affects their cacophonous machine has on wildlife and real hikers; and (3) having skipped the hard part, they can't fully appreciate where they are and don't deserve to be there. Unless you can greet heli-hikers with a smile and a wave, instead of an upraised middle finger, visit Chalice Ridge only after mid-September.

FACT

Before your trip

Be aware that Bugaboo area trailheads are infamous for car-eating porcupines. Seriously. They munch tires, hoses and fan belts. Their voracious appetite for rubber could leave you stranded. Thwart them by wrapping chicken wire around your vehicle and securing it with rocks and pieces of wood. Bugaboo Park supplies chicken wire at Bugaboo Spires trailhead, but Chalice Ridge trail-head is outside the park. So, if you're backpacking here, bring chicken wire. If you're dayhiking, you probably won't want to bother. But consider trying moth balls. It's rumoured that spreading them around and under your vehicle might be sufficient to repel the odd nocturnal opportunist that comes scavenging in daylight. Be sure to pick each ball up before you drive away.

By Vehicle
Follow the directions for Cobalt Lake (Trip 28) as far as the signed fork at 43.3 km (26.8 mi). Turn left here and reset your trip odometer to zero. Right passes Cobalt Lake trailhead on the right and ends in 3 km (1.9 mi) at Bugaboo Spires trailhead (Trip 27).

0 km (0 mi)
Turn left (south), continuing on Bugaboo FS road.

0.7 km (0.4 mi)
Turn left, cross the bridge over Bugaboo Creek and reach another fork. Bear right. Left leads in 200 meters (220 yards) to the signed left turn for the Bugaboo-Septet campground managed by the Forest Service.

1.6 km (1 mi)
The Bugaboo Spires are visible west.

1.9 km (1.2 mi)
Bear left and ascend. The road is increasingly rough and overgrown with alder. Still, a 2WD car is adequate if you're unconcerned about scratches.

3.1 km (1.9 mi)
The road widens slightly. Reluctant to drive farther? Turn around and park here.

4 km (2.5 mi)
Reach the Chalice Ridge trailhead parking area at 1600 m (5250 ft).

On Foot
If it's still here, ignore the FS sign at the trailhead. It exaggerates the elevation gain to the old trailhead, now inaccessible by vehicle, just up the road/trail.

Immediately cross a sturdy bridge over Chalice Creek and follow the road/trail south. Views are southwest up Bugaboo Creek valley to the Quintet Group and northwest to the Bugaboo Spires. In 10 minutes, gain 21 m (70 ft) to arrive at the old trailhead.

Bear left at the sign and continue ascending southeast on the road/trail. Soon switchback northeast. The grade is moderate. Like many cutblocks, the one you're hiking through is dominated by fast-growing alder. The long, rubbery limbs swoop out and swallow roads or trails in just a few seasons unless trimmed back. Brilliant fuschia fireweed also flourishes in cutblocks, and you'll see it here.

Near 1.6 km (1 mi), 1677 m (5500 ft), the road/trail levels in a **clearing**. A moderate pace should get you here in 30 minutes. Turn right (east), away from the Bugaboos, and proceed on the deteriorating road/trail into the burned, clearcut basin beneath Chalice Ridge. Within 5 minutes, stay left on the main road/trail paralleling Chalice Creek; ignore the rough trail ascending right.

Road ends and actual trail begins at about 2.4 km (1.5 mi), 1835 m (6020 ft). You've probably hiked 45 minutes so far. The trail turns sharply right (south), spurts up a grassy slope, then turns left (east) and enters **spruce forest**. With the help of some puncheon (wood punched into the mud) and footlogs, negotiate a few mucky areas where creeklets cross the trail. The ascent is still moderate.

The trail levels near the bank of **Chalice Creek** and turns right (south). You're now about an hour from the trailhead. Follow the creek upstream, but only for a few minutes. At 4.8 km (3 mi), 1884 m (6180 ft), the trail forks. Right continues south along the west bank. Turn left, drop to the creek and cross to the east bank. Enjoy a brief burst of pleasant scenery here, looking south, up-valley, toward the creek's headwaters.

From the **creek crossing**, the trail heads generally northeast, switchbacking up a very steep slope. Abundant berry bushes serve delicious snacks in late August. Glimpse the Bugaboos again as you climb. Enter **Chalice Saddle** at 6.5 km (4 mi), 2250 m (7380 ft). Total elevation gain: 650 m (2130 ft). Hiking time: about 2 hours. Open larch forest and subalpine meadows allow views northwest to the spires and glaciers in Bugaboo Park. Chalice Ridge extends left (northwest) and right (southeast).

The trail fades in the saddle and soon disappears. Metal blazes on trees indicate a route gently descending northeast 0.4 km (0.25 mi) through the saddle to **Chalice Pond**. Because it's convenient and sheltered, many people have pitched tents here. Superior camping awaits you beyond. Follow the directions below to find lonelier, more scenic, less damaging sites. Wherever you camp, leave no trace of your stay. See *Wilderness Ethics* on page 9 for details.

Roam northwest to get closer to the Bugaboos. In about 3 km (1.9 mi), top out on a 2440-m (8000-ft) bump above a couple lakelets. **Roam southeast** for airier hiking along a sharper crest, views of mountains heretofore obscured, and the option of scrambling to an unnamed 2573-m (8440-m) summit about 4 km (2.5 mi) distant.

South on Chalice Ridge

Resume climbing just beyond where the trail first entered the saddle. Soon pass treeline. Grass gives way to charcoal-coloured gravel and dirt. Within 10 minutes, approach a draw. Veer left to ascend steeply, directly onto the ridgecrest and attain views sooner. Otherwise, follow the draw south, ascending gradually, delaying views a bit longer. If you stay in the draw, proceed until it pinches closed, then ascend left to the crest. Either way, once you're on the crest, follow it south/southeast.

After 40 minutes of leisurely hiking, you'll be 2.3 km (1.4 mi) from Chalice Saddle, atop a 2515-m (8250-ft) bump on the ridge. East/northeast is the Septet Range. Look carefully to see two pairs of tarns shelved on its slopes. Lead Queen Mtn. is the dominant Septet peak. Septet Pass—a long, north-south, subalpine trough, with meadows and stands of larch—is below you (southeast). The south end of the pass drops into Frances Creek valley. Directly southeast across the upper valley is Taurus Mtn.

Continuing south along the ridge is possible and worthwhile. The farther you go, the more rugged it gets, and the more significant the ups and downs. Views improve, but the primary attraction is a heightened sense of adventure and achievement. You'll eventually be scrambling, not just hiking. Scope it out from the bump described above. If dayhiking, be sure you have sufficient daylight.

Backpackers should proceed about 15 minutes beyond the bump, into a col where scree slopes grant a 360-m (1180-ft) descent left (southeast) into 2135-m (7003-ft) **Septet Pass**. From there, begin ascending again, generally east. Cross-country travel poses no obstacles here. Having seen the Septet Range tarns from the ridgecest, you should have a strong sense of how to navigate to them.

Wondering how much time you can allow yourself to dayhike on Chalice Ridge?

Fleet feet can descend from Chalice Saddle, to where the trail turns to road, in 1 hour. Hiking the road/trail from there back to the trailhead takes speedsters 35 minutes. But before departing Chalice Saddle, pause to locate the trail. It can be tricky. Don't descend until you're sure you've found it. A blaze on a tree marks the spot.

Trip 30

Mt. Robson / Berg Lake / Snowbird Pass

Location	Mt. Robson Provincial Park
Round trip	39.2 km (24.3 mi) to Berg Lake Campground
Elevation gain	786 m (2578 ft) to Berg Lake Campground
Time required	2 to 4 days
Difficulty	Moderate
Maps	Mount Robson Park 1:125 000; Mount Robson 83 E/3; BC Parks brochure

OPINION

The highway view of 3954-m (12,970-ft) Mt. Robson is jaw-dropping. But it's the scenery west and north of this Rocky Mountain icon that inspires many hikers to return religiously. It's nonstop extraordinary. The lush rainforest along the Robson River could be in Costa Rica. The Valley of a Thousand Falls (if it's raining, count 'em) is suggestive of New Zealand's deep, green valleys. The gravelly glacial flats feel like the Yukon. And the Mist, Berg, and Robson glaciers gnawing at the flanks of the mountain are quintessential Western Canada. If you're willing to risk sensory overload, continue to Snowbird Pass and stare at a frozen sea: Coleman Glacier and 10-km (6.2-mi) long Reef Icefield.

Though the trail to Berg Lake is the most heavily traveled in the Canadian Rockies, the powerful scenery instills a sense of reverence in most hikers, which can help make the company tolerable. Because this trip is widely known, think of it as a time for stimulating encounters. We've met a hyena specialist from Berkeley, California; a couple from Valemount, B.C. with an infant and a hiking three-year-old; Jasper railroad engineers; and travellers from New Zealand, Japan and East Germany. We've sparked friendships here with people we've since hiked with many times.

It's warmer and wetter in Robson Park than in Jasper or Banff, so Berg Lake can be accessible by mid-June, up to a month earlier than most backpack trips in the range. Before mid-July, however, expect the Snowbird Pass trail to be snowbound.

Strong trekkers can flash the one-way trip to Berg Lake in 6-7 hours. After mid-July, allow an extra day for the demanding dayhike from Berg Lake to Snowbird Pass. Another excellent side trip—linking Mumm Basin, Toboggan Falls, and Hargreaves Glacier—improves considerably on the already picture-perfect view from the shore of Berg Lake.

FACT

By Vehicle

From **Jasper** townsite, drive 84 km (52 mi) west on Highway 16. From **Tete Jaune Cache** junction, drive 16 km (10 mi) east. After picking up a camping permit ($5 per person per night, no reservations required) at the visitor centre, follow the side road 2 km (1.2 mi) north to the trailhead parking lot, at 855 m (2804 ft).

On Foot

The trail is well-maintained the whole way. Initially it's broad. After walking 4.5 km (2.8 mi) northeast through a flower-dappled rainforest, with glimpses of the roaring Robson River, continue around the northeast shore of **Kinney Lake**. The path narrows here to trail width. Pass Kinney Lake Campground at 6.7 km (4.2 mi) and soon emerge onto open gravel flats. At 8 km (5 mi), cross the Robson River on a bridge. There are two more crossings of the river, both on sturdy suspension bridges. Just after the second crossing, reach Whitehorn Campground at 10.5 km (6.5 mi). It has a spacious cooking shelter. You're now in the **Valley of a Thousand Falls**. Near 11.5 km (7.1 mi) start a stiff ascent north along the rugged Robson River gorge. Ascend 450 m (1475 ft) in the next 3.5 km (2 mi). You'll pass three tremendous waterfalls: White, Falls-of-the-Pool, and 60-meter-high Emperor Falls. Take the short spur trail to pay homage to the mighty Emperor.

Emperor Falls Campground is at 15 km (9.3 mi). The terrain becomes rocky as you head northeast. Reach Marmot Campground at 17.4 km (10.8 mi), 1641 m (5382 ft), just before **Berg Lake**. The cliffs of Mt. Robson now dominate the scene. The first river of ice you'll see is Mist Glacier. Next is Berg Glacier, which occasionally calves RV-sized icebergs into the powder-blue water below, hence the name Berg Lake. Mount Robson rises 2316 m (7596 ft) directly above its southeast shore. From the lake's southwest end, follow the northwest shore, stay straight where the Hargreaves Glacier / Mumm Basin trail forks left, and reach **Berg Lake Campground** at 19.6 km (12.2 mi), 1646 m (5400 ft). You'll find a comfortable day-use shelter with a woodstove. If you want more privacy, forego quick access to the shelter and continue 0.6 km (0.4 mi) to Rearguard Campground. Robson Pass Campground is at 21.6 km (13.4 mi). Adolphus Lake Campground is farther and lonelier.

Berg Glacier and Berg Lake

The 9-km (5.6-mi) cairned route to **Snowbird Pass** heads southeast from near the park ranger cabin, which is 0.8 km (0.5 mi) north of Rearguard. It begins by crossing gravel flats to the toe of Robson Glacier. Then it climbs onto the moraine and provides astounding views of the glacier for the next 3 km (2 mi). Turning away from the glacier, the

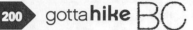

Valley of a Thousand Falls

route ascends east on the left (north) side of a creeklet through alpine meadows. Finally, ascend a steep boulder field to the 2410-m (7905-ft) pass. You will have gained 769 m (2522 ft).

The short side trip to **Toboggan Falls** starts at Berg Lake Campground and climbs northwest along the northeast side of Toboggan Creek. The trail provides ever improving views and reaches a four-way junction in 1.2 km (0.7 mi). Straight climbs steeply north, arriving at a cave and climactic vantage in another 1.2 km (0.7 mi).

Right (northeast) at the four-way junction loops 6.8 km (4.2 mi) through **Mumm Basin** and Robson Pass, back to Berg Lake Campground. The alpine basin is a wildflower garden in season and overlooks Robson Glacier. Left (southwest) at the four-way junction loops 5.1 km (3.2 mi) past a viewpoint on the lateral moraine of **Hargreaves Glacier**, back to Berg Lake Campground. Be sure to ascend the moraine to see Hargreaves lake and glacier (photo page 170).

You can visit Mumm Basin, Toboggan Falls, and Hargreaves Glacier on a grand loop. Allow a full day. Expansive views are frequent, but the way is often steep, a few sections are rough, and you must be attentive to stay on course. From Berg Lake Campground, head northeast on the main trail. Pick up the signed Mumm Basin trail at Robson Pass Campground.

Trip 31
Diana Lake / The Judge

Location	Western Rocky Mountains
Round trip	12 km (7.4 mi) for Diana Lake, plus 5.6 km (3.5 mi) for The Judge
Elevation gain	626 m (2053 ft) to Diana Lake, plus 606 m (1988 ft) to The Judge
Time required	4 to 5 hrs for Diana Lake, 7 to 9 hrs for The Judge
Difficulty	Easy to Challenging
Maps	Spillamacheen 82 K/16; Invermere FS District brochure

OPINION

Many trails, even to premier destinations, pose some kind of distress or adversity to hikers. A punishing access road. A prolonged march through an ugly clearcut. A tedious, viewless ascent. You begin to wonder: why can't it ever just be easy and pleasant? Well, once in a while, it can. It certainly is here. Everything about this hike—to Diana Lake and on up the summit ridge of The Judge—is a joy. It's all carrot and no stick.

And the carrot keeps getting sweeter. You ascend Pinnacle Creek canyon through pretty forest. The grade remains moderate—just aggressive enough that you make good progress. Avalanche paths soon allow views. Then you enter lovely subalpine meadows teeming with wildflowers. (See photo on page 171.) Larches appear. The basin opens up. And suddenly you're at Diana Lake. It takes strong hikers a mere 1½ hours.

Diana is a beauty. The 366-m (1200-ft) sheer face of Mt. Norman rises dramatically from the shore. The lake basin is lightly forested in its lower reaches. Meadows expand and trees dwindle in its upper reaches. Alpine slopes invite wandering. A gentle ascent north leads to a saddle on the ridge. You can be there within 40 minutes of leaving the lake. The entire basin is then displayed below you. The ridgecrest affords effortless, delightful walking, with views across to the main Rockies range.

Keep following the crest southeast if you want to ascend The Judge—the highpoint on Diana Lake basin's east wall. Approaching the summit block, hiking turns into scrambling. Only cool heads, stout hearts, and sure feet should continue. The steep incline and loose rock are challenging. Figure 1½ to 2 hours from the lake to the top of The Judge. You can return the way you came, or drop off the ridgecrest, aim for a point just south of the lake, and intersect the trail, thus completing a circuit of the basin.

FACT

By Vehicle
From the junction of Hwys 93 and 95 in **Radium Hot Springs**, drive Hwy 95 north 17.6 km (10.9 mi). Turn right (northeast) onto gravel Kindersley-Pinnacle FS road. It's just north of a yellow warning sign: TRUCK CROSSING. Reset your trip odometer to 0.

0 km (0 mi)
Starting northeast on Kindersley-Pinnacle FS road, departing Hwy 95.

5 km (3 mi)
Pass an elevated flume constructed in the early 1900s. It's one of the few elevated irrigation systems active in western Canada.

8.7 km (5.4 mi)
Go left (northwest) at the sign for Diana Lake. Ascend into the Pinnacle Creek drainage. Bear right at the next two forks. Both are signed for Diana Lake.

24 km (14.9 mi)
Reach the trailhead parking area, just before a washout, at 1520 m (4986 ft).

On Foot
Follow the old road upstream beside Pinnacle Creek. In 100 meters (110 yards) cross an aluminum bridge to the west bank. Bits of overgrown road lead northwest. At 1 km (0.6 mi), where the road curves left, follow the trail right (northeast) and enter forest. A moderate ascent ensues. From here on, there are no junctions. Just stay on the main trail.

At 2.5 km (1.6 mi), 1775 m (5822 ft) the trail briefly returns to the creek. It then climbs through **avalanche paths**. Wildflowers are

Ascending from Diana Lake to The Judge

Nearing the final rough ascent of The Judge

abundant here in summer. Gradually curve northwest, ascending around the southeast flank of Mt. Norman.

Cross a bridge over Pinnacle Creek at 4.4 km (2.7 mi), 1985 m (6510 ft). The grade relaxes. Proceed through subalpine meadows. About 10 minutes farther, across from broken, blocky cliffs, cross another bridge over the creek. The Judge is visible north.

Reach **Diana Lake** at 6.4 km (4 mi), 2146 m (7040 ft). Mt. Norman rises from the lake's southwest shore. The Judge is northeast. Camping is restricted to the south end of the lake, where there's an outhouse. Shortly beyond, the trail passes a private cabin. To probe the basin meadows, keep following the trail generally northwest. Rockhop the creek twice. Curve north up the gully.

An aerial view of Diana Lake basin, and a grand perspective of the main Rockies range, are your rewards for attaining the ridge ahead. The easiest way is to continue the gradual ascent north through the head of the basin to **Whitetail Pass**, a 2335-m (7660-ft) saddle. From there, turn right (southeast) and follow the crest as far as you please. The Goodsir peaks in Yoho National Park are visible north/northwest. Peaks along Kootenay Park's Rockwall are north. The Judge blocks the view northeast over Kootenay Park. Return the way you came, or complete a circuit of the basin by descending directly to the lake.

Scramblers heading for The Judge, however, can skip Whitetail Pass and opt for a steeper but more efficient route: where the basin levels and is virtually devoid of trees, go right (northeast). Top out on the ridge at 2409 m (7900 ft), a mere 15 minutes after leaving the upper basin floor. The summit is just 45 minutes farther. Turn right. Follow the crest southeast, gradually curving east.

The last easy-to-walk section of the ridgecrest is at 2561 m (8400 ft), just below the summit block. You must then carefully pick your route over loose talus and boulders to prevail over **The Judge** (2752 m / 9028 ft). The panorama is now complete. Mt. Assiniboine is visible east, way across Kootenay River valley, but it's barely recognizable from this distance.

Mt. Aeneas (Trip 32)

Trip 32

Pedley Ridge / Mount Aeneas

Location	Western Rocky Mountains
Round trip	4.2 km (2.6 mi)
Elevation gain	440 m (1444 ft)
Time required	3 to 4 hours for ridge, 8 hours for Aeneas
Difficulty	Easy
Map	Fairmont Hot Springs 82 J/5

OPINION

It's a quirk of geology that the shortest, easiest hike in this book attains the vantage point affording the most extensive panorama. Atop Pedley Ridge, on a clear day, the landmark mountains of seven other hikes in this book are discernible: Mt. Assiniboine (Trip 35 & 41), the Royal Group (Trip 34), Mt. Joffre and Russell Peak (Trip 33), the summits above Lake of the Hanging Glacier (Trip 25), and the Bugaboos (Trips 27-29). They're not just vague, distant shapes, either. They're distinct, easily identified if you've hiked those trails before coming here. What an illuminating sight. Life rarely grants you a backward glance such as this, where numerous accomplishments are visible, all at once, in bold relief. It might fluff your ego, but that's healthy now and then. A little fluffing is motivational, energizing. Fuel for your next adventure.

The reason for this unique vista is that Pedley Ridge is perched on the western edge of the Rockies but isolated by two broad valleys. East, across Kootenay River valley, is the Rockies' main range, its profile visible from Golden (north) to Waterton National Park (south). West, across Columbia River valley, are the Purcell Mountains.

All this hype about the view seems to suggest that upon attaining the ridge you should just stand and gawk. Uh-uh. After gawking, keep walking. Roam the ridge north for another hour. Or return to the pass, drop south into the basin, skirt the tarn, then scramble up Mt. Aeneas. The summit reveals the southwestern horizon, but that's not the reason to go. Do it because any significant increase in altitude vaporizes worldly cares.

North along Pedley Ridge

If you're short on time, however, or if you or members of your party are not big hikers, simply attaining the ridge can be fulfilling. The short trail is virtually switchbackless, so it's moderately steep, but vigourous children and grandparents conquer it without difficulty. Just don't stop at Pedley Pass. Complete the brief ascent northeast, out of the treed pass, to the alpine ridge, or you'll miss the show.

FACT

Before your trip
Be aware that the trailhead access road is riddled with water-bars (drainage ditches). We counted 52. They're not so deep as to prohibit 2WD cars, but if yours has low clearance you'll be banging the belly. 4WD helps little here. But high clearance helps a lot. In any vehicle, expect to crawl on the road's upper reaches.

By Vehicle
From Invermere, drive south on Hwy 93/95 for 2.8 km (1.7 mi). Turn left onto Windermere Loop Road and reset your trip odometer to 0.

0 km (0 mi)
Starting east on Windermere Loop Road from Hwy 93/95.

1 km (0.6 mi)
Stay left.

3.2 km (2 mi)
Go left onto Westroc Mine haul road. Then immediately go right onto pavement. You'll be ascending the Windermere Creek drainage.

6.5 km (4 mi)
Bear right and descend east.

11 km (6.8 mi)
Just past the mine entrance, go straight onto a narrow road.

11.3 km (7 mi)
Fork left. Right is gated.

12.8 km (7.9 mi)
Fork left. Then immediately go right onto a better two-track road.

17.4 km (10.8 mi)
Fork left (southeast). The road deteriorates and is plagued with frequent water bars.

19.3 km (12 mi)
Arrive at the parking area in a clearing. The trailhead is on the right, at 1955 m (6412 ft).

On Foot
The trail heads west but soon curves south, climbing steeply through open forest. After ascending about 10 minutes, enjoy a brief reprieve before resuming a moderate ascent. Reach **Bumpy Meadow** at 1 km (0.6 mi), 2104 m (6900 ft). Cross the meadow, then go left in front of the limestone headwall. Ascend through trees another 30 minutes. At 2 km (1.2 mi), 2256 m (7400 ft), arrive at **Pedley Pass** and a junction.

Don't go straight; it descends to Pedley Creek. Turn left (northeast). The grade is initially quite steep, but it eases about five minutes above. Mid-July through early August, expect to see a profuse display of lavendar alpine forget-me-nots, bright-yellow cinquefoil, and white mountain-avens. Crest **Pedley Ridge** at 2395 m (7856 ft), about ten minutes from the pass.

Prominently visible southwest is nearby Mt. Aeneas. Chisel Peak is slightly left of it, farther south. Across Kootenay River valley, the Mt. Assiniboine massif is north/northeast. The Royal Group (near Ralph Lake) is closer, northeast. Mt. Joffre and Russell Peak (near Limestone Lakes) are east. West, across Columbia River valley, are the Purcells, including Jumbo and Commander mountains above Lake of the Hanging Glacier. Northwest are the singular spires of Bugaboo Glacier Provincial Park.

Wandering the ridge farther north requires no directions. **Rounded Summit**, where you can survey the river valleys east and west, is a half-hour distant. You must lose and regain about 100 m (328 ft) en route.

MOUNT AENEAS

Round trip 2.4 km (1.4 mi) from Pedley Pass
Elevation gain 419 m (1374 ft) from Pedley Pass
Time required 4 hours return to Pedley Pass
Difficulty Challenging

On Foot

From the first junction in Pedley Pass, at 2256 m (7400 ft), turn right (west). Immediately go right again. In a few minutes, a basin containing a tarn is visible southwest. The route to Aeneas is through the basin, then left, up behind the sheer peak. (See photo on page 205.)

Proceed west on the trail. It quickly fades on the sparsely treed ridge. Drop left (southwest) before the base of a knob. Aim for the tarn. Scramble down steep scree. Skirt the tarn at 2274 m (7460 ft). Deeper in the basin, curve left.

A narrow west-facing couloir gives access to a plateau at 2510 m (8230 ft). That's 150 m (492 ft) below the summit of Aeneas. From the plateau, work your way up the crumbled west ridge. Top out at 2675 m (8774 ft). The panorama is similar to, although more complete than, the one visible from Pedley Ridge.

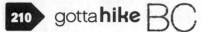

Trip 33
Limestone Lakes

Location	Height of the Rockies Provincial Park
Round trip	34 km (21 mi) plus exploring
Elevation gain	1325 m (4346 ft) plus exploring
Time required	3 days (9 hours to first lake)
Difficulty	Challenging
Maps	Kananaskis Lakes 82 J/11, Mount Abruzzi 82 J/6

OPINION

Splayed across vast alpine meadows are four lakes and a dozen pools, all hidden on a remote, high-altitude plateau, surrounded by limestone summits and a glacier. Backpackers might ask for something different, but they can't ask for more, because more doesn't exist. Not on this planet. And if you're looking for less, you'll get that here as well: very few people, no permits required, no designated campsites, no trail signs, and, for a third of the journey, no trail. Perfect.

This supernatural destination does, however, ask more of *you* than do other trips in this book. You must be physically robust. You must have well-honed routefinding skills. You must carry the topo maps and read them. You must bring a compass and use it. You must rigorously follow *Leave No Trace* guidelines. As yet, the delicate Limestone Lakes environment shows no sign of human impact; it's your responsibility to keep it that way. And, finally, you must summon the will to leave. That's the most onerous demand of all. Because unless bugs are tormenting you, the sky is pelting you, or the temperature has plummeted, it will take iron discipline to tear body and soul from this ethereal setting.

The ineffable splendor of Limestone Lakes is likely to elicit conflicting physical responses in you: vigor and lethargy, at the same time. It's weird. You're eager to bop over the next rise, spy the next lake, appreciate the next lovely surprise. You set out briskly. Yet you're slowing down. Then you're sitting down. "Ahhh, this is nice." You're eventually pulled onward, but only briefly. "Wouldn't that grassy stream-bank be wonderful to stretch out on?"

Limestone Lakes basin

So it takes you all day to wander a basin that measures just 2.5 km (1.6 mi) at its widest point. But what a day. (See photo on page 172.)

By giving the basin all the time and attention it deserves, you'll be doing the same for yourself. Fling down your pack. Take off your boots. That's the spirit. Walk barefoot in the soft grass along a shoreline. Peer into the secret world of wildflowers by narrowing your focus to a single, exquisite alpine-forget-me-not. Lie back, search the sky, feel the earth, listen to the silence. Try to keep mozying past the westernmost lake, to the edge of the basin, where you can stretch your eyeballs. The Royal Group is visible way across Palliser River valley, which you drove through to reach the trailhead.

En route to the lakes, you'll encounter a geologic phenomenon known as karst—a region of underground drainage and numerous cavities caused by dissolution of rock. That's the technical definition, but it doesn't suggest how fascinating the reality is. You'll be hiking across expansive limestone beds, some of which have a bizarre, prickly surface. Look closely. The sharply tufted rock resembles miniature mountain ranges with peaks rising 20 cm (8 in) high. Just don't fall down here, or you'll be impaled.

Though an intriguing sight and an engaging surface to walk on, karst topography presents two challenges to hikers: (1) It's fractured and fissured, so there's no surface water; it all drains downward. That can leave you thirsty, if you haven't planned ahead.

(2) Being solid rock, without so much as a bootprint to suggest the route, and having a convoluted, complex appearance, karst complicates navigation.

Actually, you'll be routefinding even before you set foot on karst. Defined trail ends where you approach Sylvan Pass. You'll have to cross the subalpine basin below the pass, negotiate the forest margin, then pick your way upward through open forest and subalpine meadows to reach the karst in the alpine zone. Fully a third of the trip to Limestone Lakes is a cross-country sojourn. You'll also find no trails or marked routes in the basin. Follow our extremely detailed directions, however, and you should only have to use your map and compass as supplementary aids, not rely on them as survival tools.

Now, where to camp? You have three good options—maybe. The basin below Sylvan Pass, at 10.5 km (6.3 mi), is the first desirable spot. It's pretty, and the creek there should be a reliable water source. It's possible to dayhike from the basin to the lakes, but that severely limits your time at the lakes. Beyond Sylvan Pass, you can't be certain of finding water until reaching the first Limestone Lake. The camping is excellent there, or anywhere else in the lakes basin. The third option—beyond the karst, but still an hour shy of the lakes—is one of the grassy ledges next to low redrock walls below the south end of Shatch Mtn. But camping there is feasible only near one of the rare seeps in the redrock. If you find one with a sufficient water flow, you're in luck. Pitch your tent. The scenery is stellar. Dayhiking to the lakes is easy. And you'll significantly reduce your impact on the lakes basin.

FACT

By Vehicle

From Kootenay National Park's south entrance at **Radium Hot Springs**, drive Hwy 93 northeast 19 km (11.8 mi). After the highway descends, turn right (southeast) onto Settlers Road. Reset your trip odometer to 0.

From **McLeod Meadows campground**, on Hwy 93, near the south end of Kootenay National Park, drive south 8 km (5 mi). Before the highway ascends, turn left (southeast) onto Settlers Road. Reset your trip odometer to 0.

0 km (0 mi)
Starting southeast on Settlers Road, departing Hwy 93.

12.6 km (7.8 mi)
Reach a junction. Go left onto Kootenay-Palliser FS road and soon cross the Kootenay River. Kootenay-Settlers FS road proceeds right (south).

14.8 km (9.2 mi)
Go right at the sign for Palliser River. Left is Cross FS road, leading to Marvel Pass trailhead (Trip 35).

Close-up of prickly limestone karst

18.8 km (11.7 mi)
Curve right and cross a bridge.

31.6 km (19.6 mi)
Stay left and descend on the main road.

35.3 km (21.9 mi)
Bear right on the main road. Little Elk FS road forks left.

37.3 km (23.1 mi)
Cross a bridge and bear left on Kootenay-Palliser FS road for Limestone Lakes, as well as the Ralph Lake (Trip 34) trailhead. To the right, Kootenay River FS road is signed for Fenwick Creek.

41.7 km (25.9 mi)
Ignore two descending left forks. Turn right for Joffre Creek and Height of the Rockies Park. Left, signed for Kootenay-Albert, leads to Ralph Lake trailhead.

49.6 km (30.8 mi)
Stay right. Pass the short trail to Palliser Canyon Falls on the left.

53.4 km (33 mi)
Cross a bridge. Mt. Joffre is visible ahead (east).

56.4 km (35 mi)
Stay right, continuing east for Joffre Creek. Pass the Queen Mary Lake horse trail on the left.

56.8 km (35.2 mi)
Follow the far left of three forks. It's a two-track road, narrow and rough, but passable in 2WD. (If you've hiked across Northover Ridge from Three Isle Lake, study the mountains ahead. You'll recognize Wakanabee Knob, in front of Warrior Mtn.)

66 km (40.9 mi)
Arrive at a horse-trail parking area signed for Height of the Rockies Park. Don't want to press your 2WD car farther? Start hiking here. High-clearance vehicles can continue. The road narrows, gets rockier, and has more potholes.

67 km (41.5 mi)
Go left and descend on the overgrown road. In 200 meters (220 yards) arrive at the road's end trailhead on a grassy bench above Joffre Creek. There's room for several vehicles. Camping is feasible here and on the bench above. The trail begins at the register box, in the far left corner of the parking area. Elevation: 1380 m (4526 ft).

On Foot
Trail to the base of Mt. Joffre
From the trail register box, descend 15 m (50 ft) to a footlog spanning Joffre Creek. Cross to the far bank. Go straight (west), away from the creek. Ascend the faint path out of the gully. In about 15 minutes, reach a **T-junction**. Left leads north up Palliser River valley. Turn right (northeast). But pause before proceeding. Take note of this unmarked junction. It's easy to miss on the way out.

Climb steep switchbacks along the edge of a low, forested ridge on the north side of Joffre Creek. About 40 minutes from the trailhead, encounter a steep, rough section. Better trail resumes 24 meters (80 ft) above.

Pass the 1.5 KM blaze (red-orange, nailed to a tree) and enter **Joffre Creek canyon**. Heading southeast, the grade is gentle to moderate. The trail returns to the creek near 1.8 km (1.1 mi). After hiking about an hour, ascend more steep stretches—probably muddy, due to horses.

At 3.5 km (2.2 mi), 1670 m (5478 ft), reach a **tributary stream**. Go straight across it to the trail on the other side. An outlier of Warrior Mtn is visible east. Mt. Northover is left (north) of the long cascade.

Proceed southeast under Warrior Mtn, through forest with meadowy undergrowth. At 4.5 km (2.8 mi), 1700 m (5576 ft), 15 minutes beyond the tributary crossing, pass a **campsite**. It's in a

Westernmost Limestone Lake. Royal Group in the distance.

small clearing with minimal views. Shallow creeklets obscure the trail here. Head south, through willows. In a few minutes, defined path is again evident. Watch for pink flagging.

Proceed straight, across a dry, rocky streambed. After crossing another washout, pass the KM 6.5 blaze at about 1780 m (5838 ft). Ascend steeply at 7 km (4.3 mi). Cross **avalanche paths**. Continue among low trees and shrubs. Water is available at a stream just past 7.5 km (4.7 mi).

Fork right at 7.7 km (4.8 mi), 1955 m (6412 ft). The grade is now moderate, on the left side of the valley. At 9 km (5.6 mi), 2165 m (7100 ft), larches are present in the forest, along with subalpine fir. The sheer wall of 3415-m (11,200-ft) **Mt. Joffre** looms just ahead (east). The trail becomes indistinct in flowery meadows. Visible southeast is the bare talus slope of 2345-m (7692-ft) Sylvan Pass. You're now 3 to 3½ hours from Limestone Lakes.

One way to reach the lakes is to attain Sylvan Pass, then traverse the unnamed, blunt, 2540-m (8331-ft) peak south of it. But that's a steeper route than necessary, entailing a substantial, but pointless, ascent and descent. Described below is a more efficient, gradual route skirting the base of the knob.

Route from the base of Mt. Joffre to Limestone Lakes

Where Mt. Joffre is first visible, keep following the trail toward it (east). Just before the KM 9.5 blaze, ignore the path forking right (southwest); it soon meanders confusingly. The main trail begins fading about 1 km (0.6 mi) before the pass. Continue the gentle ascent southeast through a **grooved meadow** bound by trees. The path soon reappears, ascending right, out of the groove. Pass the 10 KM blaze. Four of the Royal Group's eight peaks are visible behind you (northwest).

In a few minutes, enter another grooved meadow, at 2244 m (7360 ft). **Sylvan Pass basin** is visible immediately ahead (southeast). Keep working your way toward it, until you're out of the trees. At about 2265 m (7430 ft), you should be in open meadow, with an unobstructed view of the entire basin. Directly south is an **unnamed, blunt, talusy peak** right of the pass. See its northwest jutting outlier? Your immediate goal is the base of that outlier. (If it's late and/or you're tired, consider that this basin could be your last opportunity to camp near a water source until you reach Limestone Lakes.)

Pick your own cross-country route through meadow punctuated by stands of larch and subalpine fir. Generally proceed south into the basin, then curve southwest out of it. Cross a creeklet. Try to stay above the dense forest but below the steep, rocky slope of the outlier.

Approaching the **outlier**, curve south again, around it. A faint, intermittent bootbeaten path might help guide you through the trees. You want to parallel the outlier's **steep, west-facing slope**. At about 2195 m (7200 ft), near the base of the slope, pick up a narrow but distinct path leading south, up valley. The path is between where the forest thins and the rocky slope steepens.

You're now on the east side of **upper Joffre Creek valley**. The path soon fades. From here on, you must navigate without the aid of blazes, cairns or even bootprints. Proceed south, through larch-dotted, heathery meadows. Limestone outcroppings appear. Follow a depression between the **rose-coloured mound** on the left (east) and trees on the right (west). Stay about 45 meters (50 yards) from the mound.

Until about halfway up the valley, favour its east side. Keep heading south. Mt. Assiniboine is visible behind you (north). Shatch Mtn is the multi-peaked massif forming the valley's west wall. Several permanent snowfields cling to it. Aim for the south end of Shatch Mtn. Gradually leave the trees behind and continue on broad slabs of prickly karst. (Notice the ferns growing in cavities of fractured limestone.) Stay in the middle of the trough. Where the **limestone pinches out**, begin crossing to the valley's west side, still aiming for the south end of Shatch Mtn.

This "pinching out" is a discernible, **natural causeway**. It's about halfway between the unnamed, blunt peak near Sylvan Pass, and the south end of Shatch Mtn. It's also across from the midpoint of the rose-coloured mound, which forms the valley's east wall.

After crossing the causeway, work your way west (right) onto the **terraced red rock**. Proceed south along level, narrow strips of meadow. Occasionally veer right, working your way up the ledges. Ascend above the red rock, onto **grey rock**. Your general direction of travel remains south. Your goal remains the south end of Shatch Mtn.

If it's late and/or you're tired, the grassy ledges next to low redrock walls below the south end of Shatch Mtn afford comfortable, scenic camping. You can see Mt. Joffre northeast and Mt. Abruzzi southeast. But water is scarce here, perhaps unavailable. Look for seeps on the redrock walls. If you can't find an adequate dribble, you'll probably have to push on. The shore of the nearest Limestone Lake is still an hour distant. You'll spend 40 minutes of that time completing the ascent to where the lakes are first visible.

Continue hiking south up alpine slopes. Finally, crest the 2520-m (8266-ft) **ridge at the south end of Shatch Mtn** and gaze down at Limestone Lakes basin. The nearest lake, directly below, is at 2400 m (7875 ft). It's the easternmost of all the lakes and has the most polymorphic shape.

For a view of White River valley, descend southeast and continue past the east shore of the first lake, to the lip of the basin. To probe the basin and admire the other lakes, descend southwest.

Probing **Limestone Lakes basin** requires four hours. It deserves a full day or more. Start by crossing the grey, silty flats at the north end of the second lake. Then ascend gassy slopes. Curve southwest then northwest to round Shatch Mtn and reach the third and fourth lakes. Scan the cliffs northwest for mountain goats.

Exploring the rest of the Limestone Lakes and ponds requires no directions. The treeless, grassy terrain allows you to see far ahead. Let your curiosity lead you. If you continue roaming to the basin lip just beyond the westernmost lake, at 2433 m (7980 ft), you'll attain another impressive vista: northwest, across Palliser River valley, to the Royal Group.

Trip 34

Ralph and Queen Mary Lakes

Location	Height of the Rockies Provincial Park
Round trip	10 km (6.2 mi) for Ralph Lake;
	25 km (15.5 mi) for Queen Mary Lake
Elevation gain	834 m (2736 ft) to Ralph Lake;
	1644 m (5392 ft) round trip to
	Queen Mary Lake
Time required	9 hours for Ralph Lake;
	2 to 3 days for Queen Mary Lake
Difficulty	Challenging
Maps	Tangle Peak 82 J/12,
	Kananaskis Lakes 82 J/11

OPINION

Unfit hikers labouring up the wickedly steep Ralph Lake trail will sweat and whine like green logs tossed on a fire. It's hardly even a trail. Just a scurfy route, which makes it feel steeper than it is. And the ordeal of reaching the lake amplifies this destination's lonely, isolated atmosphere. It feels positively prelapsarian.

Arriving at the lake is cause for celebration. You've vanquished the rugged, taxing ascent. Admire your prize: a vast, meadowy, lake-adorned, subalpine basin, perched on the edge of the Royal Group. Ralph Lake is a spectacle: 1 km (0.6 mi) long. The Royal Group is a 9-km (5.4-mi) long massif as awesome as any in the Canadian Rockies. Each of the eight peaks is more than 3000 m (9840 ft) high. The highest is 3410-m (11,200-ft) Mt. King George. Mt. Queen Mary (3230 m / 10,600 ft) towers above Ralph Lake. Wandering to the far reaches of this pristine basin is utterly easy yet thoroughly fulfilling.

The Royal Group dazzles hikers from many distant vantage points, including Limestone Lakes (Trip 33). The Group's formidable appearance suggests impregnability. But there's a crack in the armour. Drive the long access road, grind up the Ralph Lake trail, and you're in. From there, you can continue storming the Bastille. It's possible to hike along the flanks of the Royal Group peaks, crossing two saddles before dropping to Queen Mary Lake. You'll find a com-

Ralph Lake and Mt. Queen Mary

fortable BC Parks cabin there, open to the public, free of charge. En route you'll see the Mt. Assiniboine massif northwest, and peaks shattering the sky at the southeast end of Height of the Rockies Park.

Energetic, athletic hikers should make this a dayhike. The Ralph Lake trail is more interesting, less onerous, if you're packing light. By starting early, you can go all the way to the first saddle southeast of the lake. Turn around there and you'll have fully appreciated the basin and seen most of the area's best scenery.

Queen Mary Lake, beneath Mt. Prince Henry and Mt. Prince Edward, is an inviting extension of the hike to Ralph Lake. Keep in mind that you'll be navigating cross-country. Bring a compass and the topo maps. Also, the two saddles you'll cross are very steep and rough. Lingering snowfields can make them dangerous. You'll gain 864 m (2835 ft) on the 12-km (7.4-mi) round trip between the two lakes. Allow at least three hours to go from lake to lake.

Pitching your tent in Ralph Lake basin, then dayhiking to Queen Mary Lake is viable. So is humping your whole load the entire way in one day-long push. If you choose the later, it's tempting to forgo a tent and stove, figuring that you can sleep and cook in the cabin. Just be aware that while it accommodates eight people and has wood and propane stoves, the cabin is available first come, first served, and it's accessible by a 12-km (7.4 mi) horse trail that plies Queen Mary Creek canyon, a Palliser River tributary. You won't know if equestrians are occupying the cabin until you arrive.

Also, forget about hiking the Queen Mary Creek trail. Nine challenging fords make it imprudent for bipeds.

FACT

By Vehicle

If you're approaching from **Radium Hot Springs or Kootenay National Park**, follow the directions for Limestone Lakes (Trip 33) as far as the junction of Kootenay-Palliser and Kootenay-Fenwick (from Canal Flats) FS roads at 37.3 km (23.1 mi). Go left onto the road signed for Kootenay-Palliser and Kootenay-Albert, reset your trip odometer to 0, then follow the directions (A) below.

If you're approaching from **Fernie or Cranbrook**, drive north on Hwy 93/95. Just south of Canal Flats, reach the Kootenay River bridge. From the middle of the bridge, continue north 100 meters (110 yards). Turn right onto Grainger Road, signed for Canal Flats Provincial Park. Pass the mill. In another 100 meters go right onto gravel before reaching the big yellow-orange scale. Reset your trip odometer to 0, then follow the directions (B) below.

Directions (A)

0 km (0 mi)
Starting northeast on Kootenay-Palliser FS road, from the junction of Kootenay-Palliser and Kootenay-Fenwick (from Canal Flats) FS roads.

4.2 km (2.6 mi)
Go left on Palliser-Albert FS road. Right on Joffre Creek FS road leads to the trailhead for Limestone Lakes.

5.5 km (3.4 mi)
Pass a small (two-vehicle) FS campground on the left. It's near the river, beside the bridge.

6.2 km (3.8 mi)
Bear left on the main road and cross another bridge.

8.7 km (5.4 mi)
Bear right.

12 km (7.4 mi)
Bear right, descend, and proceed along the river.

15 km (9.3 mi)
Cross a bridged creeklet.

16.2 km (10 mi)
Go left at the junction.

16.5 km (10.2 mi)
Pass a 52 KM sign.

16.9 km (10.5 mi)
The road has been closed here, near the cedar grove, due to landslides. So don't be surprised if you must park and walk about 45 minutes to the trailhead. And don't be discouraged. This road, through Albert River canyon, is more scenic than many hiking trails.

19 km (11.8 mi)
Unstable slopes here previously slumped onto the road.

21.3 km (13.2 mi)
Just before the KM 57 sign, cross a hefty bridge. Continue 150 m (165 yards) beyond the KM 57 sign, then turn right (southeast) on an overgrown road. Follow it 0.4 km (0.25 mi) to the signed trailhead parking area at 1326 m (4350 ft).

Directions (B)

0 km (0 mi)
Starting along the south end of the logging yard.

0.3 km (0.2 mi)
The road turns south toward the river. Go left, where right goes under the bridge. Ascend moderately on Kootenay River FS road, soon curving northeast.

2.4 km (1.5 mi)
Bear right. The broad, smooth road levels, then descends into the valley. A ranch is visible below.

9.1 km (5.6 mi)
Go left at the junction. Right is Kootenay-Bypass FS road. Stay on the main road.

31.7 km (19.7 mi)
Go right (west) at this Y-junction. The left fork, Settlers Road, leads to Hwy 93 and Kootenay National Park.

32.4 km (20.1 mi)
Cross a bridge over the Kootenay River.

Navigating cross-country to Queen Mary Lake

33.1 km (20.5 mi)
Before the KM 34 sign, go left (north) onto Palliser FS road. White River FS road is right.

38.7 km (24 mi)
Proceed straight (north), passing Kootenay-Fenwick FS road on the right.

48.3 km (29.9 mi)
Cross a small bridge over Fenwick Creek. In 100 meters (110 yards) pass a small FS campground on the right. It has two sites on the creek.

48.7 km (30.2 mi)
Fork left (north).

56.5 km (35 mi)
Go right at the Y-junction onto Kootenay-Palliser FS road. Reset your trip odometer to 0 and follow the directions (A) above.

On Foot
From the signed trailhead parking area, follow the overgrown skid road through a cutblock. Soon, a steep, narrow, switchback-less trail ascends southeast through forest. Gain 365 m (1200 ft) in

just 1.3 km (0.8 mi). At 1 km (0.6 mi), 1665 m (5460 ft), the trail contours east. The grade relaxes. Watch for orange western wood lilies in a creek drainage.

Reach 1762 m (5780 ft) after hiking about 1½ hours. The trail then turns northeast, into a **narrower side valley**. The view from an avalanche slope includes a cascade on the right. Ralph Lake's outlet stream is visible up-valley.

At 1920 m (6300 ft) you can see a 122-m (400-ft) cascade. Then begin another severely steep stretch. At 4 km (2.5 mi), 2076 m (6810 ft) the trail traverses beneath a cliff band. Pass a small cave, then clamber over **rock steps** (about 5 vertical meters/yards) to attain the edge of Ralph Lake basin at 2125 m (6970 ft). Swift hikers can be here in 2½ hours.

Head northeast about 15 minutes—sloshing through boggy, heathery meadows, and rockhopping across the braided outlet stream—to reach **Ralph Lake** at 5 km (3 mi), 2160 m (7085 ft). Pass a crude cabin used by outfitters just above the southwest shore.

To probe the basin, follow the faint trail southeast along the lake's south side. Reach the braided inlet stream. Beside a small cascade, begin a gentle ascent through open forest. Head toward the upper basin's west side. Follow the stream up to a tussocky meadow at the base of a talus slope. Elevation: 2256 m (7400 ft).

From a tarn on the right, pick your way through a boulder field. Choose your own route up the talus slope to the 2421-m (7940-ft) **saddle** on the southwest shoulder of Mt. Queen Mary. Looking back, you can now see more of the basin from which you've just emerged. Northwest are two lakelets. Mt. Assiniboine is visible northeast, beyond the basin.

Southeast, on the far wall of the next basin, is the saddle you must cross to reach Queen Mary Lake. Plan your route from here. Generally, you want to angle beneath cliff bands, then **traverse southeast**. As much as possible, contour at about 2225 m (7300 ft) around the head of the basin beneath Mounts Queen Mary, Prince John and Prince Henry. Then ascend, cresting the **next saddle** at 2340 m (7675 ft). Proceed southwest, picking up a faint trail descending a gully. Reach the west end of **Queen Mary Lake** at 2100 m (6888 ft). There's an outfitter's cabin on the northwest shore. Bear right, rounding the lake's west end, to reach the BC Parks cabin above the southwest shore.

Trip 35
Aurora Creek / Marvel Pass

Location	Rocky Mountains
Round trip	15 km (9.3 mi)
Elevation gain	760 m (2493 ft)
Time required	8 hours
Difficulty	Moderate
Map	Mt. Assiniboine 82 J/13

OPINION

Trekkers depart Mt. Assiniboine Provincial Park with lighter packs but fuller craniums. Hundreds of images of mountain grandeur forever flit through their minds. If they hiked over Wonder Pass, one of those images is of distant Marvel Pass. It looks fearsomely wild and beautiful. It's seldom visited only because it's way off the main trail. But scrutinizing a map reveals Marvel Pass can be a quick, easy daytrip from a remote western valley. And hiking to Marvel Pass reveals it is indeed fearsomely wild and beautiful.

Though it accesses national and provincial parkland, the trail is outside the parks. So maintenance is nil. The scarcity of boot traffic further contributes to the trail's rough, obscure character. You'll have to wade through some brush and do a little routefinding. But it's nothing that should deter a strong, intermediate hiker. Be glad the Forest Service intends to leave this a primitive route. It will heighten your sense of accomplishment, deepen your appreciation for wilderness, and deter crowds.

Within an hour of the trailhead, you'll see divinely sculpted peaks, including sharply-pointed Mt. Alcantara, spiky Eon Mtn, and sheer-walled Mt. Gloria. Start singing your alleluias. Within two-and-a-half hours, you'll be in heaven: surrounded by mountains, hiking cross-country through lightly forested subalpine meadows, to a lovely, larch-framed lake beneath Aurora Mtn. (See photo on page 172.) From the lake, continue the gentle ascent up a shoulder of Mt. Marvel. Soon, all will be revealed unto you: Marvel Creek canyon; the basin clutching Lake Gloria and Marvel Lake;

Aurora Creek and Mt. Eon

Wonder Pass; the east face of Mt. Gloria; and Mt. Assiniboine—
Matterhorn lookalike, Canadian Rockies icon, and sixth highest
peak in the range.

This ethereal setting pleads for more of your time. So consider
backpacking to Marvel Pass. Exploring both sides—the headwaters
of Aurora and Marvel creeks—could take most of a day. Venturing
north of the pass is also an option. A trail drops 340 m (1115 ft) to
Marvel Lake in Banff National Park, then climbs a heart-pounding
600 m (1968 ft) to Wonder Pass—gateway to Lake Magog in the core
of Mt. Assiniboine Provincial Park. There are no camping restrictions at Marvel Pass. Just follow *Leave No Trace* guidelines. The
parks, however, charge fees, require reservations, and constrain you
to designated campgrounds. See Trip 41 for details about Assiniboine. Call (403-762-1550) for details about Banff.

FACT

By Vehicle

From Kootenay National Park's south entrance at **Radium Hot
Springs**, drive Hwy 93 northeast 18.8 km (11.7 mi). After the highway descends, turn right (southeast) onto Settlers Road. Reset your
trip odometer to 0.

From **McLeod Meadows campground**, on Hwy 93, near the
south end of Kootenay National Park, drive south 8 km (5 mi).
Before the highway ascends, turn left (southeast) onto Settlers
Road. Reset your trip odometer to 0.

0 km (0 mi)
Starting southeast on Settlers Road, departing Hwy 93.

12.6 km (7.8 mi)
Reach a junction. Go left onto Kootenay-Palliser FS road and soon
cross the Kootenay River. Kootenay-Settlers FS road proceeds right
(south) to Canal Flats.

14.7 km (9.1 mi)
Go left (north) on Cross FS road, signed for Natural Bridge. Right
(southeast) on Palliser River FS road leads to trailheads for Ralph
Lake (Trip 34) and Limestone Lakes (Trip 33).

Mt. Assiniboine from just above Marvel Pass

17.1 km (10.6 mi)
Pass the parking area for the short trail to Natural Bridge, on the left. Proceed northeast.

21.4 km (13.3 mi)
Bear right on the main road, passing a left fork.

33 km (20.5 mi)
Bear left (north) onto Cross-Mitchell FS road.

38 km (23.6 mi)
Continue straight on the main road, ignoring the right fork. Spectacular peaks are now visible ahead.

38.5 km (23.9 mi)
Fork right (northeast) onto Aurora FS road, away from Baymag mine.

42.5 km (26.4 mi)
Cross Aurora Creek. The signed trailhead is just after the bridge, beside a cutblock on the right, at 1400 m (4592 ft). The road beyond is closed to the public.

On Foot
From the signed trailhead where the road crosses Aurora Creek, follow the trail upstream (northeast) on the creek's northwest side. The restored trail proceeds through a slash-laden cutblock. The trail should be better defined in about 0.5 km (0.3 mi) in the forest margin along the creek.

At 1.2 km (0.7 mi), 1494 m (4900 ft), cross **footbridges** to the creek's southeast bank. Soon cross a bridged tributary stream. Heading east now, angling away from Aurora Creek, the trail ascends moderately through ugly, open, lodgepole-pine forest on the valley's south side. Eon Mtn (left/north) and Mt. Alcantara (right/south) are partly visible.

About 1 hour from the trailhead, reach a **fork** at 3 km (1.9 mi), 1650 m (5412 ft). Bear right, following orange flagging. Continue ascending. The trail is sporadically indistinct. Inspiring scenery begins unfolding where the trail traverses larch-graced rocky slopes.

After hiking about 1½ hours, attain a **knoll** at 5 km (3 mi), 1940 m (6363 ft). The view includes Mt. Alcantara (southwest), Eon Mtn (northwest), and a cascade flowing from Marvel Pass (northeast).

Curve around the knoll's east edge. Follow the scant trail down to the right, through krummholz and brush. It's now just a **boot-beaten route**: overgrown, easy to lose. Keep trying to regain it. Ascend right. Look for sections of path at the base of a small, rounded ridge to the right. Watch for orange flagging and the odd cairn. Hike up-slope, onto a bench. Curve north through boulders. Upon reaching grassier slopes, the going is easy again.

At 2006 m (6580 ft), rock slabs beside upper **Aurora Creek** are a good place to rest and appreciate the panorama. You've now hiked about 2½ hours from the trailhead. Resuming generally north, the meandering trail fades in level meadow. Stay right (east) of the creek. Look for flagging ahead on a short tree, before a larch and a single silver trunk.

Favouring the right (east) side of the upper valley, ascend north, cross country. Reach Cabin Lake in **Marvel Pass** at 7.5 km (4.7 mi), 2170 m (7118 ft). Aurora Mtn rises behind the lake's southeast shore. A path rounds the northwest shore, darts uphill, then plunges into the next valley. It descends northeast, passes Owl Lake, then intersects the Bryant Creek trail in about 9 km (5.6 mi).

From the lake's west end, continue the cross-country ascent left (northwest) to a thinly forested saddle on a shoulder of Marvel Peak. Part of Mt. Assiniboine is visible northwest, behind Mt. Gloria. Keep rounding the grassy, subalpine slope. Angle upward to 2260 m (7413 ft). The view of Assiniboine quickly improves. Wonder Pass is north. Below it, you can glimpse Lake Terrapin.

If you intend to continue north, to Lake Gloria and Marvel Lake in Banff National Park, and perhaps on through Wonder Pass to Mt. Assiniboine Provincial Park, survey your route from this perch on the shoulder of Marvel Peak, high above Cabin Lake. Most of the way is visible. You can see the trail passing slim lakes in the grassy basin beneath Mt. Gloria. It descends Marvel Creek canyon, skirts the southwest end of Marvel Lake, then climbs to intersect the Wonder Pass trail.

Trip 36

Elk Lakes / Petain Basin

Location	Rocky Mountains, southeast B.C.
Round trip	22 km (13.6 mi)
Elevation gain	619 m (2030 ft)
Time required	5 to 10 hours
Difficulty	Easy to Challenging
Maps	Kananaskis Lakes 82 J/11;
	BC Parks brochure

OPINION

British Columbia's provincial parks are a national treasure. The province deserves accolades for having the will and foresight to preserve so many large tracts of wild land. The question is, do you have the will and foresight to go appreciate these precious, but often remote, provincial gifts? Begin with Elk Lakes. It's not too isolated. And the scenery is majestic.

It's worth enduring the park's long, dirt access road, even if all you do is spend an afternoon sauntering to the lakes and admiring the pyramidal limestone peaks that rise abruptly from their shores. This initial stretch of trail is as level and manicured as a city-park path—ideal for sneaker-shod children. Hike a little farther to cross impetuous Petain Creek, ascend to a flowery meadow, and behold spewing Petain Falls. (See photo on page 173.) Less-ambitious hikers turn around here. Sure-footed athletes assault the 410-m (1345-ft) headwall. Each step is a gravity-defying struggle. In places, it's a grab-the-next-root-and-haul-yourself-up scramble. Surmount it and you'll enter Petain Basin, an alpine Eden. Once again, you're striding freely—over rock slabs, across meadows—but only if you aren't knocked off your feet by the beauty of it all. Petain Glacier is just one of the enthralling sights. The temptation to lounge is the only obstacle between you and the basin's upper reaches, at 2440 m (8000 ft).

The park access road is sprinkled with Forest Service campgrounds. Take advantage of them. Come in the evening, then hit the trail early the next morning. Given a clear day, definitely start hiking

Ascending the headwall to Petain Basin, with Mt. McCuaig behind.

by 8 a.m. to see Mt. Aosta perfectly reflected in the glassy surface of Lower Elk Lake, and Mt. Fox mirrored in Upper Elk Lake. (See photo on page 173.)

Starting early also ensures you'll have time to explore Petain Basin on a dayhike. Going nonstop, strong hikers take three hours to attain the basin lip. Want more time up top? Consider backpacking part way. Enjoy a leisurely, midday start, pitch your tent at Upper Elk Lake campground, then, next morning, launch yourself over the headwall. That way you can roam the basin all day, carrying only a light daypack.

It's possible to hike to the lakes and Petain Falls from early July through October. Plan to explore Petain Basin from late July through early October.

FACT

By Vehicle

From Hwy 3, drive north on Hwy 43—signed for Elk Lakes Provincial Park. The junction is 0.4 km (0.25 mi) east of **Sparwood** and the lime-coloured World's Biggest Truck. Or it's 22.3 km (13.8 mi) west of the B.C./Alberta border. It's a 1¾-hour drive to the trailhead. You'll pass several FS campgrounds en route. For details, read *Camp Free in B.C. Volume One*, described in the back of this book.

First drive Hwy 43 north 33.5 km (20.1 mi) to Elkford. Continue 1 km (0.6 mi) north of the creek crossing and set your trip odometer to 0 where pavement ends.

0 km (0 mi)
Proceeding north on Elk River FS road, on the west side of the Elk River.

9.2 km (5.7 mi)
Krivensky Farm FS campground is on right in a meadow.

19.4 km (12 mi)
A spur road goes left 250 meters to tiny Blue Lake FS campground.

44.4 km (27.5 mi)
Cross a bridge to the river's east side. Proceed north on Kananaskis Power Line Road. There's a small, lone FS campsite here at Weary Creek.

Upper Petain Basin

45.3 km (28.1 mi)
Bear left. The road is rougher now, with a stonier surface and lots of potholes.

51 km (31.6 mi)
Bear right. Bighorn Outfitters is left.

55.5 km (34.4 mi)
Riverside FS campground is on the left. Sharp peaks are visible.

61.8 km (38.3 mi)
Tobermory Cabin is open to the public—first come, first served.

62.2 km (38.6 mi)
Go right for Elk Lakes trailhead parking. Left reaches Upper Elk River FS campground in 150 meters. Separate, treed campsites are near a broad meadow beneath peaks.

67 km (41.5 mi)
Enter Elk Lakes Provincial Park. Gated Elk Pass road is right.

67.3 km (41.7 mi)
Reach the road's end trailhead at 1729 m (5670 ft).

On Foot

The comfortable, well-maintained trail leads west from the kiosk. Pass the ranger cabin. After crossing a bridged brook, go left at the junction, into a forest of alpine fir and Englemann spruce. Reach **Lower Elk Lake** at 1 km (0.6 mi), 1740 m (5707 ft). Round the northeast shore. About 20 minutes from the trailhead, cross two sturdy bridges over the inlet stream. The trail forks just beyond. Left goes to a viewpoint. Bear right and ascend a bit.

Within 40 minutes, reach a junction at 2.6 km (1.6 mi), 1750 m (5740 ft). Stay left and you're at the northeast end of 2-km (1.2-mi) long **Upper Elk Lake**. Right crosses a bridge and goes northeast 3 km (1.9 mi) to Fox Lake and West Elk Pass, where it enters Alberta and continues into Peter Lougheed Provincial Park.

Proceed southwest along the upper lake's southeast edge. When the water is high, you'll be stepping across flooded sections of trail. Mt. Fox rises from the opposite shore. Scan the mountain's folded limestone face for spouting cascades. Reach the southeast end of the upper lake at 5 km (3.1 mi).

Walk gravel beds for the next 0.6 km (0.4 mi) to reach **Upper Elk Lake campground**. It has tent pads, a pit toilet, fire pit, and a food cache, but few if any campsites are dry when the braided Petain Creek swells with snowmelt. Remember: snow melts faster as the day warms, so the creek might keep rising into the evening.

Just past the campground, cross footlogs (or rockhop, if they're submerged) to the creek's west bank. The trail resumes southwest. Don't follow the rough route leading south from the campground. It generally follows Nivelle Creek upstream, reaching Coral Pass in 6 km (3.7 mi).

At 9 km (5.6 mi), 1835 m (6020 ft), about two hours from the trailhead, **Petain Falls** is visible. A spur trail forks left (northwest) to the base of the falls. Even if you don't want to approach the falls, briefly follow the spur into the meadow. Mid-July through early August, it explodes with wildflowers: tall, light-blue alpine forget-me-nots, yellow columbine, graceful lavender clematis on long stalks, and white spirea.

Heading to Petain Basin? Look for a **signed junction** where the waterfall was first visible. Go right (northeast) and ascend. Soon cross a rocky gorge and continue up its left (west) side. The trail rapidly deteriorates to a route and dramatically steepens. Traction is dicey even when the route is dry. If it's wet, consider aborting the attempt.

Tunnel through krummholz (stunted trees) for about 15 minutes. Negotiate a short, awkward stretch. Enjoy a brief reprieve where the ascent eases among bigger trees. Grapple with a precarious 3-meter vertical pitch, or skirt it on the right where you can hang on to krummholz. The route soon exits the trees and enters a rocky chute—the upper reaches of the gorge you crossed below. Keep powering upward, over the loose boulders.

Near 2200 m (7216 ft) a cairn indicates where to turn left, out of the chute, onto a path traversing a steep, grassy slope. Wffew. The hard part's behind you. Wildflowers are again profuse: deep purple larkspur, lavender sky pilot, purple penstemon, pink paintbrush. The hanging Castelneau Glacier is visible south. Mt. McCuaig is on the glacier's southeast edge. Keep following the narrow but well-defined path. Crest the **lip of Petain Basin** at 11 km (6.8 mi), 2287 m (7500 ft). Strong hikers can be here in 3 hours if they don't stop.

Ascend another 61 m (200 ft) over rock slabs and grass for improved glacier-views. Mt. Nivelle is visible southwest of Castelneau Glacier. Pointy Mt. Castelneau is northeast of it. A bit of Petain Glacier is visible west. Ignore the cairned route descending left (southwest) to upper Petain Creek and a treed campsite on the far bank—unless you're camping (fires prohibited). Instead, go north, cross country, up gentle, green, slabby ridges, toward the right (east) side of the basin.

The deeper you probe the basin, the more you'll see of broad Petain Glacier. Even 15 minutes makes a big difference. Mt. Petain is west. Keep ascending to see Mount Joffre southwest, rising at the upper edge of the ice.

Trip 37

Lake O'Hara Alpine Circuit

Location	Yoho National Park
Loop	9.8 to 12.4 km (6 to 7.7 mi)
Elevation gain	495 m (1625 ft)
Time required	6 to 7 hours
Difficulty	Moderate
Maps	Gem Trek Lake Louise & Yoho (1:25 000 for O'Hara region); Friends of Yoho - Yoho National Park

OPINION

Magic mushrooms. Cannabis. Tequila. Lake O'Hara. All will get you high. All are controlled substances. The difference: limitations on Lake O'Hara protect *it*, not you. Hikers experienced ineffable joy here, raved to their friends, and the onslaught began. The region's popularity was destroying it. Now there's a locked gate on the access road, a shuttle bus, and a restriction on the number of visitors. So getting here's a hassle. But it shouldn't put you off, if you're a mountain junkie. And when you arrive, it should be with an addict's obsession to complete the Alpine Circuit. A trip to O'Hara without hiking the circuit is like taking a hit but not inhaling.

Don't expect solitude, despite the Park's limitations. The buses are usually full. Which means the campground, the hut and the lodge are too. But the region's splendor transcends the crowd. Everyone is blissful, engrossed in their own communion with this bold manifestation of nature, individually touched by the captivating beauty. And of all the O'Hara trails, the Alpine Circuit is one of the least busy, because it's one of the most challenging.

Actually it's not a trail. It's a route. An acrophobe's nightmare. Catwalks, ledges and paths linked to create a loop. Mostly above treeline. Often clinging to the walls of skyscraping mountains. After a taxing grunt up to Wiwaxy Gap, the minimal but adequate route makes no serious demands. Ups and downs are few, so you can devote your energy to raving about the beauty you behold: cascades, pocket meadows, turquoise lakes, and pointy, pyramidal peaks with swooping thousand-meter cliffs and snow-filled fissures.

Yukness Ledge. Note the hiker, far right, two-thirds of the way up foreground cliff.

The Alpine Circuit should heighten your appreciation for the art of trail building. The cliffside paths were lovingly crafted by the Italian stonemason and zealous alpinist Lawrence Grassi. He was the Park warden at O'Hara for many years. His Old World heritage and his passion for these New World mountains moved him to create a remarkable walkway for all who love wilderness. An American botanist, Dr. George Link, also deserves to be remembered for his extensive mapping and trail building in the O'Hara region. He spent most of his summers here—exploring, absorbing, and making it easier for the rest of us to do the same.

To shorten the Alpine Circuit, you can eliminate the stiff ascent to Wiwaxy Gap and the Huber Ledges section to Lake Oesa, but you'd miss a lot of glory. If you're capable, ascend to Wiwaxy, descend to Oesa, then follow the Yukness Ledge route to Opabin Plateau. At the plateau, you have another opportunity to shorten the trip, this time by descending northwest back to Lake O'Hara, thus eliminating the All Souls' alpine route on Mt. Schaffer. If you only have time or stamina for one, skip the more arduous All Souls'; hike the more varied, intriguing Huber Ledges.

Cairns and paint-splotched rocks mark the Alpine Circuit. Still, bring a good map to keep yourself oriented. The trip is not inherently dangerous except in stormy weather or when lingering snow obscures the route. Because it's exposed, pack for all possibilities, from hot sun to freezing rain. Sturdy boots are a must. No scrambling is required, but you'll often be a step away from vertiginous dropoffs.

If the Alpine Circuit sounds too demanding for you, read about other Lake O'Hara region trails (Trip 38). You'll want to hike some of them anyway, if you're here a few days. For a shorter, easier introduction to the region, hike from Lake O'Hara directly to Opabin Plateau or Lake Oesa. These are less spectacular, more crowded trips, but the destinations are both on the Alpine Circuit.

Fit, experienced hikers should be able to complete the Alpine Circuit on a daytrip into O'Hara. The trick is to catch the first bus in and the last bus out: 8:30 A.M. and 6:30 P.M. A better plan is to stay overnight. With two days here, definitely devote one to the Alpine Circuit. It provides the best overview and is the most thrilling hike. Our second choice would be Lake McArthur. But you'll forego other Premier trails if you leave after two days. Stay several days if possible.

Instead of riding the shuttle bus, you could hike the Cataract Valley trail to Lake O'Hara. Don't. It's a stupid waste of time. A few up-periscope views and a couple open avalanche slopes are the paltry pleasures on this dismal, 12.8-km (8-mi) slog through forest. Pay for the bus. It buys you more hiking time in a region of surpassing scenery. You don't have a reservation and the buses are full? That's different. Then it can be worth hiking into O'Hara. Fleet-footed backpackers can scorch the trail in three hours. But you'll still need a camping permit, or a reservation at the lodge or hut.

FACT

Before your trip

Yoho Park was forced to protect the Lake O'Hara region by excluding private vehicles and limiting the number of people who enter. Hence the locked gate on the access road, and the advent of the shuttle bus. It runs mid-June through September. See the schedule below. Through the Yoho Park Visitor Centre you can reserve seats on the bus up to a month in advance of your trip. The contact numbers are listed under *Information Sources* in the back of this book. You can also just show up and hope the bus has room for you—unlikely, but possible.

If you want to stay at Lake O'Hara Lodge, check current prices and make reservations by phoning (250) 343-6418, or (403) 678-4110 in winter. The mailing address is P.O. Box 55, Lake Louise, AB T0L 1E0.

If you want to stay in Elizabeth Parker Hut, check the current price and make reservations with the Alpine Club of Canada. See *Information Sources.*

If you want to camp, check the current price and make reservations with the Yoho Park Visitor Centre. Camping permits cost $6 per person per night in 2001. The campground is open mid-June through September. Tranquil nights here are not guaranteed, for several reasons. This is a big campground. It's usually full. Everyone arrives by bus, without schlepping their gear. And most of the trails are very scenic yet not too taxing. That means lots of happy, energetic campers. It's no excuse for violating others' right to quiet, but that's the reality you should expect. So bring earplugs. And keep your own volume low. Shut up after 10 P.M. Prevent the atmosphere from degenerating to that of Harry's RV Kamp.

Maps

Buy a detailed map of the Alpine Circuit. They're available at the Yoho Park Visitor Centre in Field, and at Le Relais Day Use Shelter across from the warden cabin, near the northwest end of Lake O'Hara.

By Vehicle

From the Trans-Canada Highway, between Field and Lake Louise village, turn south onto Highway 1-A. If you're driving northeast, the turnoff is 1.6 km (1 mi) east of the lodge at Wapta Lake. If you're driving southwest, the turnoff is 3 km (2 mi) west of the signed continental divide.

From either approach, cross the railroad tracks then turn right (west). Proceed 0.8 km (0.5 mi) to the parking area. The 11-km (6.8 mi) dirt road to Lake O'Hara leads south from here; access is restricted by a locked gate. This is where you catch the shuttle bus. The Cataract Valley hiking trail to Lake O'Hara starts here too, beside the pit toilet. Mountain bikes are prohibited on the road and the trail.

By Bus

Inbound buses depart the parking lot at 8:30 A.M., 10:30 A.M., 4:30 P.M. and 7:30 P.M. Outbound buses depart Lake O'Hara Lodge at 7:30 A.M., 9:30 A.M., 3:30 P.M. and 6:30 P.M. That's Mountain Daylight Savings Time. Daytrippers should catch a morning bus, preferably the first one. Sorry, bowzer is not allowed on the bus. Dogs are just bear bait anyway. Check with the Yoho Park Visitor Centre to confirm the current bus schedule. The round-trip fare for adults is $12 (2001).

Arriving

See Lake O'Hara Region (Trip 38)

On Foot

Start where the outlet stream departs the northwest corner of Lake O'Hara, at 2035 m (6675 ft). Here's how to get there. From the lodge, hike the lakeshore trail north. From the campground, cross to the east side of the road and follow the trail heading southeast, along the right (west) side of the outlet stream, 0.5 km (0.3 mi) toward the lake. From the hut, head east to the road and continue past the warden cabin.

Cross the bridged outlet stream. Head generally east. In 300 meters (328 yards) fork left (northeast) toward Wiwaxy Gap. For the next 1.5 km (0.9 mi) climb steeply on a narrow path to emerge above treeline. Reach **Wiwaxy Gap** at 2 km (1.2 mi), 2530 m (8300 ft). It hunkers between the Wiwaxy Peaks (west) and 3368-m (11,047-ft) Mt. Huber (east). From this aerie, you can survey most of the Lake O'Hara region. North of the gap, you can see Cataract Brook valley and peaks above Kicking Horse valley.

From the gap, the route drops gradually southeast, along the cliff ledges of Mt. Huber, 1.7 km (1.1 mi) to Lake Oesa. You'll see the lake as you descend. At 3.7 km (2.3 mi) reach a rocky knoll overlooking **Lake Oesa**. The shore is 200 meters (220 yards) farther east, at 2275 m (7462 ft). The Alpine Circuit crosses the Lake Oesa trail (Trip 38) at this knoll.

North is Mt. Huber. Behind it is 3464-m (11,362-ft) Mt. Victoria, her spine arching southeast to join 3423-m (11,227-ft) Mt. Lefroy. Just over the ridge (out of sight) Victoria Glacier rumbles down toward Lake Louise. Due east is 3283-m (10,768-ft) Glacier Peak. Yukness Mtn. forms the cliffs on the south side of Lake Oesa.

Leaving Oesa, the Alpine Circuit drops to cross the outlet stream, then ascends right (west). It curves around Mt. Yukness and heads south. Contour the rock slabs and catwalks of the **Yukness Ledge route**, then descend to meadowy Opabin Plateau. Reach the east side of Hungabee Lake at 6.4 km (4 mi). Proceed southeast to reach **Opabin Lake** at 6.8 km (4.2 mi), 2285 m (7495 ft). (See photo on page 245.)

Yukness Mtn. is north, Ringrose Peak east, Hungabee Mtn. southeast, Opabin Glacier south, and Schaffer Ridge southwest. From Opabin Lake, follow the trail right (southwest), curving northwest and gently descending. Bear left (northwest) at the fork as you pass Hungabee Lake again, this time on its west side.

Reach a junction at 7.7 km (4.8 mi). Straight (north) descends 1.4 km (0.9 mi) directly back to Lake O'Hara. Left on the lakeshore trail leads to Lake O'Hara Lodge, for a total loop distance of 9.8 km (6.1 mi).

Want to continue the Alpine Circuit to additional lofty viewpoints? Go left at the 7.7-km (4.8-mi) junction. Cross a creek and immediately turn right (north) on a spur trail. Reach **Opabin Prospect** at 8.4 km (5.2 mi). It overlooks Mary Lake and Lake O'Hara. The Wiwaxy Peaks are north. Mt. Huber is northeast.

From Opabin Prospect, curve south to a junction at 8.8 km (5.5 mi). Right descends steeply north on the West Opabin trail. In 1 km (0.6 mi) it reaches another junction just north of Mary Lake. Right leads to Lake O'Hara in a few minutes. Left on the lakeshore trail leads northwest to Lake O'Hara Lodge, for a total loop distance of 10.2 km (6.3 mi).

Want to continue the Alpine Circuit to additional lofty viewpoints? Proceed straight (southwest) at the 8.8-km (5.5-mi) junction, onto the **All Souls' alpine route**. It curves northwest, traversing the nose of Mt. Schaffer. It's a rugged, rocky route providing yet another perspective of the Lake O'Hara region. Ascend 275 m (900 ft) in 1 km (0.6 mi) to All Souls' Prospect, at 2475 m (8118 ft). The route then descends steeply to reach Schaffer Lake at 10.9 km (6.8 mi), 2215 m (7265 ft).

Still have energy to pursue views? Just before **Schaffer Lake**, turn right (northeast) on the rocky Big Larches trail. In 1.1 km (0.7 mi), turn left. Soon after, go right to reach Le Relais Day Use Shelter, across from the warden cabin, near the northwest end of Lake O'Hara. Total loop distance: 12.4 km (7.7 mi).

Had enough views? Here's a more pastoral return that's a few minutes shorter. Ignore the Big Larches trail and continue the final 100 meters (110 yards) to Schaffer Lake. Turn right and follow the **Alpine Meadows trail** north. At Elizabeth Parker Hut, go right (east). Soon after, bear left to reach Le Relais Day Use Shelter, across from the warden cabin, near the northwest end of Lake O'Hara.

Trip 38

Lake O'Hara Region

Location	Yoho National Park
Round trips	5.8 km (3.6 mi) to 14.2 km (8.8 mi)
Elevation gain	240 m (787 ft) to 495 m (1625 ft)
Time required	3 to 7 hours
Difficulty	Moderate
Maps	Gem Trek Lake Louise & Yoho (1:25 000 for O'Hara region); Friends of Yoho - Yoho National Park

OPINION

The Lake O'Hara region bristles with as many options as a Swiss Army knife. A superior network of trails leads to a dozen alpine lakes from 15 minutes to 2 hours away. You can camp, bunk in an alpine hut, or splurge on feather-bed comfort at the lodge. And the peaks walling in this hikers' holy land are immensely beautiful. Base yourself here for several Premier daytrips.

The region has five hiking areas: (1) Lake Oesa cirque; (2) Opabin Plateau; (3) Lake McArthur cirque; (4) Odaray Grandview and Prospect, which might still be closed due to grizzly bear activity; and (5) Duchesnay Basin, containing Linda and Cathedral lakes.

You'll hit Lake Oesa and Opabin Plateau on the lofty, thrilling Alpine Circuit (Trip 37). Hiking it should be a priority for anyone fit, experienced, and up for a challenge. Make the other areas your secondary choices. You can visit Lake Oesa or Opabin Plateau separately, without linking them via the Alpine Circuit. If the Odaray Plateau and Prospect trails are open, plan three days at Lake O'Hara. If you hike slowly, or prefer to limit your hiking to five hours a day, allow four days to fully appreciate the region.

Lake Oesa is a turquoise gem set beneath the other side of the same stunning massif that makes Lake Louise so photogenic. The best view of Oesa is from above, on the Alpine Circuit, which also skirts its shore. But even by itself, Oesa is an essential excursion for any first-time O'Hara visitor.

Adorned with small meadows, stands of alpine larch, and picturesque tarns, Opabin Plateau is in a hanging valley beneath Yukness

Lake O'Hara Region

Mtn. and Schaffer Ridge. Ideally, you should drop to the plateau after a clockwise trip around the Alpine Circuit. For a more thorough, relaxed exploration, hike here directly. Opabin has an intimate, pastoral charm. It's lovely, but less spectacular than the rugged Lake Oesa cirque.

The half-day hike to Lake McArthur should be number two on your to-do list, after the Alpine Circuit. This 1.5-km (1-mi) long lake is an opulent blue jewel resting in the cleavage of awesome Mt. Biddle, Mt. Schaffer and Park Mtn. Their sheer cliffs rise more than 600 m (2000 ft) from the water. The lake's 85-m (280-ft) depth creates the intense blue colour. If the trails are open to Odaray Grandview or Prospect, include them in your trip to the lake. Forget this whole area, however, if you see a posted grizzly-bear warning. Even when there are no warnings, stay alert. You're in prime grizzly habitat here. Make noise. Hike in a group. The louder you are, and the bigger your group, the safer you'll be. Read the *Bears* section for further suggestions.

Odaray Grandview is the only trailside vantage where you can see Morning Glory Lakes, Linda Lake, Lake McArthur, Lake O'Hara and Lake Oesa, all at once. The view east, of the Great Divide peaks, is as magnificent as any mountain scene in the range. Though Odaray Prospect is near the impressive, sheer east wall of Odaray Mtn., the view northwest over Duchesnay Basin to Cathedral Mtn. is not unique for the Rockies. It's the Grandview panorama and Odaray Highline vistas that make this trip premier.

Duchesnay Basin is less compelling than other areas in the Lake O'Hara region, because it's lower—more forested, less alpine. Morning Glory and Cathedral Lakes are here. Probing the basin you'll get a wonderful view east over Linda Lake to Mt. Huber and Mt. Victoria. Above the basin, Cathedral Prospect grants a fine perspective southeast of the entire Lake O'Hara region, including the ledges of the Alpine Circuit. But Duchesnay Basin alone doesn't justify the time and expense of busing into O'Hara. Considered separately, the basin rates no higher than outstanding. So hike here only on a multi-day visit to O'Hara, when you can also enjoy the premier trails.

FACT

Before your trip

Make reservations at the lodge, hut or campground, as well as for the bus trip into the region. For details, see Lake O'Hara Alpine Circuit (Trip 37).

Keep in mind that grizzly bears frequent the Lake O'Hara region, particularly the southwest corner. Bear encounters have increased as the number of people visiting O'Hara has risen. Consequently the Odaray Prospect and Plateau trails, and the McArthur Creek trail to McArthur Pass were closed for years. Check the current status of these trails by phoning the Yoho Park Visitor Centre at (250) 343-6433. Ask about other possible closures. If caught hiking a closed trail, you could be fined up to $2000.

Maps

See Lake O'Hara Alpine Circuit (Trip 37).

By Vehicle

See Lake O'Hara Alpine Circuit (Trip 37).

By Bus

See Lake O'Hara Alpine Circuit (Trip 37).

Arriving

If you're staying at **Lake O'Hara Lodge**, it's at road's end. The bus will take you all the way there. If you're staying in **Elizabeth Parker Hut**, get off the bus at Le Relais Day Use Shelter, near the northwest end of Lake O'Hara, across the road from the warden cabin, a short way before the lodge. From the trail sign on the west side of the road, ascend gently southwest to a junction at 0.3 km (0.2 mi). Stay right and soon reach the hut at 0.5 km (0.3 mi). If you're **camping**, get off the bus at the campground. It's 0.8 km (0.5 mi) before Lake O'Hara.

Opabin Plateau

LAKE OESA

Round trip	5.8 km (3.6 mi)
Elevation gain	240 m (787 ft)
Time required	3 hours
Difficulty	Easy

Start where the outlet stream departs the northwest corner of Lake O'Hara, at 2035 m (6675 ft). Here's how to get there. From the lodge, head north on the lakeshore trail. From the campground, cross to the east side of the road, pick up the trail heading southeast, and follow it along the right (west) side of the outlet stream 0.5 km (0.3 mi) toward the lake. From the hut, head east to the road and continue past the warden cabin.

Cross the bridged outlet stream. Head generally east. In 300 meters (328 yards) the Wiwaxy Gap trail forks left (northeast). Continue straight, along the lakeshore. At 0.7 km (0.4 mi) turn left (north) onto the Lake Oesa trail. Ascend 65 m (215 ft) before the trail turns east again and the grade eases.

Pass small Lake Victoria and the shortcut to the Yukness Ledge route, both on your right, at about 2.4 km (1.5 mi). Proceed straight (southeast) deeper into the cirque. At 2.9 km (1.8 mi) reach a rocky knoll overlooking **Lake Oesa**. The shore is 200 meters (220 yards) farther east, at 2275 m (7462 ft). The Alpine Circuit route (Trip 37) crosses the Lake Oesa trail at the knoll.

North is 3368-m (11,047-ft) Mt. Huber. Behind it is 3464-m (11,362-ft) Mt. Victoria, her spine arching southeast to join 3423-m (11,227-ft) Mt. Lefroy. Just over the ridge (out of sight) Victoria Glacier rumbles down toward Lake Louise. Due east is 3283-m (10,768-ft) Glacier Peak. Yukness Mtn. forms the cliffs on the south side of Lake Oesa.

Instead of returning directly to Lake O'Hara, if you're up for a challenge and a few more hours of hiking, read the Alpine Circuit description then ascend the Yukness Ledge route.

OPABIN PLATEAU

Loop	7.2 km (4.5 mi)
Elevation gain	250 m (820 ft)
Time required	3 hours
Difficulty	Easy

Start in front of Lake O'Hara lodge, at 2035 m (6675 ft). Head southeast on the lakeshore trail. In 0.7 km (0.4 mi), a trail forks right (south). Proceed straight along the shore for the more moderate ascent to Opabin Plateau. At 1.1 km (0.7 mi) turn right (southeast) on the East Opabin trail and start climbing.

At 2.2 km (1.4 mi) the trail forks. Go left (southeast) and soon enter the east side of the plateau. Pass the first of the tiny **Moor Lakes**. At 3 km (1.9 mi), near the northeast end of Hungabee Lake, you might notice the Yukness Ledge route intersecting from the left. It's part of the Alpine Circuit (Trip 37). To sample it and attain broader views, turn left and ascend. After about 0.5 km (0.3 mi) the route contours on the ledge. Continue another 0.5 km (0.3 mi) if you're comfortable doing so.

Beyond where the route intersected your trail, proceed southeast. Reach **Opabin Lake** at 3.4 km (2.1 mi), 2285 m (7495 ft). Yukness Mtn. is north, Ringrose Peak east, Hungabee Mtn. southeast, Opabin Glacier south, and Schaffer Ridge southwest. From Opabin Lake, follow the trail right (southwest), curving northwest and gently descending. Bear left (northwest) at the fork as you pass Hungabee Lake again, this time on its west side.

Reach a junction at 4.3 km (2.7 mi). Straight (north) descends 1.4 km (0.9 mi) directly back to Lake O'Hara, rejoining the trail you originally ascended to Opabin Plateau. To vary your return and attain a viewpoint, go left at this junction, cross a creek, then immediately turn right (north) on a spur trail leading 0.6 km (0.4 mi) to **Opabin Prospect**. It overlooks Mary Lake and Lake O'Hara. The Wiwaxy Peaks are north. Mt. Huber is northeast.

From Opabin Prospect, curve south 0.4 km (0.25 mi) to a junction. Turn right and descend steeply north on the West Opabin trail. In 1 km (0.6 mi) you'll be just north of Mary Lake, at another junction. Turn right to reach Lake O'Hara in a few minutes. Then turn left, onto the lakeshore trail, and follow it northwest back to Lake O'Hara Lodge, where your total loop distance is 7.2 km (4.5 mi).

LAKE MCARTHUR

Round trip	7 km (4.3 mi)
Elevation change	315-m (1033-ft) gain; 100-m (330-ft) loss
Time required	3 hours
Difficulty	Easy

From the trail sign on the west side of the road, across from the warden cabin, near the northwest end of Lake O'Hara, ascend gently southwest to a junction at 0.3 km (0.2 mi). Stay right and soon enter alpine meadows. At the junction beside **Elizabeth Parker Hut**, turn left (south) and begin ascending through forest. At 1.6 km (1 mi) reach **Schaffer Lake** and many junctions.

Round the right (west) side of Schaffer Lake. At its south shore the trail forks. Right leads southwest to McArthur Pass in 0.4 km (0.25 mi). Go left (south) onto the high cutoff trail through larch forest toward Lake McArthur. The stone steps ascending the cliff bands on this trail were built by Lawrence Grassi, who created the Alpine Circuit.

At the next junction, right descends to **McArthur Pass**. Go left again, continuing the ascent around Mt. Schaffer's west shoulder. Reach the trail's 2350-m (7710-ft) highpoint at 3 km (1.9 mi). **Lake McArthur** is visible ahead. The trail drops to reach the north shore at 3.5 km (2.2 mi), 2250 m (7380 ft).

ODARAY GRANDVIEW AND PROSPECT

Loops	6.5 km (4 mi) or 9.5 km (6 mi)
Elevation gain	290 m (950 ft) to 655 m (2150 ft)
Time required	3 to 6 hours
Difficulty	Moderate

If these trails are still closed to due to grizzly bear activity, don't even think about hiking here. Before setting out, check the current status at the warden cabin.

From the trail sign on the west side of the road, across from the warden cabin, near the northwest end of Lake O'Hara, ascend gently southwest to a junction at 0.3 km (0.2 mi). Stay right and soon enter alpine meadows. At the junction beside **Elizabeth Parker Hut**, turn right and cross the stream. In a few minutes reach another junction, at 0.7 km (0.4 mi). Right (northwest) leads to Morning Glory and Linda lakes. Turn left and ascend generally west into forest on the Odaray Plateau trail.

At 1.4 km (0.9 mi) the trail forks. Go right and ascend northwest. At 2.2 km (1.4 mi), ascend left. Reach **Odaray Prospect** at 2.6 km (1.6 mi), 2285 m (7495 ft). Cathedral Mountain is north, across forested, lake-splashed Duchesnay Basin. The small, emerald Morning Glory Lakes are beneath the 1150-m (3772-ft) east face of Odaray Mtn. Proceed left (south), traversing the high, west side of Odaray Plateau.

Reach a four-way junction at 3.4 km (2.1 mi). Right is the rugged route northwest to **Odaray Grandview**. It ascends 205 m (672 ft) in 1.1 km (0.7 mi), topping out at 2530 m (8300 ft). It's a demanding scramble over talus, requiring stamina and off-trail experience.

Left (east) at the four-way junction soon leads to a fork. Go left over the Odaray Plateau to Elizabeth Parker Hut, or right to Schaffer Lake.

Proceed straight (south) at the four-way junction, onto Odaray Highline trail. At 4 km (2.5 mi) you can look southwest and see twin-peaked Mt. Goodsir, highest mountain in Yoho Park. Reach a junction in **McArthur Pass**, at 4.5 km (2.8 mi), 2220 m (7282 ft).

From the McArthur Pass junction, left (northeast) leads to Schaffer Lake. By rounding the west shore, then taking the middle trail north, you can pass Elizabeth Parker Hut and return to the warden cabin at Lake O'Hara, completing a 6.5-km (4-mi) loop.

To extend this hike to **Lake McArthur**—a gain of 60 m (197 ft) in 1.2 km (0.75 mi)—bear right at the 4.5-km (2.8-mi) McArthur Pass junction. A few minutes farther, turn right and descend through open forest to another junction. Right descends southwest into the Ottertail River valley. Go left on the Lower McArthur trail to reach the lake.

Leaving Lake McArthur, go left (northeast) via the high cutoff trail. It ascends, then traverses the west shoulder of Mt. Schaffer. Reach a fork 1.1 km (0.7 mi) from the lake. Go right and descend to Schaffer Lake. By rounding the west shore, then taking the middle trail north, you can pass Elizabeth Parker Hut and return to the warden cabin at Lake O'Hara, completing a 9.5-km (6-mi) loop.

DUCHESNAY BASIN

Round trip	13 km (8.1 mi) from O'Hara Campground
Elevation gain	300 m (984 ft)
Time required	5 to 6 hours
Difficulty	Easy to Cathedral Lakes, Challenging to Cathedral Prospect

You're entering the most remote area in the Lake O'Hara region. Make noise frequently to warn bears of your presence.

Starting at Elizabeth Parker Hut

At the junction beside the hut, turn right and cross the stream. In a few minutes reach another junction. Go right (northwest). After a gentle ascent to a highpoint, drop southwest to a junction at 2.5 km (1.6 mi), near **Morning Glory Lakes**. Left climbs to Odaray Prospect. Turn right (northwest). Quickly reach a fork and bear left.

Ascend to the south shore of **Linda Lake** and a 3-way junction at about 3.5 km (2.2 mi). Go left 0.4 km (0.25 mi) to a junction near the lake's southwest corner. Now follow the directions two paragraphs below, from the 3.9-km (2.4-mi) junction.

Starting at Lake O'Hara Campground

From the north end of the campground, follow the trail northwest 1.6 km (1 mi) through forest to a junction. Right (east) leads to the road. Turn left (west) and reach a 4-way junction at 2.4 km (1.5 mi). Left (south) leads to Morning Glory Lakes in 0.7 km (0.4 mi). Right is the Cataract Brook trail, leading 6.7 km (4.2 mi) north to the parking lot near the Trans-Canada Highway. Proceed straight (west) to reach a T-junction at 3.2 km (2 mi), near the east side of **Linda Lake**. Elevation: 2090 m (6855 ft). You can turn left or right to circle the lake. Go right, around the north shore, for a view south over the lake to 3159-m (10,362-ft) Odaray Mtn.

Curve around Linda Lake to a junction near its southwest corner at 3.9 km (2.4 mi). Turn right on the Duchesnay Basin trail, heading northwest through tree-lined subalpine meadows. Pass between the lower **Cathedral Lakes** at 5 km (3.1 mi).

At 5.7 km (3.5 mi) ignore the unmaintained Last Larch Prospect route forking left, marked by red dots on trees. For Cathedral Prospect, 165 m (540 ft) above, go right (northwest) on a cairned trail also marked by red and orange paint on trees. Ascend the southeast spine of Consummation Peak, then curve northeast. The trail deteriorates to a rough, rocky route, but offers broad views. Reach **Cathedral Prospect** at 6.5 km (4 mi), 2315 m (7593 ft).

Visible below are the lakes of Duchesnay Basin. Above and beyond them (south) is Odaray Mtn. Southeast, you can see most of the Lake O'Hara region, including the ledges of the Alpine Circuit. North, slightly below you, 0.4 km (0.25 mi) into Cathedral Basin cirque, is tiny Monica Lake. There you can ogle cliffs zooming up from meadows.

Retrace your steps back to Lake O'Hara Campground. It's a bit shorter and adds variety if you stay right at Linda Lake to curve around its south shore. Bear left at the next fork to reach the T-junction where you first saw Linda Lake. Turn right (east) and you're again on familiar ground.

Trip 39

Goodsir Pass

Location	Yoho National Park
Round trip	29 km (18 mi) by bike;
	plus 21.4 km (13.3 mi) on foot
Elevation gain	335 m (1100 ft) by bike;
	plus 775 m (2542 ft) on foot
Time required	9 to 10 hours
Difficulty	Moderate
Maps	Lake Louise 82 N/8, Mount Goodsir 82 N/1;
	Gem Trek Lake Louise & Yoho; Friends of
	Yoho - Yoho National Park

OPINION

Goodsir Pass is too far from any trailhead to be a reasonable day-hike destination. But if you're a serious outdoor athlete, you can get there in a single day with the help of your iron steed. You'll find the pass extraordinary, the accomplishment exhilarating.

The pass—among the most spectacular in the Canadian Rockies—is a vast, rock-strewn, flower-dappled, alpine meadow beneath soaring Sharp Mtn., Sentry Peak, and Mt. Goodsir. The twin-towered Goodsir is the highest mountain in Yoho Park. This is as close as you'll get to it on a trail. It rises an astonishing 1950 m (6400 ft) from the creekbed below its northeast face. (See photo on page 174.)

If Goodsir Pass were easier to reach, it would be too popular for its own good. For visual impact it rivals the Ramparts in Jasper National Park, or a chunk of the Ten Peaks rising above Moraine Lake in Banff Park. But access is sufficiently inconvenient to discourage the multitudes. So it's possible you'll be here alone, which will greatly enhance the experience.

The first 14.5 km (9 mi) are on a fire road. It makes for lousy hiking but fun biking. The grade is gentle, gaining only 360 m (1180 ft), and views are frequent. Then the trail and the hard work begin. You'll hike 10.7 km (6.6 mi) and gain 770 m (2525 ft), almost entirely in forest, before entering Goodsir Pass. Allow yourself a couple hours at the pass, so you can wander farther into it and appreciate the magnificent scenery. With even more time and energy, you could roam the open slopes north of the pass.

Easy cycling on a fire road gets you to the trail.

Ascending the fire road, you'll see the peaks of the Ottertail Range, across the Ottertail River valley. Visible are 3319-m (10,886-ft) Mt. Vaux, 3133-m (10,276-ft) Mt. Ennis, and 2911-m (9810-ft) Allan Peak. Get a good look on the way up, because on the way down gravity will pull you into a screaming descent.

FACT
Read *Backcountry Permits* (page 6) for details about camping fees and reservations.

By Vehicle
Drive the Trans-Canada Highway through Yoho Park 8.4 km (5.2 mi) southwest of Field to the Ottertail fire road parking area on the left (south) side of the highway, at 1195 m (3920 ft). This is 150 meters (165 yards) northeast of the Ottertail River bridge.

By Bike
Follow the fire road gently ascending the Ottertail River valley. Your general direction of travel will be southeast all the way to McArthur Creek. There's little elevation gain the first 3.2 km (2 mi). The road then climbs moderately to about the 5-km (3-mi) point. After that, you can coast downhill for 1 km (0.6 mi). Cross **Float Creek bridge** at 6.2 km (3.8 mi). A short, switchbacking ascent is followed by a level stretch. Near 10 km (6 mi), the road ascends, pulling farther away from the river.

Goodsir Pass

At 14.5 km (9 mi), 1480 m (4855 ft), reach a junction beyond which bicycles are prohibited. Left (north) ascends to McArthur Pass. Park your bike in the trees and proceed for Goodsir Pass.

On Foot

Bear right (southeast) at the junction and immediately cross McArthur Creek bridge. Pass a campground at 14.8 km (9.2 mi) and, a few minutes farther, McArthur Creek warden cabin. At 15.5 km (9.6 mi) cross the **Ottertail River bridge**. Just beyond is a junction. Straight leads directly to the pass. Left is a 2-km (1.2-mi) detour to Ottertail Falls. After the falls viewpoint, the spur trail rejoins the main trail to the pass. If you're on a daytrip, it makes sense to leave the falls until you return from the pass. See if you have time and energy for it then.

Ignoring the falls for now and continuing directly to the pass, you'll reach the southern spur trail to the falls in about 10 minutes. Proceed straight, ascending steeply. The trail drops then regains the lost elevation to enter the pass.

Just before the pass, attain a view across the valley to the 3562-m (11,683-ft) South Tower and 3525-m (11,562-ft) North Tower of Mt. Goodsir. On their southeast side, Sentry Peak continues the rugged chain.

Reach the northwest end of 2210-m (7250-ft) **Goodsir Pass** at 25.2 km (15.6 mi). Sharp Mtn. rises south of the pass.

Trip 40
Iceline / Whaleback

Location	Yoho National Park
Round trip or Loops	12.8 km (8 mi) to 27 km (16.7 mi)
Elevation gain	690 m (2265 ft)
	+ 305 m (1000 ft) for Whaleback
Time required	5 to 10 hours, or overnight
Difficulty	Moderate
Maps	Gem Trek Lake Louise & Yoho;
	Friends of Yoho - Yoho National Park

OPINION

"One day's exposure to mountains is better than a cartload of books." John Muir said it. Yoho proves it. The park is smaller than others in the Canadian Rockies yet has the heaviest concentration of high-impact scenery. You'll survey a big chunk of it from the Iceline.

After a stiff climb past treeline, the trail undulates over rugged glacial moraine. Daly Glacier and 380-m (1246-ft) Takakkaw Falls are visible across the valley. *Takakkaw*, by the way, is a Stoney Indian word meaning *magnificent*. Emerald Glacier and the 800-m (2625-ft) west face of The Vice President are beside you. Fred Flintstone chaise lounges—rock slabs—invite you to sprawl and stare.

The Iceline's quick access to postcard scenery is no secret, so you won't be alone here. And, like most trails aiming for the alpine zone, this one's steep, but you might not notice. Bombardment by dazzling sights is a natural pain reliever.

Many people hike the Iceline out and back, as far as the highpoint. It's a 12.8 km (7.9 mi) round trip. Others about-face earlier, satisfied with the vantage beneath Emerald Glacier. You can also choose one of two loops. Neither includes any additional "must see" sights, but both reveal more of the area:

(1) Drop past Lake Celeste on the old Highline trail, then descend to Yoho Valley for the return. You'll quickly exit the realm of rock and ice, pass through meadows, and enter forest. This loop is 4.5 km (2.8 mi) longer than a round trip to the highpoint.

(2) Continue northwest on the Iceline into Little Yoho Valley, then descend to Yoho Valley for the return. You'll see another tarn, the

Striding the Iceline. Daly Glacier in the distance.

pyramids of The Vice President and President from their north sides, and the pretty subalpine meadows of Little Yoho. This loop is 8.5 km (5.3 mi) longer than a round trip to the highpoint, yet adds only 30 m (100 ft) of elevation gain.

A further extension—detouring from Little Yoho up to Kiwetinok Pass—is also possible for swift dayhikers, but few include that unless backpacking. The trail ascends the magnificently garbled slopes of Mt. Kerr. It feels like a *Journey to the Center of the Earth*. Only a few cairns indicate the way near the top.

It's more impressive, however, to attain the stupendous 2210-m (7250-ft) Whaleback vantage than to see Little Yoho or Kiwetinok. From there you can survey the stupendous topography walling in Yoho Valley. The highlights are Yoho Glacier, Glacier des Poilus, and Waputik Icefield. If you're a strong hiker, consider a one-day, 27-km (16.7-mi) loop gaining 995 m (3265 ft) that includes the Iceline, a short up-and-back detour to the Iceline highpoint, the descent past Lake Celeste, the Whaleback traverse, crossing the top of 80-m (262-ft) Twin Falls, and a gently-graded return via Yoho Valley.

If you're backpacking, the logical first-night refuge is Little Yoho Valley, at the campground or Alpine Club hut (reservations: 403-678-3200). That's only 10.4 km (6.4 mi) via the Iceline, so after arriving you should have time to bounce up to Kiwetinok Pass. Next day, complete the trip by traversing the Whaleback, descending to the base of Twin Falls, then hiking out Yoho Valley for a total of 19.1 km (11.8 mi).

FACT

Before your trip

Read *Backcountry Permits* (page 6) for details about camping fees and reservations. If you want to stay in the Stanley Mitchell Hut, make reservations with the Alpine Club of Canada. If you want to stay in the Whiskey Jack Youth Hostel (at the trailhead), make reservations with Lake Louise International Hostel. The contact numbers for both are listed under *Information Sources* in the back of this book. If you want to stay in the Twin Falls Chalet, make reservations by calling (403) 228-7079.

By Vehicle

From the Yoho Park Visitor Centre, in Field, B.C., drive the Trans-Canada Highway northeast 3.7 km (2.3 mi). Or, from the Alberta-B.C. boundary on the Great Divide, drive the Trans-Canada southwest 12.5 km (7.8 mi). From either approach, turn north on Yoho Valley Road. Follow it 12.5 km (7.8 mi) to the Whiskey Jack Youth Hostel parking lot, on the left. Elevation: 1520 m (4985 ft).

Meet the Vice President, on the Iceline

Northwest over the Whaleback, toward Waterfall Valley

On Foot

Ascend the Yoho Pass trail through forest. Keep right at the 1-km (0.6-mi) and 1.2-km (0.7-mi) forks. At 2.5 km (1.6 mi) turn right again, onto the Iceline trail. Left leads south to Yoho lake and pass.

The Iceline ascends northwest, soon emerging from trees. Traverse rocky slopes with **Emerald Glacier** left (west) above you. Hop across a couple streams. The trail undulates over moraine, ascending steadily to a junction at 5.7 km (3.5 mi). Left continues northwest over the Iceline highpoint, then into Little Yoho Valley. Right (north) descends past Lake Celeste.

ICELINE HIGHPOINT: 12.8-KM (8-MI) ROUND TRIP

From the 5.7-km (3.5-mi) junction, stay left and proceed northwest to the 2210-m (7250-ft) highpoint on a moraine at 6.4 km (4 mi). Having climbed 690 m (2265 ft) from the trailhead, you're now in a rocky amphitheatre beneath Emerald Glacier. The 3066-m (10,059-ft) Vice President is visible southwest. Northwest, across the Little Yoho Valley, are Whaleback Mtn (right) and Isolated Peak (left). Return the way you came.

ICELINE / LITTLE YOHO VALLEY / YOHO VALLEY: 21.3-KM (13.2-MI) LOOP

From the 6.4-km (4-mi) highpoint, descend to a blue tarn chilled by ice slabs. The trail heads generally northwest. Enter subalpine forest near 8.5 km (5.3 mi). The north side of the President Range is visible south.

Reach a junction at 10.2 km (6.3 mi), 2075 m (6805 ft), near a bridge over Little Yoho River. The faint trail left (southwest) heads upstream to Kiwetinok lake and pass. In 1 km it becomes a cairned route over loose rock. Total gain to the pass: 375 m (1230 ft) in 2.5 km (1.6 mi). At the 10.2-km (6.3-mi) junction, cross the bridge to reach **Little Yoho Campground** in 200 meters (220 yards).

Stanley Mitchell Alpine Club Hut is a few minutes farther right (east), at 10.7 km (6.6 mi). From there, the trail descends east, staying above the river's north side.

At 13.7 km (8.5 mi), the right fork ascends past Lake Celeste. Stay straight. At 13.8 km (8.6 mi), the left fork ascends the Whaleback. Stay straight again. At 14.3 km (8.9 mi), the left fork leads past Marpole Lake to Twin Falls Chalet. Stay straight again.

Intersect the **Yoho Valley trail** at 15.9 km (9.9 mi). Left leads to Twin Falls Chalet. Right heads down valley southeast to the trailhead at 20.3 km (12.6 mi), near Takakkaw Falls. From there it's a 1-km (0.6-mi) road-walk south to the Whiskey Jack Youth Hostel parking lot.

ICELINE / LAKE CELESTE / WHALEBACK / YOHO VALLEY: 19.1-KM (11.8-MI) LOOP

At the 5.7-km (3.5-mi) junction, turn right and descend into subalpine forest. Round the east side of small **Lake Celeste**. Immediately after crossing the bridged Little Yoho River, intersect the **Little Yoho River trail**, above the north bank, at 9.7 km (6 mi). Left (west) ascends into Little Yoho Valley. Turn right. In 100 meters (110 yards), go left to ascend the Whaleback. If you're returning to your vehicle now, straight leads to Yoho Valley. Soon stay straight again, then intersect the Yoho Valley trail at 11.9 km (7.4 mi). Go right (southeast) 4.4 km (2.7 mi) to the trailhead near Takakkaw Falls.

Continuing to the Whaleback, the trail climbs north, gaining 305 m (1000 ft) in 2.1 km (1.3 mi) via tight switchbacks. Crest the **Whaleback ridge** at 16 km (9.9 mi), 2210 m (7250 ft). Visible south are The President and The Vice President. West, above Kiwetinok Pass, are Mts. Kerr and Pollinger. Northwest are Waterfall Valley and Glacier des Poilus. North are Yoho Peak and Yoho Glacier. Northeast are Mt. Balfour and Trolltinder Mtn. East is Waputik Icefield. Southeast is Mt. Niles.

Proceeding north-northeast, a gentle descent of the Whaleback leads to a bridge over Twin Falls Creek at 17.6 km (10.9 mi). An unmarked route left (northwest) into Waterfall Valley is 100 meters (110 yards) farther. Continuing past the lip of **Twin Falls**, the main trail heads north through open forest along the edge of the escarpment clutching the falls. It then descends steeply east to a junction at 20.5 km (12.7 mi), 1800 m (5905 ft). Right 100 meters (110 yards) is Twin Falls Chalet; just beyond is the base of Twin Falls. Bear left (east). Pass Twin Falls Campground at 22 km (13.6 mi). Intersect the **Yoho Valley trail** at 22.2 km (13.8 mi).

At the 22.2-km (13.8-mi) junction, left (north) leads 2.3 km (1.4 mi) to a view of Yoho River and Glacier. Turn right and begin the gently-graded descent of Yoho Valley, southeast to the trailhead.

Pass the only major junction on the way out at 24.3 km (15.1 mi). Right (west) ascends Little Yoho Valley. Stay straight. Reach the parking lot at 28.7 km (17.8 mi), near Takakkaw Falls. From there it's a 1-km (0.6-mi) road-walk south to the Whiskey Jack Youth Hostel parking lot.

Trip 41

Mt. Assiniboine Region

Location	Banff National Park / Mt. Assiniboine Provincial Park, Rocky Mountains
Distance	55 km (34 mi) circuit; 56.4 km (35 mi) shuttle trip
Elevation gain	622 m (2040 ft) for circuit; 482 m (1580 ft) for shuttle trip
Time required	3 to 6 days
Difficulty	Moderate
Maps	Mount Assiniboine 82 J/13; Gem Trek Banff & Mt. Assiniboine; BC Parks brochure

OPINION

St. Peter's is not Rome. Disneyworld is not Florida. Mt. Assiniboine is not Mt. Assiniboine Provincial Park. Landmarks often deceive. Overshadowed by a dominating mountain, the scenery in this enchanting park is more marvelously varied than you might think. That's why it's premier backpacking country. Your enjoyment isn't limited to seeing the namesake peak. It's only one of many powerful sights.

Ravishing Lakes Park would be an equally apt name. Seven of them are clustered beneath a classic Northern Rockies massif. And the massif comprises a dozen eminent peaks. Though Mt. Assiniboine is one of them, even if its top were lopped off, the remaining scene would still be Sierra Club calendar material. Meadows are another salient feature of the Park. You'll hike through vast expanses of green alpine carpet here.

The high-voltage scenery, however, is concentrated near the southeast corner of the roughly triangular-shaped park. Naturally, that's where most of the trails lead and where a trail network has developed. So despite competition for your attention, you'll see the famous mountain—assuming the visibility's good. And Mt. Assiniboine's icon status is justified. A pyramidal, grand poohba's hat, it resembles Switzerland's Matterhorn. But it's only the Canadian Rockies' seventh highest peak—3618 m (11,867 ft)—a statistic that belies how frequently and far away *The Boine* is visible and recognizable. You can see it from Pedley Ridge (Trip 32) and the ridge above Ralph Lake (Trip 34).

Mt. Assiniboine looms above Lake Magog

Most backpackers visiting the park share the same initial destination: Lake Magog, in the basin north of The Boine. Strong hikers can tag Magog on a weekend—one long day in, one long day out. Too fast. Give yourself at least a third day for a side trip. Ignore the nearby ridges and lakes and you'll leave with a limited impression of the Park.

An excursion to Nub Peak is de rigeur. From the summit of this modest mountain, you can see Elizabeth, Wedgwood, Cerulean, Sunburst, Magog, Gog and Og lakes, as well as The Boine and its attendant peaks. Mounts Ball, Temple and Hector are even visible way north.

Dayhiking from Magog to Windy Ridge is also a compelling option, for the wildflower display in the meadows en route, and for the supreme vantage on top. It reveals Og Valley, the Goodsirs in Yoho Park, Kootenay's Rockwall and, of course, The Boine massif. It should also satisfy your curiosity about Valley of the Rocks and Brewster Creek valley. Windy Ridge is among the highest trail-accessible points in the mountain parks.

Og Meadows are a fine viewing platform and a wildflower garden in season. They're on the way to Og Lake or Windy Ridge. The easiest excursion is to Sunburst and Cerulean lakes. To escape the Magog melee, head for Ferro Pass and check out the mountainous wall behind Wedgwood Lake. But don't hike to Wedgwood. The low-level trail linking it with Lake Magog is pointless, entailing a muddy, 305-m (1000-ft) descent through forest, which you'll really regret on the return.

Be sure to see why Wonder Pass deserves its name. It grants an awesome view of vast, turquoise Marvel Lake beneath gargantuan, glacier-clogged peaks: Aye Mtn., Eon Mtn., Mt. Gloria, and Aurora Mtn. On a dayhike to Wonder Pass from Magog, include the spur trail to Wonder viewpoint and be as moved as when you first glimpsed The Boine.

Choose between two approaches to Magog. Both are long, neither is difficult. Both begin in Alberta. One is over Citadel Pass, the other up Bryant Creek. Forget about entering via Simpson River in Kootenay National Park.

The optimal gateway is Citadel Pass. Try to arrange a shuttle, so you can trek one-way through Assiniboine Park. Start at Sunshine Village in Banff Park, cross Citadel Pass, and arrive at Lake Magog in 29 km (18 mi). The choice of exits is easy: cruise through Wonder Pass then drop past Marvel Lake. Sunshine Village is higher than the other recommended trailhead, and the scenery is inspirational, making this a less demanding hike even though it's longer.

Bryant Creek offers the easiest, quickest access. You don't have to pay for the shuttle up to Sunshine Village. You can hike a circuit, returning via Wonder Pass and Marvel Lake. But you must endure a monotonous four- to six-hour trudge starting at Mt. Shark trailhead. Only at Bryant Creek warden cabin does the insipid forest back off and let you see the mountains. If you come this way, hike over Assiniboine Pass first. It poses a less taxing ascent than Marvel Lake to Wonder Pass, and it climaxes with a dead-on view of The Boine.

The wondrous view from Wonder Pass invites exploration of Marvel Pass. It's perched at the head of three alpine valleys and is surrounded by captivating mountains. The easiest way to reach it, however, is not as an excursion from this trip. Via Aurora Creek, Marvel Pass is a dayhike. Read Trip 35 for details.

Finally, a request. Please respect the reverie of fellow Magogites. The campground is huge and often full. Never yell—day or night. Be rock quiet after 10 P.M. Anyone who hikes this far is entitled to tranquility. If your loud, obnoxious behaviour disturbs others here, you deserve whatever retribution they choose to inflict.

FACT

Cycling is no longer permitted on the Bryant Creek trail. You can still ride the short distance to Trail Centre, from the Mt. Shark trailhead, but it's not worth the trouble.

Hunting is permitted during September. If hiking here then, be aware and be bright, or avoid these areas: west of Cerulean Lake, between Og Lake and Citadel Pass.

Before your trip

If you want to stay in Bryant Creek shelter, the Bryant Creek campgrounds, or the campground at Howard Douglas Lake (northwest of Citadel Pass), make reservations with the Banff Info Centre. In 2001 it cost $15 per night per person to stay in the shelter.

You don't need reservations to camp in Mt. Assiniboine Provincial Park, but it does cost $5 per person per night at Lake Magog or Og Lake. Bring money to pay the warden. Mitchell Meadows Campground, between Cerulean Lake and Ferro Pass, is free. Fires are prohibited in the core area, so pack a stove.

The four Naiset Cabins near Lake Magog accommodate a total of 30 people on a first come, first served basis. The fee was $15 per person per night in 2001. Even if you find an empty bunk, you'll need a sleeping bag, mattress, and stove. But the cabins are often full, so pack a tent too, or risk ending up with your ass in a boine.

If you want to stay in Mt. Assiniboine Lodge, check the current price and make reservations on their web site at www. canadianrockies.net\assiniboine. You can also phone (403) 678-2883, or e-mail assinil@telusplanet.net.

By Vehicle—Bryant Creek approach

From the Trans-Canada Highway, just southeast of Banff Park's East Gate, turn into Canmore. From here, the trailhead is more than 40 km (24.8 mi) distant, mostly via good, gravel road. Through downtown follow signs directing you toward the Nordic Centre and the Spray Lakes. Proceed onto the Smith-Dorrien/Spray Trail (Highway 742). Drive south through Kananaskis Country, past the south end of Spray Lakes reservoir. Turn right (west) on Watridge logging road, signed for Mt. Engadine Lodge, and continue 5.3 km (3.3 mi) to Mt. Shark trailhead at 1770 m (5805 ft).

By Vehicle and Bus—Citadel Pass approach

Drive the Trans-Canada Highway east 21 km (13 mi) from Castle Junction, or west 9 km (5.6 mi) from Banff townsite. Turn south onto the signed Sunshine Village road. Drive 9 km (5.6 mi) to the parking lot at the gondola station. The gondola does not operate in summer. To reach **Sunshine Village**, at 2200 m (7215 ft), you must hike the restricted-use access road, or ride the shuttle operated by White Mountain Adventures. To make reservations, call (403) 678-4099 or 1-800-408-0005. A round trip cost $18 in 2001. It's $10 for a one-way ride down. Service is available June 20 through September 30. White Mountain also offers service from Banff. Check the current schedule at the Banff Info Centre.

On Foot

MT. SHARK TRAILHEAD TO LAKE MAGOG VIA BRYANT CREEK & ASSINIBOINE PASS

One way	27.5 km (17 mi)
Elevation gain	480 m (1575 ft)
Time required	1 to 1½ days
Difficulty	Moderate

Head generally west-southwest on an old logging road. At 3.7 km (2.3 mi) stay straight where the spur trail to Watridge Lake forks left. Near 5 km (3 mi) begin a steady descent to the Spray River bridge, crossed at 6 km (3.7 mi), 1700 m (5576 ft). Arrive at a junction just beyond. Turn right (northwest). The Palliser Pass trail parallels the Spray River left (south).

At 6.7 km (4.2 mi) cross the Bryant Creek bridge at Trail Centre junction, near the southwest corner of Spray Lakes Reservoir. Bear left (northwest). Right leads northeast to Canyon Dam.

Big Springs Campground is at 9.7 km (6 mi). Reach a junction at 12 km (7.4 mi). Left is the **Owl Lake trail** (described below) heading southwest to Marvel Pass (also accessed via Aurora Creek trail—Trip 35). Proceed straight (northwest). At 13 km (8 mi) reach another junction. Stay straight again. Left leads 0.6 km (0.4 mi) to Marvel Lake Campground and reaches the northeast shore of the lake in 1.6 km (1 mi).

At 13.6 km (8.4 mi) a spur trail left leads 200 meters (220 yards) to Bryant Creek shelter. Stay straight (northwest). At 14.3 km (8.9 mi) arrive at **Bryant Creek warden cabin** and a junction. McBride's Camp is about 150 meters (165 yards) behind the warden cabin. Left (southwest), the Wonder Pass trail climbs above the northwest shore of Marvel Lake. Stay straight, continuing northwest up Bryant Creek valley, toward Assiniboine Pass. This stretch can be muddy, but the willow and dwarf birch trees allow views.

At 17.3 km (10.7 mi) bear right on the hikers' trail veering north, away from Bryant Creek. The horse trail fords the creek and continues straight. At 17.7 km (11 mi) cross Allenby Creek. At 20 km (12.4 mi) the trail forking right leads north over Allenby Pass, then down through the forested Brewster Creek valley to eventually reach the Trans-Canada Highway. Stay straight and traverse rocky slopes west. At 22.4 km (14 mi) stay right where the horse trail merges from the left. Switchback steeply to crest **Assiniboine Pass** at 23 km (14.3 mi), 2180 m (7150 ft).

Proceeding through Ass Pass, encounter a posted map where you cross into B.C. and Mt. Assiniboine Provincial Park. Enter O'Brien Meadows at 23.5 km (14.6 mi). The Boine is visible ahead, above the forest. Approaching the core area, pay attention to the junctions; it will make subsequent daytrips easier.

At 25.5 km (15.8 mi) reach a junction. Right is the **Og Lake trail** north through Og Valley, then northwest over Citadel Pass to Sunshine Village. Stay left for Lake Magog. At 25.8 km (16 mi), the left fork leads 200 meters (220 yards) to Mt. Assiniboine Lodge, and 0.7 km (0.4 mi) farther to the Naiset Cabins. Stay straight for Lake Magog.

At 26 km (16.1 mi) the Nub Peak trail forks right (west). Stay left, above the shore of Lake Magog. At 27.2 km (16.9 mi) reach another junction. Right leads 0.4 km (0.25 mi) to Sunburst Lake. Left leads back to the Naiset Cabins. Stay straight. Reach Lake Magog Campground at 27.5 km (17 mi).

LAKE MAGOG TO MT. SHARK TRAILHEAD
VIA WONDER PASS

One way	27.5 km (17 mi)
Elevation gain	230 m (755 ft)
Time required	1 to 1½ days
Difficulty	Moderate

Leaving Lake Magog Campground, follow the trail northeast 200 meters (220 yards) to a junction. Left leads to Sunburst Lakes. Turn right on the trail to the Naiset Cabins and skirt the lake's north shore. At 29.1 km (18 mi) pass a spur trail left to the lodge. Soon pass the cabins. Follow the trail on a gentle ascent beside tiny Gog Creek, through meadows and forest sprinkled with larch. Cross the creek at 2.3 km (1.4 mi). At 2.6 km (1.6 mi) stay straight (southeast) where a spur trail forks right 100 meters (110 yards) to small Gog Lake.

The grade steepens until cresting **Wonder Pass** at 4.3 km (2.7 mi), 2395 m (7855 ft). Looking northwest, you can see Og Valley and beyond to Citadel Pass. The trail curves south and enters Banff Park. Visible ahead (southwest to south) are Aye Mtn. with ice-clad Eon Mtn. above it, Mt. Gloria, and Lake Gloria. Long, turquoise Marvel Lake extends northeast, far below the pass. Lake Terrapin is the little

Mt. Gloria, Eon and Aye mtns., above Lake Gloria, from Wonder Pass trail

one, between Lake Gloria and Marvel Lake. Marvel Peak is southeast, above Marvel Lake.

If you're dayhiking to Wonder Pass from Lake Magog, proceed to about 5 km (3.1 mi). Near the last rise, before the larches, follow the cairned spur trail left. It leads about 1 km (0.6 mi) to **Wonder viewpoint**, an open slope where you can better survey the surrounding lakes and mountains. Don't stop at the plateau with a partial view. Skirt that small rise, then drop to the more open viewpoint.

Continuing on the main trail through Wonder Pass, begin a long, steep, switchbacking descent south. Views improve below. Reach a junction at 7.6 km (4.7 mi). The right fork keeps dropping to the southwest end of **Marvel Lake**, then crosses a creek and begins ascending south to Marvel Pass. Stay left (northeast) and descend more gradually now, through forest and across rocky avalanche paths, above the northwest shore of Marvel Lake.

At 12 km (7.5 mi) a spur trail forks right (south) to Marvel Lake's northeast end. Stay left. Cross Bryant Creek bridge at 13 km (8 mi), then cross meadows. At 13.3 km (8.2 mi), 1845 m (6052 ft), intersect the **Bryant Creek trail** near the warden cabin. Turn right and switch to auto pilot for the final 14.3 km (8.9 mi) on a broad, smooth, mostly-level path to Mt. Shark trailhead. The total distance from Lake Magog Campground is 27.5 km (17 mi).

SUNSHINE VILLAGE TO LAKE MAGOG VIA CITADEL PASS

One way	29 km (18 mi)
Elevation change	450-m (1475-ft) gain; 427-m (1400-ft) loss
Time required	1 to 1½ days
Difficulty	Moderate

From Sunshine Village ski lodge at 2195 m (7200 ft), go south 200 meters (220 yards) to the Parks Canada cabin. Just south of it, turn left onto the well-groomed, gravel path. You'll be gently ascending. Go right at the first junction. In another 5-7 minutes, reach the next junction, 1.2 km (0.7 mi) from Sunshine Village. Go left (southeast) on the narrower path for Citadel Pass.

Mt. Howard Douglas (left, northeast) is the grey mountain with a ski lift on its bare chest. Behind it is Brewster Creek Valley. You'll start descending 45 minutes into the hike—one of many downs and ups. Soon regain 145 m (480 ft). If the wildflower show hasn't slowed you, you'll reach a 2385-m (7820-ft) shoulder of **Quartz Hill** in 1¼ hours, having hiked 5 km (3 mi) from Sunshine Village. The 3618-m (11,867-ft) horn of Mt. Assiniboine is visible ahead. The first lake beneath you is Howard Douglas (labeled Sundown on some maps). Descend to reach the shore at 2280 m (7480 ft).

After the deeply rutted, narrow trail to Howard Douglas Lake, the path improves through meadows with a scattering of trees. You'll ascend 100 m (330 ft) and pass another lake before reaching **Citadel Pass** at 9.3 km (5.8 mi), 2360 m (7740 ft).

Entering Mt. Assiniboine Provincial Park, carry full water bottles; sections of trail ahead are dry. The gradual descent southeast through meadows steepens in a gully. After losing about 305 m (1000 ft), reach a junction at 12.8 km (7.9 mi). Right (south) descends to Porcupine Campground. From there, head southeast nearly 2 km (1.2 mi) to rejoin the main trail. Most hikers bear left at the 12.8-km (7.9-mi) junction, staying higher on the direct, main trail to Lake Magog.

Head southeast, contouring a grassy slope through Golden Valley. Near 15.5 km (9.6 mi) stay straight (southeast) where the lower trail from Porcupine Campground enters on the right. In **Valley of the Rocks**, the trail wiggles for a couple kilometers through a hilly forest studded with a chaotic array of boulders. Reach **Og Lake** and campground in subalpine meadows at 22.3 km (13.8 mi), 2060 m (6757 ft). Og Mtn. (northeast) and Cave Mtn. (southeast) are near the Banff Park boundary. Mt. Magog and The Boine are visible south.

Head south through Og Meadows. Ignore the **Og Pass trail** entering from the left. Also ignore the Sunburst Lake horse trail entering from the right. Ascend to join the Assiniboine Pass trail, at 27 km

(16.7 mi). Turn right (south). Approaching the core area, pay attention to the junctions; it will make subsequent daytrips easier.

At 18 km (11.2 mi), the left fork leads 200 meters (220 yards) to Mt. Assiniboine Lodge, and 0.7 km (0.4 mi) farther to the Naiset Cabins. Stay straight for **Lake Magog**. At 18.2 km (11.3 mi) the Nub Peak trail forks right (west). Stay left, above the shore of Lake Magog. At 19.4 km (12 mi) reach another junction. Right leads 0.4 km (0.25 mi) to Sunburst Lake. Left leads back to the Naiset Cabins. Stay straight. Reach Lake Magog Campground at 29 km (18 mi).

SUNBURST, CERULEAN & ELIZABETH LAKES

Circuit	8 km (5 mi)
Elevation gain	135 m (443 ft)
Time required	2 to 3 hours
Difficulty	Easy

From the north edge of Lake Magog Campground, follow the trail northwest 0.4 km (0.25 mi) to a junction. Stay left to reach Sunburst Lake at 0.8 km (0.5 mi). Round the north shore. Reach the northeast end of Cerulean Lake at 1.4 km (0.9 mi). There's a junction at 1.6 km (1 mi). Left is the low route to Ferro Pass and Wedgwood Lake. Turn right for the high route detouring to Elizabeth Lake.

Climb to a junction at 2 km (1.2 mi), 2300 m (7545 ft). The right fork ascends Nub Peak. Bear left and descend to Elizabeth Lake. Reach the west end of the lake and cross the bridged outlet stream at 2.5 km (1.6 mi). Descend open forest to intersect the Ferro Pass trail at 4 km (2.5 mi). Turn left to loop back to Cerulean Lake.

Reach Cerulean Lake's southwest shore at 5.5 km (3.4 mi). Follow the trail northeast along the shore. At the junction where you previously ascended to Elizabeth Lake, turn right (southeast) to pass Sunburst Lake and return to Lake Magog Campground.

NUB PEAK

Round trip	11.6 km (7.2 mi)
Elevation gain	578 m (1896 ft)
Time required	4 hours
Difficulty	Moderate

From Lake Magog Campground, head north on the Assiniboine Pass trail. Keep straight at the left fork to Sunburst and Cerulean lakes. At 1.4 km (0.9 mi) turn left for Nub Peak. Head northwest across meadow. At the next junctions, stay left, then right. Ascend through subalpine forest. Crest Nub Ridge at 3.6 km (2.2 mi). The view is dominated by The Boine massif. The rest of the area is visible as well, including Wedgwood Lake cirque, Sunburst and Cerulean lakes, and Lake Magog.

The trail follows the ridgecrest northwest to a saddle, where you have a choice: (1) follow the trail descending left (west) to Cerulean or Elizabeth lakes, or (2) continue another 2 km (1.2 mi) to the 2743-m (8997-ft) summit of Nub Peak for an expanded view.

Turning west at the saddle, descend about 75 m (245 ft) in 0.7 km (0.4 mi) to a junction on a forested divide. Right drops north to Elizabeth Lake, left drops south to Cerulean Lake.

To scramble up Nub Peak, follow the route angling right from the saddle. Ascend the Nublet, drop to the ridge, then work your way up to the summit.

WINDY RIDGE

Round trip	17.4 km (10.8 mi)
Elevation gain	470 m (1542 ft)
Time required	5 hours
Difficulty	Moderate

From Lake Magog Campground, head north on the Assiniboine Pass trail. Proceed straight through the next three junctions. At 2 km (1.2 mi) reach another junction where you turn left on the Citadel Pass trail.

Ignore the Sunburst Lake horse trail entering from the left. Just beyond, turn right onto the Og Pass trail. Head north through Og Meadows. At 3 km (1.9 mi) bear left where the Assiniboine Pass horse trail forks right.

At 4.7 km (2.9 mi) begin the forested climb northeast to Og Pass. The ascent eases in the undulating pass. At 6.5 km (4 mi) reach a junction. Right continues east through Og Pass, then descends southeast to intersect the Allenby Pass trail. Turn left (north) for Windy Ridge.

Ascend through alpine larch, cross a prolific alpine flower garden with a panoramic view, and continue up a steep talus slope. Crest Windy Ridge, a saddle on Og Mtn., at 8.7 km (5.4 mi), 2635 m (8643 ft). On the east side, 427 vertical meters (1400 ft) straight below, is a blue tarn in a hanging valley. You can also see northeast down forested Brewster Valley. Look for Halfway Cabin on the edge of a meadow.

FERRO PASS

Round trip	18.6 km (11.5 mi)
Elevation gain	275 m (900 ft)
Time required	5 hours
Difficulty	Moderate

Follow the directions above (past Sunburst, Cerulean and Elizabeth lakes) to intersect the Ferro Pass trail at 4 km (2.5 mi). Turn right and continue descending generally northwest through forest. Cross the bridge over Nestor Creek at 5.7 km (3.5 mi), 1995 m (6544 ft), and arrive at Mitchell Meadows Campground.

Ascend west, then northwest, through forest and across avalanche swaths. Steep switchbacks begin at 8.5 km (5.3 mi) in the final bid to reach larch-graced Ferro Pass at 9.3 km (5.8 mi), 2270 m (7446 ft).

Ferro Pass is between Nestor Peak (northeast) and Indian Peak (west). Southeast is Wedgwood Lake, backed by (left to right) 3030-m (9938-ft) Wedgwood Peak, 3190-m (10,463-ft) The Marshall, and 2972-m (9748-ft) Mt. Watson. Northwest is Rock Lake, beneath Simpson Ridge (right).

Trip 42
The Rockwall

Location	Kootenay National Park
Shuttle trip	54.8 km (34 mi) one way
Elevation change	1490-m (4887-ft) gain, 1440-m (4730-ft) loss
Time required	3 to 4 days
Difficulty	Challenging
Maps	Mount Goodsir 82 N/1;
	Gem Trek Kootenay National Park; The
	Adventure Map The Rockwall 1:50,000

OPINION

The Rockwall trail is a thrilling, demanding roller coaster. Thigh-throbbing ascents to climactic vistas are followed by long knee-crunching swoops into forest. The trail slams up against stone monoliths, glides through meadows, dips under glaciers, and whips past lakes and waterfalls. It's as challenging a backpack trip as any in the Canadian Rockies, as rewarding as any in the world. Get buffed for this four-day trek, so it will fulfill you rather than waste you.

Despite its ups and downs, the trail is frequently above or near treeline, beside the sheer limestone cliffs of the 35-km (22-mi) Rockwall on the Great Divide. This solid eastern face of the Vermilion Range is broken only once along its length—at tight Wolverine Pass. The Rockwall is a fantastic sight, more than compensating for the strenuous effort necessary to admire it.

Driving through Kootenay Park, south of Marble Canyon, glimpses of pulse-quickening summits are few and fleeting—unlike in Banff, Jasper and Yoho parks. Only a couple tantalizing peaks are visible from Highway 93. They're far up the forested valleys to the west. They're part of the Rockwall. To enter this sequestered realm of mountain majesty, you must commit to one of those long approaches.

By starting at the Floe Lake trailhead and hiking the Rockwall trail northwest, you'll dispatch the stiffer climbs on the first half of the journey. At a race pace you can finish in three days: one afternoon, two full days, and one morning. Floe Lake, beneath 1000-m (3330-ft) cliffs, is a

The Rockwall and Floe Lake, from just below Numa Pass

gorgeous setting for your first night. (See photo on page 161.) The camp-ground is of front-country quality, highly manicured and organized, with gravel tent pads, gravel paths, picnic tables, plus the standard outhouses and bear poles. Purists wish it were smaller, more rough-hewn, but we should all give the Park credit for crowd control. On your next night, stay at Tumbling Creek Campground. Shoot for Helmet Falls Campground your last night. The waterfall plunges 365 m (1197 ft), making it one of Canada's highest. If you need more time to complete the trip, spend your second night at Numa Creek Campground, below the steep ascent to Tumbling Pass.

If you return to the highway via Helmet and Ochre creeks, you'll complete a 54-km (33.5-mi) one-way trip. Some backpackers extend this to a four- to six-day trek by proceeding north over Goodsir Pass (Trip 39) into Yoho Park, then up McArthur Creek to Lake O'Hara, for a total of 67 km (41.5 mi). We don't recommend it. The most efficient way to visit Goodsir Pass is on a half-day hike from the Helmet Falls Campground. And Lake O'Hara (Trips 37 and 38) offers enough premier hiking to deserve a pilgrimage exclusively to that region. The descent from Goodsir Pass to the Ottertail River is largely through viewless forest. To reach Lake O'Hara from there, you must ascend densely forested McArthur Creek valley, which supports a healthy population of grizzlies.

Try to allow enough time on your Rockwall journey to include the half-day hike from Helmet Falls to vast, lonely, lovely Goodsir Pass, where you'll see the twin-horned Goodsir Towers. This 8-km (5-mi) round-trip excursion entails a 450-m (1475-ft) ascent. Continue northwest through the pass for a direct view of the Goodsirs, which rise 1950 m (6400 ft) from Goodsir Creek.

Don't have time for the entire Rockwall? Dayhike to Floe Lake (21 km / 13 mi round trip with a gain of 715 m / 2350 ft). If you have more energy, flame on to Numa Pass. Though the lake is a captivating sight, the view from the pass is catapulting. High in the flower-dappled alpine tundra, you'll marvel at the continuous cliffs of the Rockwall. Alpine larch trees—some unusually big—are profuse between Floe Lake and Numa Pass. In late September they turn electric gold, as if plugged in (photo on page 174).

FACT

Before your trip

Read *Backcountry Permits* (page 6) for details about camping fees and reservations. If you plan to extend this hike to Lake O'Hara, read the *Before Your Trip* section under Trip 37 and make the required reservations. Also check with the Yoho Visitor Centre about the status of the McArthur Creek trail. Hiking has been and might still be prohibited to preserve the habitat for resident grizzlies.

By Vehicle

Drive Highway 93 through Kootenay Park to the Floe Lake / Hawk Creek trailhead parking area, on the west side of the highway. It's 22.5 km (14 mi) south of the Banff-Kootenay boundary, or 71 km (44 mi) north of Kootenay Park's West Gate at Radium. Elevation: 1325 m (4346 ft). The Paint Pots trailhead is 13 km (8 mi) farther northwest, at 1450 m (4756 ft). If arranging a shuttle, leave one car there.

On Foot

After descending south to a bridge over the Vermilion River, the trail turns right (northwest). At 1.7 km (1.1 mi) cross the bridge over Floe Creek. The trail then turns southwest—the general direction of travel nearly all the way to the lake. Climb gradually, then steeply, gaining 152 m (500 ft) through dense forest.

The trail contours for just over 1 km (0.6 mi) before starting a short, moderate ascent near 6 km (3.7 mi). Soon attain a view back northeast across the Vermilion River valley to the Ball Range. At 8 km (5 mi), begin a 2-km (1.2-mi) section of steep switchbacks heading northwest. Proceed through a subalpine meadow ringed with alpine larch to reach **Floe Lake** at 10.5 km (6.5 mi), 2040 m (6690 ft).

Tumbling Pass

Just before the warden cabin near Floe Lake's northeast shore, the Rockwall trail ascends northwest. It's another 2.7 km (1.7 mi) from the lake to 2355-m (7724-ft) Numa Pass. That's a gain of 315 m (1033 ft), most of which you'll endure in the final kilometer. On top, you can see sharply pyramidal Foster Peak (southwest), Numa Mtn. (northeast), and Tumbling Pass (northwest, beyond the Numa Creek drainage).

Numa Pass is the Rockwall trail's highest point. From there, drop 830 m (2722 ft) down the north side of the pass into lush Numa Creek basin. Numa Creek Campground is at 20.3 km (12.6 mi). You'll intersect the Numa Creek trail just beyond, at 20.7 km (12.8 mi).

Turn left (west) to continue on the Rockwall trail. Right immediately crosses a tributary and follows Numa Creek downstream 6.6 km (4.1 mi) to the highway.

From Numa Creek basin, the Rockwall trail climbs steeply west, then northwest, gaining 725 m (2380 ft) to reach **Tumbling Pass** at 25.5 km (15.8 mi), 2250 m (7380 ft). Left (west) is Tumbling Glacier, flowing off Mt. Gray. You'll cross subalpine meadows scattered with larches and parallel a terminal moraine. After a bit more than a kilometer, begin a rapid descent north. Reach **Tumbling Creek** and a significant junction at 27.8 km (17.2 mi), 1890 m (6200 ft).

Straight (northeast), staying on the right (east) bank, is the Tumbling Creek trail. It descends the valley to reach Highway 93 in 10.7 km (6.6 mi).

Turn left (west) and cross the bridge to reach Tumbling Creek Campground. (Kootenay Park has struggled to maintain a bridge here; several have washed away in high water or collapsed under heavy snow.) Proceed through the campground to where the Rockwall trail begins a switchbacking ascent northwest. Wolverine Pass is 3.5 km (2.2 mi) distant.

At 31 km (19.2 mi) reach the southeast side of the open, meadowy Wolverine Plateau. In 300 meters (328 yards) a trail forks left (west) through the narrow cleft of 2195-m (7200-ft) **Wolverine Pass**, between Mts. Gray and Drysdale. A short way into the pass, B.C.'s Purcell Range is visible west. This break in the Rockwall is not obvious until you're directly across from it.

Where the Wolverine Pass trail forks left (west), the Rockwall trail ascends gently north through 2241-m (7350-ft) **Rockwall Pass**. You're in meadowlands here, with the nearby Rockwall escarpment constantly in view. It rises 670 m (2200 ft) above you. After a mostly level 1.6 km (1 mi), the trail descends steeply to cross a bridged stream at 35.6 km (22 mi). It then climbs 250 m (820 ft) over a shoulder of Limestone Peak before angling west and descending again. You'll hear the roar of 365-m (1200-ft) **Helmet Falls** (photo on page 163) crashing into the broad amphitheatre created by Sharp Mtn. (northwest), Helmet Mtn. (west) and Limestone Peak (southeast). Helmet Falls Campground is at 39.7 km (24.6 mi), 1760 m (5773 ft).

Beyond the campground and warden cabin, there's a junction at 40.3 km (25 mi). To reach the highway and the Paint Pots trailhead, bear right (east) and descend along the north side of Helmet Creek. To visit Goodsir Pass or extend your trek into Yoho Park, ascend left (north).

Descending **Helmet Creek valley**, cross a bridge at 42.6 km (26.4 mi) to the south side of the creek. Cross another bridge over Helmet Creek's east end, at 48 km (29.8 mi). A few minutes farther cross Ochre Creek and reach a junction with the **Ochre Creek trail** at 48.3 km (30 mi). Left (north) ascends to Ottertail Pass. Go right (southeast).

At 51 km (31.6 mi) stay left (east) where the Tumbling Creek trail forks right (west), crosses Ochre Creek and passes Ochre Creek Campground. At 53.4 km (33.1 mi) turn right (south) where a trail to Marble Canyon bears left (east). Your trail then leaves the forest and passes the large paint pots (ochre beds). At a fork where straight (northeast) leads to Marble Canyon, turn right and immediately cross the Vermilion River suspension bridge. In a couple minutes arrive at the highway and the Paint Pots trailhead parking lot, having completed a 54.8-km (34-mi) journey.

Heading for **Goodsir Pass** or Yoho Park? From the 40.3-km (25-mi) junction on the north side of Helmet Creek, fork left (north) on the Goodsir Pass trail. It gains 450 m (1476 ft) in 4 km (2.5 mi) to crest the pass at 2210 m (7250 ft). Directly south above the larch-fringed, meadowy pass is 3049-m (10,000-ft) Sharp Mtn. Soaring southwest behind it is 3267-m (10,716-ft) Sentry Peak. West are the twin towers of Mt. Goodsir. The south tower is 3562 m (11,683 ft), the north tower is 3525 m (11,562 ft). Northwest of the pass, the trail enters Yoho Park. About 2 km (1.2 mi) through the pass, as you start descending, attain a closer view across Goodsir Creek to the northeast face of the Goodsir Towers.

From the Kootenay-Yoho boundary, the trail descends steadily through dense forest to Goodsir Creek. Near 50.5 km (31 mi), stay left (west) where a trail detours right (north) to Ottertail Falls. Stay left again in 10 minutes, just before the Ottertail River bridge. Near 53 km (33 mi) pass the **McArthur Creek** warden cabin. McArthur Creek Campground is just beyond. A few minutes farther, cross the McArthur Creek bridge and arrive at a junction. Straight ahead the Ottertail River fire road (Trip 39) leads northwest 16.2 km (10 mi) to the Trans-Canada Highway. Right leads north to McArthur Pass and Lake O'Hara.

Trip 43
Hudson Bay Mountain

Location	Hudson Bay Range, near Smithers
Round trip	4 km (2.2 mi) to 9 km (5.6 mi)
	314 m (1030 ft) to 1076 m (3530 ft)
Elevation gain	284 m (930 ft) to 980 m (3214 ft)
Time required	3 to 7 hours
Difficulty	Easy to Challenging
Maps	Smithers 93 L/14; Great Trails in the Bulkley Valley

OPINION

Hudson Bay Mountain's allure is due in part to its multiple per-sonalities. Climb the steep route up Glacier Gulch and you'll meet a snarling, icy peak baring its teeth and spitting a boulder-shattering meltwater torrent down at you. Hike the other side, to Crater Lake, and you'll meet a meadowy mountain as innocent as a flower child, its countenance so gentle that locals call it "the prairie." (See photo on page 175.)

Glacier Gulch takes only half a day but consumes a full day's energy. It begins with a short walk to a waterfall. A rough trail then climbs at a demanding grade high above the falls. Finally, an even steeper route leads through chaotic rubble, beside a thundering stream, into the craggy cirque sheltering Hudson Bay Glacier. On the access road, approaching the trailhead, crane your neck over your car dashboard, lift your eyes, and you can see the glacier; you'd swear it's straight up. Standing at the foot of the glacier, look-ing back down, your suspicion is confirmed. This is as vertical, challenging and exciting as a hiking trail gets.

For Crater Lake, you don't even need hiking boots. Runners will do. Starting just below treeline at a ski area, the trail ascends gently across an alpine carpet of grass and heather. The southwest horizon, crowded with heavily ice-capped Hazelton and Coast range peaks, is in constant view. July through early August, the greenery underfoot erupts with wildflowers. Suddenly, there's the lake: shoved into the belly of the mountain. This half-day hike is as blissfully stress-free and pastorally beautiful as any in the province.

Ascending rugged route into Glacier Basin

Stretch the Crater Lake trip into a full day's adventure by aiming for the 2576-m (8450-ft) summit. It's steep, rugged, trailless, requires lots of tiresome boulder hopping, but is easier than Glacier Gulch. Soon you're rewarded with a cliff-edge view of Smithers far below. Attain the ragged summit ridge and you'll peer pop-eyed

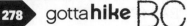
over a sheer headwall down on Hudson Bay Glacier. This is the kind of airy, thrilling perch that motivates rock climbers. You're high above where hikers' progress is halted in Glacier Gulch. If you already explored the gulch, you've now visually completed the loop.

The Glacier Gulch and Crater Lake trails are each only a couple kilometers long. Junctions are few. And it's only another couple kilometers from Crater Lake to the summit.

FACT

By Vehicle
This bonus trip is not in southern B.C. It's near Smithers, which is between Prince Rupert and Prince George, on Hwy 16.

Hudson Bay Mountain via Glacier Gulch

0 km (0 mi)
In Smithers, drive Hwy 16 northwest from Toronto Street. This junction has the last traffic lights before leaving town. There's also a Taco Bell and KFC here.

2.8 km (1.7 mi)
Bear left at the Y-junction onto Lake Kathlyn Road. Immediately after, stay on the main road where Proctor forks left.

4.2 km (2.6 mi)
Ascend left, toward the mountains, on the unsigned road. Beach Road continues straight. (Kathlyn Glacier is now visible. The trail ascends just left of it.)

5.1 km (3.2 mi)
Go left onto Glacier Gulch Road.

6.8 km (4.2 mi)
Stay straight on pavement and keep ascending. Davidson Road (dirt) forks right.

6.9 km (4.3 mi)
Pavement ends. Proceed straight on the better dirt road.

9.3 km (5.8 mi)
Arrive at Twin Falls day-use area and Glacier Gulch trailhead. Elevation: 750 m (2460 ft).

Summit of Hudson Bay Mountain

Hudson Bay Mountain via Crater Lake

0 km (0 mi)
From Hwy 16 in Smithers, turn southwest onto King Street (one street southeast of Main). Follow the ski-area signs.

0.7 km (0.4 mi)
Turn left onto Railway Avenue.

4.7 km (2.9 mi)
Pavement ends.

6.2 km (3.8 mi)
Proceed straight, uphill.

7.4 km (4.6 mi)
Bear right.

11.3 km (7 mi)
Stay straight on the main road, passing the turnoff to the cross-country ski area.

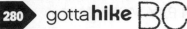

16 km (10 mi)
Turn right, toward the downhill ski area. The road is steep for 6 km (3.7 mi). Left leads to the small FS campground at Dennis Lake. To get there, bear left on McDonell Lake FS road at 21.8 km (13.5 mi), then descend the spur at 29.5 km (18.3 mi).

22.2 km (14 mi)
Arrive at the downhill ski-area's first parking lot.

23 km (14.3 mi)
Arrive at the road's end parking area, among chalets, just before the green T-bar. There's room for about six vehicles here, at 1500 m (4920 ft).

On Foot
<u>Hudson Bay Mountain via Glacier Gulch</u>
From the upper (left) side of the parking lot, follow the signed Glacier Gulch trail. It's initially a broad, rocky path. In a few minutes, fork left at a sign. Soon reach the stream below the waterfall. Scramble across the rock on the left to resume on the trail.

Though it switchbacks, the trail is steep. It climbs through fern, devil's club, salmonberry, and lovely forest. About 20 minutes up, the waterfall's second cascade is visible. At a moderate pace, you'll break out of the trees in 45 minutes.

Continue through krummholz (dwarfed trees) to a rockslide. About 20 meters (yards) beyond, look for cairns. Stay on the lower route. Ignore the bootbeaten trail left. The lower route crosses more rock slabs, so it's a bit easier than the higher route on scree. But both routes are rough, aggressively ascending the rockslide beside the raging creek. Follow flagging and cairns while gaining the next 152 m (500 ft). Reach the glacier's snout at 2 km (2.1 mi), 1585 m (5200 ft), in about 1¾ hours.

It's possible to probe deeper into the cirque of Hudson Bay Mountain. At 1677 m (5500 ft), you'll have climbed 927 m (3040 ft) from the trailhead.

<u>Hudson Bay Mountain via Crater Lake</u>
Follow the T-bar cable uphill. Just before the second T-bar pole, angle left on a rough road, toward Hudson Bay Mountain. Walk the road for a few hundred meters. Where the road peters, go left on the well-defined trail along a creeklet.

After gaining 140 m (460 ft), the grade eases. Within 20 minutes, you're in the open. This expansive, fairly level meadowland is known locally as "the prairie." In summer, wildflowers burst through the grass. Among them are lavender fleabane, fuschia lousewort (resembling a loon's beak), pink and orange paintbrush, deep-purple monkshood, king gentian, white valerian, and bright-yellow arnica and cinquefoil. The Howser Range (southeast) and the Hazelton Range (southwest) fill the horizon. At 2 km (1.2 mi) the trail fades on a rocky bluff overlooking Crater Lake. The lake is at 1814 m (5950 ft). Dropping to the shore is quick and easy.

You can resume the ascent of Hudson Bay Mountain by following the trail around the right (northeast) side of the crater, just above the lake. But it leads to rougher terrain (bigger, looser rock) than you'll encounter going more directly up the ridge. So, from the rocky bluff where Crater Lake is first visible, bear right (north) along the low, green ridge. Then ascend onto the middle ridge (grass and black rock). Where it appears most comfortable to do so, head northwest, toward the highest black-rock ridge. Attain the ridgecrest at 2104 m (6900 ft), about 1½ hours after departing the trailhead. Here, you can look southwest down a canyon to Smithers.

Continue ascending the ridgeline. It provides ever-improving views and leads directly to the mountaintop. Pick your route according to where you find the surest footing. Attain a minor summit (2480 m / 8134 ft) after hiking about 3¼ hours. Scramble 91 m (300 ft) higher for a more complete panorama and to sign your name in the summit-cairn register crowning 2576-m (8450-ft) Hudson Bay Mountain. Distance from the trailhead: 4.5 km (2.8 mi). Elevation gain: 1076 m (3530 ft).

PREPARING FOR YOUR HIKE

Hiking in the mountains is an adventure. Adventure involves risk. But the rewards are worth it. Just be ready for more adventure than you expect. The weather here is constantly changing. Even on a warm, sunny day, pack for rain or snow. Injury is always a possibility. On a long dayhike, be equipped to spend the night out. If you respect the power of wilderness by being prepared, you'll decrease the risk, increase your comfort and enjoyment, and come away fulfilled, yearning for more.

The following recommendations will help you know what's best to pack for mountain conditions. If you don't own or can't afford some of the things listed, make do with what you have. Just be sure to bring warm clothing that insulates when wet. Cotton is terrible. Wool is good. Lighter, softer, synthetic fabrics are better. When upgrading or buying new equipment, consult this section so you don't waste money on something inefficient or inappropriate.

Rain or snow can hit the high country on any summer day.

THE FIRST THING TO PACK

Even with all the right gear, you're ill-equipped without physical fitness. If the weather turns grim, the physical capability to get out of the wilderness fast might keep you from being stuck in a life-threatening situation. If you're fit, and a companion gets injured, you can race for help. Besides, if you're not overweight or easily exhausted, you'll have more fun. You'll be able to hike farther, reach more spectacular scenery, and leave crowds behind. So if you're out of shape, work on it. Everything else you'll need is easier to acquire.

TRAVEL LIGHT

Weight is critical when backpacking. The lighter you travel, the easier and more pleasant the journey. Carrying too much can sour your opinion of an otherwise great trip. Some people are mules; they can shoulder everything they want. If you'd rather be a thoroughbred, reduce your load and get lighter gear. You might have to sacrifice a little luxury at the campsite in order to be more agile, fleet-footed and comfortable on the trail, but you'll be a happier hiker.

Weigh your pack when it's empty. Switching to a newer, lighter model might shave a couple pounds off your burden. A palatial dome tent is probably overdoing it. Check out the smaller, lighter, anthropomorphic designs. A down sleeping bag will weigh less, stuff smaller and last longer than a synthetic-filled bag that has the same temperature rating. You can also cut weight and volume with a shorter, inflatable sleeping-pad instead of a full-length one made of thick foam. Forget that heavy, bulky, fleece jacket. If you get really cold at camp, you can dive into your bag. And on any trek less than four days, it's possible to pack only real food and leave all that clunky cooking equipment at home. Try it. Hot meals aren't necessary. Playing outdoor chef and dishwasher is a time-consuming ordeal. It also makes it harder to leave no trace of your visit, and it can attract bears. Select the right foods and you'll find they weigh no more than a stove, fuel, pots, and freeze-dried meals.

These reductions long ago revitalized our interest in backpacking. Now we revel in going light. Lighter equipment is more expensive because the materials are finer quality and the craftsmanship superior. But it's definitely worth it. Consult reputable backpacking stores for specific brands.

Glacier Crest (Trip 18) from just below Perley Rock (Trip 19)

UNNECESSARY STUFF

It's amazing how much unnecessary stuff a lot of hikers carry. We once encountered two men labouring up a trail, bound for a distant, backcountry lake, pushing wheelbarrows piled with camping "necessities." They had a cooler, tackle box, hatchet, lawn chairs, even a radio. They also had sore hands, aching spines, and a new appreciation for backpacks and minimal loads. Unless you're in terrific shape, have a high pain threshold, or don't mind creeping along at a slug's pace, think about everything you pack. Jettisoning preconceptions will lighten your load.

Do you really need the entire guidebook? Take notes, or photocopy the pages of your book. Carrying the whole thing is like lugging a rock in your pack.

A cassette player, even a tiny one, is questionable, and not just because of the added weight. Toting tunes into the outdoors will deny you the delight of birdsong, windsong, riversong. Wearing headphones blunts your awareness, increasing the likelihood of a bear encounter. Subjecting campers to unwanted music can ignite a feud.

An extra pair of shoes? No way. Even river sandals are heavy. For in-camp comfort, bring a pair of beach flip-flops. The cheap,

$1.99-cent variety are almost weightless, and their treadless soles are easy on the environment.

Jeans are ridiculous. They're heavy, restrictive, and don't insulate. Cotton sweatpants are almost as bad. Anything 100% cotton is a mistake, as explained below.

LAYERING WITH SYNTHETICS

Don't just wear a T-shirt and throw a heavy sweatshirt in your pack. Cotton kills. It quickly gets soaked and takes way too long to dry. Wet clothing saps your body heat and could lead to hypothermia, a leading cause of death in the outdoors. Your mountain clothes should be made of synthetic fabrics that wick sweat away from your skin, insulate when wet, and dry rapidly. Even your hiking shorts and underwear should be at least partly synthetic. Sports bras should be entirely synthetic.

There are now lots of alternatives to the soggy T-shirt. Many outdoor clothing companies offer short-sleeve shirts in superior, synthetic versions. Unlike cotton T-shirts, sweat-soaked synthetics can dry during a rest break.

For warmth, several synthetic layers are more efficient than a single parka. Your body temperature varies constantly on the trail in response to the weather and your activity level. With only one warm garment, it's either on or off, roast or freeze. Layers allow you to fine tune for optimal comfort.

In addition to a synthetic short-sleeve shirt, it's smart to pack two long-sleeve tops of different fabric weights: one thin, one thick. Wear the thin one for cool-weather hiking. It'll be damp when you stop for a break, so change into the thick one. When you start again, put the thin one back on. The idea is to always keep your thick top dry in case you really need it to stay warm. Covered by a rain shell (jacket), these two tops can provide enough warmth on summer hikes. You can always wear your short-sleeve shirt like a vest over a long-sleeve top. For more warmth on the trail, try a fleece vest. For more warmth in camp, try a down vest or down sweater. Don't hike in down clothing; it'll get soaked and be useless.

For your legs, bring a pair of tights or long underwear, both if you're going overnight. Choose tights made of synthetic insulating material, with a small percentage of lycra for stretchiness. These are warmer and more durable than the all-lycra or nylon/lycra tights runners wear. You'll find tights way more efficient than pants. They stretch and conform to your body movements. They're lighter and insulate better. You can wear them for hours in a drizzle and not feel damp. If you're too modest to sport this sleek look, just wear shorts over them. Shorts also protect tights from snagging when you sit down.

RAINGEAR

You need a full set of raingear: pants, and a shell (jacket) with a hood. Fabrics that are both waterproof and breathable are best, because they shed rain and vent perspiration vapor.

Wearing coated nylon, you can end up as damp from sweat as you would from rain. If you can't afford technical raingear, use a poncho. It allows enough air circulation so you won't get sweat soaked.

Raingear is useful even when it's not raining. A shell and pants, worn over insulating layers, will shed wind, retain body heat, and keep you much warmer.

BOOTS AND SOCKS

Lightweight fabric boots with even a little ankle support are more stable and safer than runners. But all-leather or highly technical leather/fabric boots offer superior comfort and performance. For serious hiking, they're a necessity. Here are a few points to remember while shopping for a pair.

If it's a rugged, quality boot, a light- or medium-weight pair should be adequate for most hiking conditions. Heavy boots will slow you down, just like an overweight pack. But you want boots with hard, protective toes, or you'll risk a broken or sprained digit.

Lateral support stops ankle injuries. Stiff shanks keep your feet from tiring. Grippy outsoles prevent slipping and falling. And sufficient cushioning lessens the pain of a long day on the trail.

Out of the box, boots should be waterproof or at least very water resistant, although you'll have to treat them often to retain their repellency. Boots with lots of seams allow water to seep in as they age. A full rand (wrap-around bumper) adds an extra measure of water protection.

The key consideration is comfort. Make sure your boots don't hurt. you wait to find out until after a day of hiking, it's too late; you're stuck with them. So before handing over your cash, ask the retailer if, after wearing them in a shopping mall, you can exchange them if they don't feel right. A half-hour of mall walking is a helpful test.

Socks are important too. To keep your feet dry, warm and happy, wear wool, thick acrylic, or wool/acrylic-blend socks. Cotton socks retain sweat, cause blisters, and are especially bad if your boots aren't waterproof. It's usually best to wear two pairs of socks, with a thinner, synthetic pair next to your feet to wick away moisture and reduce friction, minimizing the chance of blisters.

GLOVES AND HATS

Always bring gloves and a hat. You've probably heard it, and it's true: your body loses most of its heat through your head and extremities. Cover them if you get chilled. Carry thin, synthetic gloves to wear while hiking. Don't worry if they get wet, but keep a pair of thicker fleece gloves dry in your pack. A fleece hat, or at least a thick headband that covers your ears, adds a lot of warmth and weighs little. A hat with a long brim is required equipment to shade your eyes and protect your face.

TREKKING POLES

Long, steep ascents and descents in the mountians make trekking poles vital. Hiking with poles is easier, more enjoyable, and less punishing to your body. If you're constantly pounding the trails, poles could add years to your mountain life.

Working on a previous guidebook, we once hiked for a month without poles. Both of us developed knee pain. The next summer we used Leki trekking poles every day for three months and our knees were never strained. We felt like four-legged animals. We were more sure-footed. Our speed and endurance increased.

Studies show that during a typical 8-hour hike you'll transfer more than 250 tons of pressure to a pair of trekking poles. When going downhill, poles significantly reduce stress to your knees, as well as your lower back, heel and forefoot. They alleviate knee strain when you're going uphill too, because you're climbing with your arms and shoulders, not just your legs. Poles also improve your posture. They keep you more upright, which gives you greater lung capacity and allows more efficient breathing.

Crossing Petain Creek, heading for upper Petain Basin (Trip 36)

The heavier your pack, the more you'll appreciate the support of trekking poles. You'll find them especially helpful for crossing unbridged streams, traversing steep slopes, and negotiating muddy, rooty, rough stretches of trail. Poles prevent ankle sprains—a common hiking injury. By making you more stable, they actually help you relax, boosting your sense of security and confidence.

We rarely see others using poles. Yet on every trail, someone asks about ours.

They typically initiate the conversation with an idiotic quip: "So where are your skis? Ha ha ha!" A few people carry those big, heavy, gnarled wood staffs, which are a joke. Some hike with old ski poles, which are better, but not nearly as good as poles designed specifically for trekking. To get the full benefit, invest in a pair of true trekking poles made of aircraft-quality aluminum, with adjustable, telescoping shafts and anti-shock springs.

FIRST AID

Someone in your hiking party should carry a first-aid kit. Pre-packaged kits look handy, but they're expensive, and some are inadequate. If you make your own you'll be more familiar with the contents. Include an anti-bacterial ointment; pain pills with ibuprofen, and a few with codeine for agonizing injuries; regular bandages; several sizes of butterfly bandages; a couple bandages big enough to hold a serious laceration together; rolls of sterile gauze and absorbant pads to staunch bleeding; adhesive tape; tiny fold-up scissors or a small knife; and a compact first-aid manual. Whether your kit is store bought or homemade, check the expiration dates on your medications every year and replace them as needed.

Instead of the old elastic bandages for wrapping sprains, we now carry neoprene ankle and knee bands. They slip on instantly, require no special wrapping technique, keep the injured joint warmer, and stay in place better. They're so convenient, we sometimes slip them on for extra support on long, steep descents.

BANDANAS

A bandana will be the most versatile item in your pack. You can use it to blow your nose, mop your brow, or improvise a beanie. It makes a colorful headband that'll keep sweat or hair out of your eyes. It serves as a bandage or sling in a medical emergency. Worn as a neckerchief, it prevents a sunburned neck. If you soak it in water, then drape it around your neck, it'll help keep you from overheating. Worn Lawrence-of-Arabia style under a hat, it shades both sides of your face, as well as your neck. For an air-conditioning effect, soak it in water then don it a la' Lawrence. When shooing away mosquitoes, flicking a bandana is less tiresome than flailing your arms. Always bring at least two bandanas on a dayhike, more when you're backpacking.

SMALL AND ESSENTIAL

Take matches in a plastic bag, so they're sure to stay dry. It's good to have a Bic lighter, too. A fire starter, such as Optimus Firelighter or Coghlan FireSticks, might help you get a fire going in an emergency when everything is wet. Buy the finger-size wands, not the type for a barbecue.

Pack an emergency survival bag on dayhikes. One fits into the palm of your hand and could help you survive a cold night without a sleeping bag or tent. The ultralight, metallic fabric reflects your body heat back at you. Look for the survival bags you crawl into; they're more efficient than survival blankets.

Also bring several plastic bags in various sizes. Use the small ones for packing out garbage. A couple large trash bags could be used to improvise a shelter.

A headlamp or flashlight, and extra batteries, are often helpful and can be necessary for safety. You'll need one to stay on the trail if a crisis forces you to hike at night. Learn to use a compass and never hike without one. Most people find bug repellent indispensable. For those dreaded blisters, pack Moleskin or Spenco jell. Cut it with the knife or scissors you should have in your first-aid kit.

Wear sunglasses for protection against glare and wind. A few hours in the elements can strain your eyes and even cause a headache. People who don't wear sunglasses are more prone to cataracts later in life. Also bring sunscreen and a hat with a brim. High-altitude sun can fry you fast. Those holes in the ozone layer aren't shrinking.

And don't forget to pack lots of thought-provoking questions to ask your companions. Hiking stimulates meaningful conversation.

KEEPING IT ALL DRY

Most packs are not waterproof, or even very water resistant. To protect your gear from rain, bag it in plastic bags and use a pack cover for your backpack. Rain is a constant likelihood, so you might as well start hiking with everything in bags. That's easier than wrestling with it in a storm. For added assurance, Aqua-Quest waterproof nylon organizers are superior to plastic bags.

WATER

Drink water frequently. Keeping your body hydrated is essential. If you're thirsty, you're probably not performing at optimal efficiency. But be aware of giardia lamblia, a waterborne parasite that causes severe gastrointestinal distress. It's transported through animal and human feces, so never poop or pee near water. To be safe, assume giardia is present in all surface water. Don't drink any water unless it's directly from a source you're certain is pure, like a glacier or spring, or until you've boiled, disinfected or filtered it. Boiling is an immense hassle. Killing giardia with iodine tablets can be tricky, and it makes the water smell and taste awful unless you use neutralizing pills. Carrying a small, light filter (some weigh only 240 grams / 8 ounces) is the most practical solution. Safewater

Anywhere filter bottles are ideal. To strain out giardia cysts, your filter must have an absolute pore size of 4 microns or less. To strain out cryptosporidium cysts, which are increasingly common and cause physical symptoms identical to giardiasis, your filter must have an absolute pore size of 2 microns or less. Iodine has no effect on crypto.

BODY FUEL

When planning meals, keep energy and nutrition foremost in mind. During a six-hour hike, you'll burn 1800 to 3000 calories, depending on terrain, pace, body size, and pack weight. You'll be stronger, and therefore safer and happier, if you fill up on high-octane body fuel. A few candy bars and a white-flour bun with a slab of cheese or meat on it won't get you very far up the trail. Refined sugars give you a brief spurt that quickly fizzles. Too much protein or fat will make you feel sluggish and drag you down.

For sustained exercise, like hiking, you need a little protein and fat to function normally and give you that satisfying full feeling. Most people can sustain athletic effort longer by eating some protein in the morning and a smaller portion during the day. In the evening, eat protein to aid muscle repair.

How much protein and fat you should eat depends on the speed of your metabolism. Both are hard to digest. Your body takes three or four hours to assimilate them, compared to one or two hours for carbohydrates. That's why, while hiking, a carbo-heavy diet is optimal. It ensures your blood supply keeps hustling oxygen to your legs, instead of being diverted to your stomach.

For athletic performance, the American and Canadian Dietetic Association recommends that 60 to 65% of your total energy come from carbos, less than 25% from fat, and 15% from protein. They also say refined carbos and sugars should account for no more than 10% of your total carbo calories. Toiling muscles crave the glycogen your body manufactures from complex carbos. Yet your body has limited carbo storage capacity. So your carbo intake should be constant. That means loading your pack with plant foods made of whole-wheat flour, rice, corn, oats, legumes, nuts, seeds, fruit and vegetables.

You'll find natural- or health-food stores are reliable sources of hiking food. They even stock energy bars, which are superior to candy bars because they're rich in complex carbos and lower in fat.

Filtering water in the Valhallas

Whether dayhiking or backpacking, always bring extra energy bars for emergencies. We rely on and recommend **greens+** bars because they're highly nutritious.

On dayhikes, carry fresh or dried fruit; whole-grain pita bread filled with tabouli, hummus, or avocado, cucumbers and sprouts; whole-grain cookies made with natural sweeteners (brown-rice syrup, organic cane-sugar, fruit juice, raw honey); or whole-grain crackers. We often pack a bag of organic-corn or mixed-grain tortilla chips prepared in expeller-pressed safflower or canola oil. Take marinated tofu (high in protein) that's been pressed, baked, and vacuum-packed. It's delicious and lasts about three days. Omnivores might like hard-boiled eggs. But don't rely on cheese for protein. Beyond small amounts, it's unhealthy.

For a backpacking breakfast, try spreading butter, maple syrup and cinnamon on hearty, whole-grain bread or in pita pockets. Or why not whole-grain cookies in the morning? They're like cereal, only more convenient. The backpacking lunch menu is the same as for dayhiking. For dinner, try bean salad, rice with stir-fried vegetables, or pasta with dressing and steamed veggies, all cooked at home and sealed in plastic. Cold bean burritos you make ahead of time are great too. Fresh veggies that travel well include carrots and bell peppers.

Real meals are heavier than freeze-dried, but they make up for it by eliminating the weight of cooking equipment and the bother of cooking and cleaning. Plus they're tastier, more filling, cheaper, and better for you.

Most backpackers carry a stove. In addition to using it to cook meals, they say it'll help warm them in an emergency. True enough. Warm liquids can help revive someone slipping into hypothermia. But we prefer to reduce our load and go without, risking the small chance that we'll ever need a stove. In case our survival depends on it, we carry tiny, lightweight fire starters to help us light a fire.

Fresh food tends to be too heavy, bulky and perishable for trips longer than four days. Then it makes sense to pack a stove and freeze-dried food. Other fast-and-easy options are soup mixes, lentils, and quick-cooking pasta or brown rice. But for shorter trips, don't adhere blindly to tradition. Carry a stove only if cooking significantly increases your enjoyment.

INFORMATION SOURCES

Within the province, instead of phoning long distance, dial Inquiry BC: 1-800-663-7867. Tell them the phone number of the FS or BC Parks office you're calling. They'll connect you at no charge.

For on-line information about BC provincial parks, go to www.elp.gov.bc.ca/bcparks/

For on-line information about FS regions, go to www.for.gov.bc.ca/mof/regdis.htm

The hours of operation for most FS offices are Monday through Friday, 8 A.M. to 12 noon, and 1 P.M. to 4:30 P.M. BC Parks offices are open 8:30 A.M. to 4:30 P.M.

VANCOUVER ISLAND

Strathcona Provincial Park
Ministry of Environment,
Lands and Parks
1812 Miracle Beach Drive
Black Creek, BC V9J 1K1
phone (250) 337-2400
fax (250) 337-5695

**Capital Regional District
Parks,** for East Sooke Coast
490 Atkins Avenue
Victoria, BC V9B 2Z8
phone (250) 478.3344
fax (250) 478.5416
Website www.crd.bc.ca/parks

B.C. COAST MOUNTAINS

**Garibaldi and Tantalus
provincial parks**
District Manager,
Box 220, Brackendale, B.C. V0N 1H0
phone (604) 898-3678
fax (604) 898-4171

Cathedral Provincial Park
District Manager
B.C. Parks Okanagan
P.O. Box 399, Summerland, BC
V0H 1Z0 Canada
phone (250) 494-6500

**Western Canada Wilderness
Committee**
227 Abbott Street
Vancouver, BC V6B 2K7
phone (604) 683-8220;
1-800-661-9453
fax (604) 683-8229
www.wildernesscommittee.org

Stein Valley Provincial Park
1210 McGill Road
Kamloops, BC V2C 6N6
phone (250) 851-3000

SELKIRK & PURCELL MOUNTAINS

**Mount Revelstoke and
Glacier National Parks**
PO Box 350, 301B 3rd Street West
Revelstoke, BC V0E 2S0
phone (250) 837-7500
fax (250) 837-7536

Arrow Forest District
845 Columbia Avenue
Castlegar, BC V1N 1H3
phone (250) 365-8600

**Kokanee Glacier and
Valhalla provincial parks**
mail RR 3, S-8, C-5
Nelson, BC V1L 5P6
visit 4750 Hwy 3A, 19 km
(12 mi) NE of Nelson
phone (250) 825-3500

Nelson Forest Region
518 Lake Street
Nelson, BC V1L 4C6
phone (250) 354-6200

**Columbia Forest
Service District**
Box 9158, RPO #3
1761 Big Eddy Road
Revelstoke, BC V0E 2S0
phone (250) 837-7611

Invermere FS District
Box 189, 625 4th Street
Invermere, BC V0A 1K0
phone (250) 342-4200

**Kootenay Lake
Forest District**
mail 1907 Ridgewood Rd, RR1
Nelson, BC V1L 5P4
phone (250) 825-1100
visit Hwy 3A, 6.5 km (4 mi)
NE of Nelson

Valhalla Society
Box 329, 307 6th Avenue
New Denver, BC V0G 1S0
phone (250) 358-2333

CANADIAN ROCKIES

Alpine Club of Canada
P.O. Box 2040, Canmore, AB T0L 0M0
phone (403) 678-3200
fax (403) 678-3224
website www.culturenet.ca/acc/
e-mail alpclub@telusplanet.net
Membership fees vary for each section, starting at $43 annually for a
single person to $79 for a family. The cost per night to stay in a Class A
hut is $17.50 (2001) per person. Non-members must pay $24.
Contact the club for current specifics and reservations.

Banff Information Centre
Box 900, Banff, AB T0L 0C0
phone (403) 762-1550 for brochures, general information, and
backcountry reservations
phone (403) 762-1460 for trail information   **fax** (403) 762-1551
website www.worldweb.com/parkscanada-banff/
e-mail banff_vrc@pch.gc.ca
Open daily 8 A.M. to 8 P.M. July and August;
8 A.M. to 5 P.M. June, September, and October through May.

Kootenay Information Centre
Box 220, Radium Hot Springs, B.C. V0A 1M0
(located in hot springs complex)
phone (250) 347-9615 for general information   **fax** (250) 347-9980
phone (250) 347-9505 for backcountry reservations
website www.worldweb.com/
parkscanada-kootenay/
e-mail kootenay_reception@pch.gc.ca
Open daily 9 A.M. to 5 P.M. mid-May through late June; 9 A.M. to 7 P.M.
late June through early Sept.; 9 A.M. to 5 P.M. Sept. through mid-Oct.

Lake Louise International Hostel
Village Road, P.O. Box 115,
Lake Louise, AB T0L 1E0
phone (403) 522-2200   **fax** (403) 522-2253
e-mail llouise@telusplanet.net
Make reservations with this office for the Whiskey Jack Hostel
in Yoho Valley.

Assiniboine and Elk Lakes provincial parks
6188 Wasa Lake Park Drive
Box 118, Wasa, B.C. V0B 2K0
phone (250) 422-4200
fax (250) 422-3326
website www.elp.gov.bc.ca/bcparks/

Mt. Robson Provincial Park Visitor Centre
Box 579, Valemount, B.C. V0E 2Z0
phone (250) 566-4325 **fax** (250) 566-9777
website www.elp.gov.bc.ca/bcparks/
Open daily 8 A.M. to 8 P.M. in summer

Yoho National Park Visitor Centre
Box 99, Field, B.C. V0A 1G0
phone (250) 343-6433 for Lake O'Hara bus & camping reservations
phone (250) 343-6783 for all other areas of the park **fax** (250) 343-6012
website www.worldweb.com/parkscanada-yoho/
e-mail yoho_info@pch.gc.ca
Open daily 9 A.M. to 5 P.M. May 15 through late June; 9 A.M. to 7 P.M.
late June through Aug. 30; 9 A.M. to 5 P.M. Aug. 31 through late Sept.;
9 A.M. to 4 P.M. late fall through mid-May.

Taking notes in the Coast Mountains

INDEX
Cities, towns and villages are in bold. Photo pages are in bold.

The Authors

Besides each other, hiking is Skye and Lake's greatest passion. Their second date was a 32-km (20-mi) dayhike in Arizona. Since then, they've never stopped for long. In celebration of 20 years of adventurous travel together, they changed their names from Kathy and Craig Copeland.

Skye and Lake have trekked through much of the world's vertical topography, including the Himalayas, Pyrenees, Alps, Dolomites, Sierra, North Cascades, and Rockies, as well as the mountains of New Zealand and the canyons of the American Southwest. They moved from the U.S. to Canada so they could live near the Canadian Rockies, the range that inspired their highly unconventional *Don't Waste Your Time*® hiking guidebook series. *Camp Free in B.C.* was their next book. Then they devoted two years to hiking the North Cascades, the subject of their second *Don't Waste Your Time*® guidebook. Following that, they explored southwest British Columbia and wrote *Don't Waste Your Time*® *in the B.C. Coast Mountains*. While living on Kootenay Lake, between B.C.'s Purcell and Selkirk mountains, they hiked those ranges and wrote *Don't Waste Your Time*® *in the West Kootenays*.

Having completed *Gotta Hike*® *B.C.*, Skye and Lake intend to live up to their new name by continuing to wander the world. They're currently researching and writing a hiking guidebook to southern Utah canyon country.

The authors at Grizzly Creek, en route to Bald Mountain (Trip 21).

Other titles from Voice in the Wilderness Press

Look for these and other titles in outdoor shops and book stores. You can also order them through AdventurousTraveler.com (1-800-282-3963), MEC (1-888-847-0770), or www.chapters.ca. Visit **www.wild.bc.ca** for book excerpts, photos, and prices.

PREMIER   **OUTSTANDING**   **WORTHWHILE**   **DON'T DO**

The Don't Waste Your Time® *hiking guidebook series rates and reviews trails to help you get the most from magnificent wilderness areas. Route descriptions are comprehensive. Includes shoulder-season trips for more hiking opportunities. Offers wisdom on mountain travel.*

Don't Waste Your Time® in the BC Coast Mountains
    ISBN 0-9698016-3-7   1999 edition, 288 pages
72 hikes in southwest BC, including Vancouver's North Shore mountains, Garibaldi Provincial Park, and the Whistler-Pemberton region.

Don't Waste Your Time® in the Canadian Rockies
    ISBN 0-9698016-4-5   2000 edition, 392 pages
125 hikes in Banff, Jasper, Kootenay, Yoho and Waterton national parks, plus Mt. Robson and Mt. Assiniboine provincial parks.

Don't Waste Your Time® in the North Cascades
    ISBN 0-89997-182-2   2000 edition, 364 pages
110 hikes in southern BC and northern Washington. Includes North Cascades National Park, Mt. Baker and Glacier Peak wilderness areas, plus BC's Manning and Cathedral parks.

Don't Waste Your Time® in the West Kootenays
    ISBN 0-9698016-9-6   2000 edition, 344 pages
68 hikes in the Selkirk and west Purcell ranges of southeast B.C. Includes Valhalla, Kokanee Glacier, Goat Range, and St. Mary's Alpine provincial parks.

More titles on next page

Camp Free in B.C. Volume I
   ISBN 0-9698016-7-x   1999, 3rd edition, 416 pages
Precise directions to over 260 official, free campgrounds
accessible by two-wheel drive. Covers southern BC, from
Trans-Canada Hwy 1 to the U.S. border, from Vancouver
Island to the Rocky Mountains.

Camp Free in B.C. Volume II
   ISBN: 0-9698016-6-1   1999, 1st edition, 368 pages
Precise directions to over 225 official, free campgrounds
accessible by two-wheel drive. Covers central BC, from
Trans-Canada Hwy 1, north past Highway 16. Follow
exciting backroads through the Shuswap Highlands,
East Cariboo, and Chilcotin. Includes sites near Terrace,
Smithers, and Prince George.

Gotta Hike® B.C. Volume I
   ISBN 0-9698016-8-8   2001 1st edition, 312 pages,
   16 pages of colour photos
The only book you need to enjoy the most spectacular,
exhilarating hikes in southern BC. Discerning trail reviews
help you choose your trip. Detailed route descriptions
keep you on the path. Includes dayhikes and backpack
trips. Covers Vancouver Island, Coast Mountains, Selkirks,
Purcells, and Canadian Rockies.

Bears Beware! Warning Calls You Can
   Make to Avoid an Encounter
   ISBN 0-9698016-5-3   1998 edition, audio cassette
30 minutes that could save your life. Find out why pepper
spray, talking, and bells are not enough. Follow these
strategies for safer hiking and camping in bear country.

What's Your Opinion?

A guidebook continues to evolve, like the landscapes it describes.
Please contribute to the evolution of this book by answering the following
questions. Mail them, on a separate sheet of paper, to **Voice in the
Wilderness Press, Box 30, Riondel, BC V0B 2B0 Canada.** Or e-mail us
at: **explore@wild.bc.ca** Thanks. We value your comments.

1. How experienced a hiker are you, and how often do you hike?

2. What did you like most about this book?

3. What did you like least about this book?

4. Were any of the directions inaccurate or difficult to follow?
   If so, which trip? Please explain.